C000063461

Toward the Outside

Toward the Outside

○ ○ ○ ○

Concepts and Themes in Emmanuel Levinas

Michael B. Smith

Duquesne University Press
Pittsburgh, Pennsylvania

Copyright © 2005 Duquesne University Press
All Rights Reserved

This book, or parts thereof, may not be used or reproduced
in any manner whatsoever without the written permission of the Publisher,
except in the case of short quotations in critical reviews or articles.

This book is published by

DUQUESNE UNIVERSITY PRESS
600 Forbes Avenue
Pittsburgh, Pennsylvania 15282

Library of Congress Cataloging in Publication Data

Smith, Michael B. (Michael Bradley), 1940–
    Toward the outside: concepts and themes in Emmanuel Levinas/by Michael
B. Smith.
        p. cm.
    Includes bibliographical references and index.
    ISBN 0-8207-0368-0 (hardcover: alk. paper) — ISBN 0-8207-0369-9
(pbk.: alk. paper)
    1. Lévinas, Emmanuel. I. Title.
    B2430.L484S65 2005
    194—dc22   2004023893

∞ Printed on acid-free paper.
Published in the United States of America.

For Helen

CONTENTS

ACKNOWLEDGMENTS

I wish to thank Dean Chaitram Singh of Berry College for recommending my sabbatical leave in the spring of 2001, which allowed me to write some of the early material from which this book developed; Susan Wadsworth-Booth for her editorial encouragement and reassurance along the way; and Mary Groeninger for her numerous stylistic improvements.

ABBREVIATIONS

Levinas

AAT   *Alterity and Transcendence*. Trans. M. B. Smith. New York: Columbia University Press, 2000.

AE   *Autrement qu'être ou au-delà de l'essence*. Dordrecht: Kluwer Academic, 1988.

AT   *Alterity et transcendence*. With an introduction by Pierre Hayat. NP [Montpellier]: Fata Morgana, 1995.

BPW   *Basic Philosophical Writings*. Ed. A. Peperzak, S. Critchley and R. Bernasconi. Bloomington: Indiana University Press, 1996.

BTV   *Beyond the Verse: Talmudic Readings and Lectures*. Trans. G. D. Mole. Bloomington and Indianapolis: Indiana University Press, 1994.

CPP   *Collected Philosophical Papers*. Trans. A. Lingis. Pittsburgh: Duquesne University Press, 1998.

DD   *De Dieu qui vient à l'idée*. Paris: J. Vrin, 1986.

DE   *Discovering Existence with Husserl*. Trans. and ed. R. A. Cohen and M. B. Smith. Evanston: Northwestern University Press, 1989.

DF   *Difficult Freedom: Essays on Judaism*. Trans. S. Hand. London: The Athlone Press, 1990.

DL   *Difficile Liberté*. 3rd ed., Biblio-essais. Paris: Albin Michel, 1976.

DLE   *De l'évasion*. With notes and introduction by J. Rolland. N. P. [Montpellier]: Fata Morgana, 1982.

DSS   *Du sacré au saint.* Paris: Éditions de Minuit, 1977.

EAE   *Existence & Existents.* Trans. A. Lingis with a foreword
       R. Bernasconi. Pittsburgh: Duquesne University Press,
       2001.

EAI   *Ethics and Infinity: Conversations with Philippe Nemo.*
       Trans. R. A. Cohen. Pittsburgh: Duquesne University
       Press, 1985.

EDE   *En décourvrant l'existence avec Husserl et Heidegger.*
       Paris: Vrin, 2nd Edition, 1988 [1967].

EE   *De l'existence à l'existant.* Paris: Vrin, 1986.

EI   *Éthique et infini: Dialogues avec Philippe Némo.* Paris:
       Librairie Arthème Fayard et Radio-France, 1982.

EN   *Entre nous: Essais sur le penser-à-l'autre.* Paris: Bernard
       Grasset, 1991.

ENN   *Entre nous: on thinking-of-the-other.* Trans. Michael B.
       Smith. New York: Columbia University Press, 1998.

GDT   *God, Death, and Time.* Ed. J. Rolland and trans. B. Bergo.
       Stanford: Stanford University Press, 2000.

HS   *Hors Sujet.* N. P. [Montpellier]: Fata Morgana, 1987.

HAH   *Humanisme de l'autre homme.* Biblio-essais. Montpellier:
       Fata Morgana, 1972.

IDI   *L'intrigue de l'infini.* Ed. A.-M. Lescourret. Paris: Flam-
       marion, 1994.

IH   *Les Imprévues de l'histoire.* N.P. [Montpellier]: Fata
       Morgana, 1994.

IRB   *Is it Righteous to Be? Interviews with Emmanuel Levinas.*
       Ed. Jill Robbins. Stanford: Stanford University Press,
       2001.

LR   *The Levinas Reader.* Ed. S. Hand. Oxford: Basil Blackwell,
       1987.

NLT   *Nouvelles lectures talmudiques.* Paris: Les Éditions de
       Minuit, 1996.

NP   *Noms Propres.* Biblio-essais. Montpellier: Fata Morgana,
       1987.

NTR   *Nine Talmudic Readings.* Trans. A. Aronowicz. Bloomington & Indianapolis: Indiana University Press, 1990.

NeTR *New Talmudic Readings.* Trans. R. A. Cohen. Pittsburgh: Duquesne University Press, 1999.

OE   *On Escape/De l'évasion.* Trans. B. Bergo: Stanford: Stanford University Press, 2003.

OB   *Otherwise than Being or Beyond Essence.* Trans. A. Lingis. Pittsburgh: Duquesne University Press, 1998.

OG   *Of God Who Comes to Mind.* Trans. B. Bergo. Stanford: Stanford University Press, 1998.

OS   *Outside the Subject.* Trans. M. B. Smith. Stanford: Stanford University Press, 1993.

PN   *Proper Names.* Trans. M. B. Smith. Stanford: Stanford University Press, 1996.

QEV *Emmanuel Lévinas: Qui êtes-vous?* Interview by François Poirié. Lyon: La Manufacture, 1987.

TA   *Le temps et l'autre.* Paris: Quadrige/Presses Universitaires de France, 1985.

TO   *Time and the Other [and additional essays].* Trans. R. Cohen. Pittsburgh: Duquesne University Press, 1987.

TAI   *Totality and Infinity.* Trans. A. Lingis. Pittsburgh: Duquesne University Press, 1969.

THI   *Théorie de l'intuition dans la phénoménologie de Husserl.* Paris: Alcan, 1930.

TTI   *The Theory of Intuition in Husserl's Phenomenology.* 2nd ed. Trans. A. Orianne. Evanston: Northwestern University Press, 1995.

TI   *Totalité et infini.* 4th ed. Boston: Martinus Nijhoff, 1984.

TN   *In the Time of the Nations.* Trans. M. B. Smith. Bloomington and Indianapolis: Indiana University Press, 1994.

Other Authors

A   *Adieu.* Jacques Derrida. Paris: Editions Galilée, 1997.

AEL   *Adieu to Emmanuel Levinas.* Jacques Derrida. Trans.
        P.-A. Brault and M. Naas. Stanford: Stanford University
        Press, 1999.

AQS   *Autrement que savoir: Emmanuel Levinas. Les entretiens
        du Centre Sèvres, avec les études de Guy Petitdemange
        et Jacques Rolland.* Paris: Éditions Osiris, 1988.

DLT   *De l'idée de transcendance à la question du langage:
        L'itinéraire philosophique de Lévinas.* Étienne Feron.
        Grenoble: Jérôme Millon, 1992.

E   *Elevations: The Height of the Good in Rosenzweig and
        Levinas.* Richard A. Cohen. Chicago and London: The
        University of Chicago Press, 1994.

ED   *L'écriture et la différence.* Jacques Derrida. Paris: Editions
        du Seuil, 1967.

EL   *Emmanuel Levinas* (biography) Anne-Marie Lescourret.
        Paris: Flammarion, 1994.

ELVT   *Emmanuel Lévinas: la vie et la trace.* Salomon Malka.
        Paris: JC Lattès, 2002.

ELSA   *Emmanuel Levinas et la socialité de l'argent.* Roger
        Burggraeve. Louvain: Peeters, 1997.

EM   *Emmanuel Levinas: The Problem of Ethical Metaphysics.*
        2nd ed. Edith Wyschogrod. New York: Fordham University
        Press, 2000.

LL   *Lire Lévinas.* 2nd ed. Salomon Malka. Paris: Les Éditions
        du Cerf, 1989.

PA   *Parcours de l'autrement: Lecture d'Émmanuel Lévinas.*
        Jacques Rolland. Paris: Presses Universitaires de France,
        2000.

PT   *Positivité et transcendance, suivi de Lévinas et la phénom-
        énologie.* Ed. J.-L. Marion. Paris: Presses Universitaires
        de France, 2000.

RL   *Re-Reading Levinas*. Ed. R. Bernasconi and S. Critchley. Bloomington and Indianapolis: Indiana University Press, 1991.

WD   *Writing and Difference*. Jacques Derrida. Trans. A Bass. Chicago: The University of Chicago Press, 1978.

INTRODUCTION

The overall movement of Levinas's philosophy is toward "the outside." By this I do not mean to make a statement about the development of his philosophy, but about its constant polarity at every stage. This movement dominates his entire philosophy, and is already present in his first original work, "De l'évasion" ("On Escape"), in 1935. His philosophy is a metaphysics, structured and sustained by that movement of transcendence: transcendence being the movement of the self (or "same") toward the outside (the "other" or alterity). The "I" is understood as interiority itself. Like an organism in the natural world, it has its inner economy. This theme is developed in a preliminary way in the essay "The *I* and the Totality," then a few years later in his first major work, *Totality and Infinity: An Essay on Exteriority* (1961), with its extensive analysis of the inside ("Interiority and Economy") and the outside ("Exteriority and the Face"). The analysis continues in the same direction, albeit with important modifications, in Levinas's last major work, *Otherwise than Being or Beyond Essence* (1974), the last section of which is titled "Outside."

This philosophy goes against the contemporary grain for a number of reasons, first, by being a metaphysics. Kant declared the metaphysical project hopelessly beyond the reach of human understanding. More recently, contemporary philosophers (particularly, but not exclusively, Heideggerians), would reject the inside/outside dichotomy as being too compromised by its long metaphysical and theological past to have a promising future. Not only "the inner man," but subjectivity altogether, is seen by some as an anachronism.[1] So much for continental philosophy. In this country the triumph of scientism, the current form of naturalism, has so dominated philosophical discussion as to have made metaphysical speculation seem, to many, an idle pastime. Nevertheless, Levinas's philosophy has the attraction for me of renewing humanistic thought, not by appeals to the aesthetic or cultural domains, but by reviving and deepening the ethical intuitions that lie dormant within humanism itself.[2]

The present study will follow this centrifugal movement in Levinas's philosophy, exploring its presuppositions and implications, the critique it has both given and received with respect to other philosophies, and the avenues it opens up for future research and reflection. As such, it may be helpful in orienting readers of this important and original thinker. It does not give special emphasis to either side of Levinas's work, the philosophical or the Judaic. The distinction, though real, is less dramatic than one might suppose, since Levinas's texts on Judaism are charged with philosophical significance. The relationship between these two aspects of his work will be one of the issues this introduction will address. The only claim to originality that such a work as this may have is in the way I have allowed my own interests to guide my approach to the texts of Levinas, putting questions to them that may differ from those whose interests are either more specialized or informed by a different background.

I suppose that Levinas's thought presents a coherent whole, finding the points of articulation between the philosophical and the Judaic facets of Levinas's œuvre, which one commentator has described as a diptych, one panel of which contains essentially philosophical texts, the other "religious" or "Jewish" ones.[3] If I therefore refer to Levinas's "thought," this is not to be construed as a lesser category than philosophy, but rather as a broader one, embracing all aspects of reflection, even those that may for historically contingent reasons be routinely excluded from the domain of philosophy proper.[4]

Biographical Note

Emmanuel Levinas was born in Kovno (or Kaunus), Lithuania, which was still Russian, in 1906. His parents spoke Yiddish to each other and Russian to the children (Emmanuel and his two younger brothers Boris and Aminadab). He received Hebrew lessons beginning at age six. Forced to leave Kovno in 1915, the family moved to Kharkov, in the Ukraine, then back to Kovno in 1919, after the German defeat. This border life, at the crossroads of so many different nationalities and beliefs, constituted Levinas's first milieu. "The extinction of these crossroads was brought about by the bureaucrats of ideas who called nations and classes to arms, imposed a global perspective and introduced categories that differentiated members of the community according to the simplistic categories of culture, language, religion, politics . . . It is precisely that spontaneous openness to the foreigner that constitutes the 'hidden treasure' of the literature of the crossroads."[5] Levinas's antitotalitarian instinct and sense of the rich complexity of sociality may have roots in these early years of human confluence. Marie-Anne Lescourret sums up the tenor of his 17-year-old existence in the following terms.

> Levinas learned to appreciate spiritually that which disdains him existentially; he learned to live not within the ever resolved dialectical contradiction, but within the coexistence of opposites; and this will be the dominant note of his whole life. He claims as his philosophical ancestors on one hand Biblical texts read in the light of Lithuanian Judaism, and on the other Russian literature. He stands from the start beneath a double cultural allegiance, the twofold nature of which is increased both by the foreignness of these

traditions to those of Western Europe and by the contradiction in which they stand to each other. He is a Jew among Christians, a Litvak among Jews, a Russo-phone among speakers of Yiddish, at once enlightened and observant, rationalist and sensitive to pathos, pan-humanist and banished. . . .[6]

The next phase of Levinas's career was that of a university student.[7] He was accepted at the University of Strasbourg in 1923, after having been turned down by several German universities. His university thesis, *The Theory of Intuition in Husserl's Phenomenology*, was directed by Maurice Pradines; and it occasioned his research trip to Freiburg, Germany, where he studied under Husserl himself. He also took courses with Husserl's successor Martin Heidegger, for whose work, *Being and Time*, published two years earlier, Levinas had an immediate and abiding admiration, despite that philosopher's subsequent lamentable turn toward Nazism.

Levinas stopped short of the *agrégation*, a public, competitive examination that gives access to university teaching in France. It would have meant learning enough Greek to pass the examination, as well as the expense of further studies rather than employment, which the young Lithuanian who had just married could ill afford. Instead he worked as a teacher-monitor-secretary for the École Normale Israélite Universelle (the ENIU), a Jewish organization that prepared teachers for the Alliance Israéite Universelle (AIU), the most important mission of which was to maintain schools to teach reading, arithmetic, French culture and history in Morocco, Tunisia, Iran, Turkey and the Near East. Levinas worked there for nine years until the outbreak of the Second World War. He received French citizenship in 1931 and fulfilled his military obligation in 1932. He volunteered for military service in 1939. During the war he was immediately taken prisoner, along with the other French officers of his regiment, and spent four years in a work camp — not for Jews, which he almost certainly would not have survived, but for French officers. His camp was liberated by the United States Army.[8] At his release he learned that his brothers and parents in Lithuania had been killed. His wife and daughter Simone were saved by being hidden in a monastery.

After the war Levinas became the director of the École Normale Israélite, as well as the cofounder of the Colloquium of Jewish Intellectuals, a group that played an important role in providing a forum for thought on the problems posed to Judaism by modernity. His academic career proceeded: in 1961, the year of publication of his doctoral thesis (*doctorat d'état*), *Totalité et infini*, he was assigned a position as professor at the University of Poitiers; then, in 1967, at Nanterre (one of the branches of the University of Paris); and finally in 1973 at the Sorbonne (Paris IV). He retired in 1976, but continued to publish, lecture and conduct occasional seminars. He also continued to grant interviews in the living room of his apartment in the 16th *arrondissement*, and to give his weekly talmudic lesson, every Saturday at noon, at the synagogue of the École Normale Israélite Orientale. Levinas died in Paris on December 25, 1995.

Preliminary Characterization of Levinas's Philosophy

Essentialism

There is a sense in which Levinas's philosophy may be said to be essentialist. First, it is essentialist in that meaning, or essence, is primary. While there are important differences between Levinas's essentialism and Plato's idealism, Levinas, true to the spirit of the phenomenology of Edmund Husserl, sees his philosophical project as one of finding meaning: the meaning of life, of death, of being. We shall have more to say about this essentialist aspect of Levinas's philosophy, which is discernable in his account of perception (in chapter 3 of *Otherwise than Being*), his theory of language as essentially metaphorical (in the essay "Meaning and

Sense"), and his analysis of the meaning of temporality. This affinity with an essentialist form of thought makes Levinas closer to idealism than realism.

It must be noted that in drawing attention to an essentialism in Levinas's thought I am not using the term "essence" in the special sense in which Levinas himself uses the term — as a verbal meaning of being, or his equivalent of Heidegger's *Sein*, as he explains in his introductory note to *Otherwise than Being*. If I were to adopt his usage, I would speak rather of the "eidetic" nature of his philosophy.

I am not unaware of the apparent oddity of characterizing as "essentialist" a philosopher who is usually classed (along with Heidegger and Sartre) as an "existential" phenomenologist. But the fact is that Husserl's phenomenology began by making abstraction from ontological questions altogether, insisting as it did on the equal rights of all data. Levinas's philosophical career traverses existentialism but does not dwell there. Perhaps the most "existential" moments of Levinas's writings are in his early work, *De l'existence à l'existant*, and in the choice of themes in section 2 of *Totality and Infinity*. Another relevant consideration is that the best known existentialists have been, unlike Levinas, atheists, with the exception of the movement's putative father, Kierkegaard, and Gabriel Marcel. This may be more than a historically contingent circumstance: essentialism, an admittedly vague classifier, would seem *prima facie* to be more amenable to religious thought than existentialism for philosophical reasons — if we accept Sartre's dictum that for existentialists existence precedes essence. But further discussion along the lines of such vague generalization would be fruitless.

The Relationship Between the Religious and the Philosophical

Since both religion and philosophy attempt to find meaning in life, or, as some might prefer to say, assign it a meaning, it will be important to define the relationship between religion and philosophy in Levinas. This is especially true since already there are signs of a controversy forming about whether Levinas is primarily a philosopher or a religious (Jewish) thinker.

In his attempt to get at the essence of religion (see the end of chapter 3 in *Otherwise than Being*), Levinas develops a theoretical view of the relationship between philosophy and religion. Even more specifically, he pursues an inquiry into the essence of Judaism, or an interpretation of Judaism. (Is not such an attempt to be expected of the thoughtful heritors of every religious tradition?) There is also a body of texts, the talmudic readings, in which Levinas does not attempt to view Judaism from above, but to pursue a certain hermeneutic practice that is within the tradition of talmudic interpretation and commentary. In the realization of these talmudic readings many of the ideas subsequently developed within the more purely theoretical format of philosophical writing are given a first exposure. Perhaps for Levinas the creative moment was favored by the more welcoming milieu of fellow Jewish intellectuals. This circumstance might give rise to the view that Levinas's philosophy is no more than a very sophisticated and elaborate theological apologetics for his religious beliefs, cast in philosophical form. I am convinced that this view would be mistaken; nor am I alone in rejecting it. A recent study of Levinas justifies its approach in the following terms. "If I have adopted the policy of reading Levinas in a strictly philosophical way, and of bracketing the Judaism that he professes openly, and in which I have no competency, it is because his major works are truly philosophical and certainly not a simple transposition of any sort of Jewish theology into a pseudo-philosophical discourse." An admirably clear and unexceptionable position, up to this point at least. But the author (Étienne Feron) goes further, and draws support for his approach from Levinas himself, in the distinction the latter makes between "signification" and "sens" (the former being a meaning based on a particular cultural orientation, and the latter a "sense" prior to history: contextless, an-archic or without beginning). "Moreover, in keeping with the distinction Levinas himself established between cultural meanings and *sense*, understood as the fundamental orientation that marks all meaning, I am convinced that a properly philosophical attitude is characterized by the fact that its questioning has a sense and a significance that transcend the cultural situation in which it unfolds."[9]

The problem with this is that it reduces Judaism to a cultural manifestation (which it is **also**, but not **only**, for Levinas), and grants philosophy an atemporal status that it certainly does not enjoy in Levinas, being unmistakably "Greek," and (however transcendent it may be in intent) historically determined. In fact, the text in Levinas to which Feron refers us (in a footnote to the above-quoted text) is "Meaning and Sense," and that essay's thesis is precisely that "before culture and aesthetics, meaning is situated in the ethical, presupposed by all culture and all meaning."[10] If this is the case, Judaism has at least as good a claim to giving access to that primordial *sens* as philosophy — and possibly a better one.

More will be said, in its place, on the topic of religion and philosophy as institutions in Levinas, and of the way in which they are relativized within his writings. One issue deserves preliminary mention: Levinas's view that there was, or is, creation, and that the human being is a created being, or creature. This premise was not considered to be an intrusion of the religious into the philosophical realm among the philosophers of earlier periods, since the question of origins was viewed as a legitimate area of philosophical speculation, and creation seemed to be a viable alternative, perhaps even the only alternative, to the eternity of the world, which was Aristotle's position. Since the advent of evolutionary theory, an opposition between "creationism" and "evolution" has developed. As far as I know, there is no mention of this opposition in Levinas's work at all. My surmise is that

Levinas correctly perceived that evolution is not an answer to the problem of "the" origin at all in any absolute, philosophical sense, but just to the problem of the origin of species. Although Levinas denounces the error of those who think of creation in ontological terms (and *a fortiori* in terms of the creation of matter), it is clear that he views humans as in some sense creatures of God.

These matters have contributed to an aura of controversy surrounding Levinas. It is a largely inarticulate controversy, if I may be permitted that paradoxical formulation. It is as if Levinas's mode of discourse, using as it does such terms as "transcendence," "the Good," "the infinite" and even "God" — placed it off limits to the "tough minded" tribe of philosophers. And there are other signals of alarm. Levinas has attracted the interest of an ever growing number of individuals who do not have a particularly strong background in philosophy but feel attracted by a certain urgency in the texts or a relevance to their lives — an interest that academic philosophers may find suspect, prompting them to conclude that texts attracting such attention may be suspect as well.

I hope that my drawing attention to these circumstances will not be taken as a gesture to win sympathy for the thinker whose work I have undertaken to introduce. My motivation is in fact quite different. After considerable research and reflection I have come to believe that what is most distinctive — and perhaps most valuable and original as well — about this thinker's work is the mixture of the philosophical and the hermeneutic or interpretive mode that it offers. The latter mode is deeply interrelated to the Judaic aspect of his work.

Levinas himself drew attention to the two categories into which his writings could be classified: his philosophical and his "confessional" writing, as he was amused to call them — the latter category comprising his four volumes of talmudic readings, but also his anthology of essays and articles, *Difficult Freedom*. The approach I follow in the present study features the interplay between these two aspects of Levinas's work as they clarify and complete each other. Given the conditions of thought, i.e. the general intellectual situation, of many contemporary readers, this double appurtenance may be particularly welcome. I, too, have felt the inner tension, the "underlying rending of a world attached to both the philosophers and the prophets" to which Levinas refers,[11] and which he believed characterizes our age. A careful reading of the relationship between eschatology and philosophy in the preface to *Totality and Infinity* will reveal Levinas's extraordinary philosophical project to be no less than a critique of the whole of Western philosophy, by establishing the primacy of the infinite in relation to the totality.[12]

The infinite and transcendence are the two key terms that mediate Levinas's project. I will follow the working out of this revision of the philosophical tradition presently. Suffice it to say that the *déchirement*, the inner rending, may indeed have been overcome independently in the philosophical and the Judaic writings; in my own experience of the texts, however, I find it helpful to follow the progress and modalities of this novel and challenging resolution in both registers in tandem, and to be able to weave my way between the two. They complement each other like light and warmth.[13] Salomon Malka describes the Jewish/philosophical relation in Levinas's works as follows.

> It is that infinite conversation between philosophy and Judaism that constitutes Levinas's work, giving it its power of universality. His personal approach has the double effect of giving his philosophy its specific tone because it is imbued with Judaism, and his Judaism a particular tenor because imbued with philosophy. The two universes touch and nourish one another without overlapping.[14]

It is possible to distinguish three stages in Levinas's thought with respect to ontology. Setting out from the existentialist-inspired *il y a* (the "there is")[15] of the earlier pieces, we move on to the opposition between totality and infinity, and finally to a characterization of being that makes it possible to envisage a "beyond being." But ontology is not primary in Levinas's philosophy because his thought is centered on the meaning of transcendence, and that meaning is described as the relation between the *moi* and the other person, a relation designated as different than all other relations — if it can even be said to be a relation. An important part of this study will therefore focus on that "relation," the main traits of which are asymmetry, diachrony, infinity, and an-archy.

For the purposes of exposition, I shall begin already in this introduction by presenting in a simplified, and therefore not entirely accurate way, a few of the most salient features of Levinas's philosophy, without regard for the developmental periods I have just mentioned.

Two Realms

There are two realms: being, and otherwise than being.[16] The rule (or *arche*), of being is the *conatus essendi*, a Latin expression used by Spinoza to designate the "effort to be" and frequently used by Levinas. Since this is the realm of being, Levinas refers to it as the domain of ontology. This effort to be is characterized by hardness, competition, simultaneity and strife; there is a tendency for physical objects to resist change from the outside, to continue being whatever they are, if only by "passive resistance." On the vital level, this takes the form of the struggle for survival. On the specifically human level, egotism and possessiveness are added. Yet the human — that is, human subjectivity — is, or can be, a movement of transcendence toward otherwise than being. The self, which is essentially first-personal, is referred to as the *moi* and is "riveted" to its identity and anchored in being; the *soi* (or Self) or the *un* (the "one") is that subjectivity which is not absorbed by being, but is rather obsessed by, and hostage to, the other (person). It is responsible for the other, even though there has been no freely assumed responsibility. This responsibility is prior to any conscious taking up of the other on my part. The *moi*, or selfish self, is said to be "denucleated" or hollowed out by the other as it becomes transformed into a "for-the-other," or *soi*. The *soi* is in turn inspired but also beleaguered by the other.

Otherwise than being is not non-being, or nothingness, or a being otherwise. Its positive characterization is problematic, and will be discussed further in chapter 3, "Saying/Said."

Relations Between the Two Realms

Transcendence, which begins by being the movement of the subject toward an outside, or objectivity, eventually reveals itself as metaphysical: the movement from being to otherwise than being. Other in a stronger sense than the other of objects is the otherness of the other person, as revealed through the Face. The realm of the otherwise than being is distinguished by being **anarchic**, i.e. without *arche* — arche understood as beginning, rule or principle. It is "a past that never was present." It is the locus (although locus is here used improperly, as neither time nor place pertain properly to this realm, and even the term realm must be taken figuratively) of God, the Infinite, and subjectivity.

It is in the area of social philosophy, or what Levinas calls sociality, that the relation between being and otherwise than being is the most available for scrutiny. Levinas's shorthand or symbolic representation of this relation is the relation between love and justice. Justice is necessary in order to carry out the intentions of love in the world of sociality.

The Other, and Ethics

Ethics is the relationship between the other person and one-self. The relation to the other is **asymmetric**: the other is always greater than me. Although it may seem that this relation of the couple (the I-Thou relationship, to use Martin Buber's term) is first or primary, Levinas points out on several occasions that the **third party** is already present in the face of the other. The relation to the other is non-indifference, potentially love, while the consideration of the third party brings with it the need for jus-tice — which necessitates and justifies various institutions, such as courts of law and human rights. Justice remains itself justified by the love of the other that is at its basis. The relation between the other and the one (in *Totality and Infinity* between the other and the same) is called "proximity." It is described in terms that are ethical and affective.

This is Not an Ethics of Resolve, or Willpower

In most discussions of morality, the will plays an important, perhaps the most important role. Temptation as a force that tests the resolve and sets the stage for a spiritual battle seems to be absent from Levinas's considerations. This is because the "intrigue of the infinite" that he describes and analyzes is prior to the domain of the will and of freedom.

> Freedom is put into question by the other, and is revealed to be unjustified, only when it knows itself to be unjust. Its knowing itself to be unjust is not something added on to spontaneous and free consciousness, which would be present to itself and know itself to be, *in addition*, guilty. A new situation is created; con-sciousness's presence to itself acquires a different modality, its positions collapse. To put it in purely formal terms, the same does not recover its priority over the other, it does not rest peaceably in itself, is no longer the principle.[17]

Rather than as an ethics of willpower or strength, it would be more appropriate to speak in terms of an ethics of weakness or of sensitivity and exposure. The imperative "Thou shalt not kill" that Levinas discerns in the face of the other is an imperative dictated by vulnerability and weakness, making it impossible to be aggressive. "Our age," writes Levinas on the occasion of the second anniversary of the death of his friend Jacob Gordin, "certainly no longer needs to be convinced of the value of non-violence. But perhaps it lacks a new reflection on passivity, on a certain weakness that is not cowardice, a certain patience that we must not preach to others, and within which the *moi* must restrict itself and that cannot be treated in negative terms as simply the reverse side of finitude."[18]

Although I have chosen the point of view of the master trope of interiority/exteriority, it is not my ambition in the following chapters to survey Levinas's philosophy from above in a startlingly new way. Not that such an overview is impossible or undesirable; but my hope is rather to open the work, to identify points of possible entry, to unravel certain texts along the lines of the questions I would like to put to them. My selection, in part 1, of a few key concepts and binary oppositions that run through the work will function as those points of possible entry. This approach has two features to recommend itself: it cannot be seen as in any way suggesting that the texts themselves, which are extremely rich in conceptual connotation, do not say incomparably well what they have to say; and it invites the reader to the task of elaborating his or her own interpretation, on the basis of further questions.

I also have my own interests, biases and predilections, clearly reflected in the themes that I have chosen in part 2. My first dealings with Levinas's texts were those of a translator. A translation is always a first interpretation. It is therefore with great pleasure that I can now allow myself, in the form of commentary (part 3), to interpret certain selected texts in a more personal way, and with fewer formal constraints than those of translator.

By and large the following texts, under rubrics that still bear the mark of classifiers for ongoing research, remain philologically close to the body of the work that Levinas has left us. Others in the field have focused their efforts more directly on the transmission or critical examination of the philosophical arguments and teachings of Levinas. My condition may bear more affinities with the diremption of the women (and Apollodorus) who, at the beginning and the end of the *Phaedo*, cling with less composure than the others to the body of Socrates.[19] This predilection for the signifier over the signified, less common in the philosophical than the literary or esthetic fields, may be more justifiable now, since the departure of the "signifier" himself. Because my previous role has been predominantly that of translator, this closeness to the text is habitual with me. The result drifts between interpretation and analysis: a freed translation, the movements of which become ever broader, more ex-centric.

Because of the inevitable distance that separates Levinas's French expression from the English reader and because of a well-founded preference in philosophical translations for literalness to the greatest degree possible, I sometimes prefer the technique of paraphrasing the original text fairly closely, hoping thereby to bridge the gap translation leaves and to naturalize Levinas's thought more thoroughly.

Unless otherwise attributed, all translations are my own. Levinas occasionally uses italics for emphasis, as is the custom in French. I have scrupulously retained them in translation. It is useful, however, for me to emphasize certain words in the quoted material when interpreting Levinas. I have therefore used **bold type** for my emphasis, which may not be otherwise indicated in each instance.

In the conclusion, which regroups and intensifies my questions and tries to resolve some of them, I venture a few ideas within the more tenuously associated realm of a Levinasian "unthought." Part of the role of a great author is to "authorize," or make possible, beyond what he or she has authored. This statement should not be construed as implying that my prolongations or innovations are to be read as speaking in the name of Levinas, of course, but merely as the grateful recognition of indebtedness.

PART ONE

Concepts

No philosopher begins entirely anew. In a sense, by taking as my point of departure an analysis of selected concepts, I begin with what is least specific to this thinker. But not only does every philosopher come to a much labored vineyard, so that his originality is manifested largely by his choice of available concepts; even those that are rejected often have a determinative influence on what is to come. Thus, Levinas's early rejection of the all-inclusiveness of "being" (see below, chapter 15) eventually led him to his most original, most controversial and difficult concept, namely that of an "otherwise-than-being."[1]

The following sets of binary oppositions will afford us strategic points of entry into Levinas's thought. Seldom if ever do the concepts taken up from the tradition remain unchanged. Some of them, such as **Totality/Infinity**, are far from being diametrical oppositions; others — **Sacred/Holy** for example, are not commonly distinguished. Since it is within the linguistically polarized space of these opposing concepts that Levinas's most intense philosophical developments unfold, it is from them that this study sets out.

Concepts or ideas? The Talmudist scholar David Banon, in an article devoted to Levinas's concept of "the face" as it relates to

the interpretation of the meaning of Abraham's binding of Isaac
in Genesis 22, rejects the term "concept," preferring "idea." He
prefers the latter "[i]nsofar as the concept is what allows us to
give an account of the real, of the entirety of the real, and to grasp
it by absorbing it within a network of relations; whereas certain
dimensions of reality cannot be assimilated or converted into
knowledge because they exceed this type of relation."[2] This terminological scruple, obviously laden with philosophical consequences, is already interpretive, and ultimately linked with Levinas's
view of the direction taken by the Western philosophical tradition, and the advantage it gives to the relation of immanence over
transcendence. Since my concern here is not — at the outset at
least — to speak from within Levinas's mode of thought, but to
highlight the articulations between that thought and the conceptual landscape within which it unfolded in France during the last
century, I will retain the more neutral term here.[3]

The **Totality/Infinity** distinction is followed by that of **Same/
Other**, which is probably the most fundamental element of
Levinas's entire problematics. His later philosophy becomes
increasingly centered upon language **(Saying/Said)**, and what
would seem to be, by definition, an insurmountable difficulty: the
expression of the ineffable. Levinas has characterized philosophy
itself as "an indiscretion with regard to the unsayable."[4] **Being/
beyond** (or otherwise than) **Being**, takes up many of the same
difficulties on an ontological plane. The **Person/Thing** dichotomy
will occasion an exploration of Martin Buber's contribution, and
also help situate Levinas's thought within the spectrum of current philosophy, particularly physicalism. **Ontology/Metaphysics**
brings the discussion to Levinas's rejection of both pre- and post-
Heideggerian ontology, while the last chapter of this section, the
Sacred/Holy (or Sacred/Saintly), takes us to the heart of Levinas's
religious and ethical thought.

1. TOTALITY/INFINITY

The fundamental importance of this opposition is reflected in the title of Levinas's major 1961 work *Totality and Infinity*. Although the opposition between totality and infinity is not a dialectical one in the Hegelian sense, it would be a mistake, as the French philosopher Pierre Hayat warns us, to think that Levinas is inviting us to choose between infinity and totality.[5] This chapter begins with a synopsis of two short pieces by Levinas on "totality" and "infinity" as independent concepts in the history of philosophy, before moving on to the specific way in which they are used by Levinas and their role in his philosophy.

Two Short, Formal Treatments: The Entries in the Encyclopaedia Universalis

In 1968 Levinas wrote two articles to be included in the *Encyclopaedia Universalis*: "Totalité et totalisation" and "Infini."[6] Pierre Hayat suggests that they may be read "as a response, perhaps, to the reproach that Levinas makes an overly personal, and slightly equivocal use of the categories of totality and infinity."[7] These two succinct treatments of totality and infinity will prove useful in leading off our consideration of each of these important philosophical concepts in the philosophy of Levinas. The fact that they were written about midway between the publication of Levinas's two major works (*Totality and Infinity*, 1961 and *Otherwise than Being or Beyond Essence*, 1974) makes them particularly valuable in gaining insight into the movement of his thought in this interim period.

"Totality and Totalization"

"Totality and Totalization" begins with a quick summary of Kantian and Aristotelian views on the subject, then moves on to the idea of an extrapolation from empirical totalities to the abstract notion of an all-inclusive totality that leaves nothing outside. Levinas traces the relationship between the totality that vision can encompass and the purely logical thought of totality — an empty generality, the pure thought of the thinkable. The logical totality is subject to both analysis and synthesis, which move toward — and stop at — some smallest or largest, respectively. But may such analyses not go beyond the province of the true or untrue? asks Levinas. Here he is thinking of the true or untrue as that which does or does not correspond to the way things are in the spatiotemporal world.

This further opposition — that of thought as restricted to and modeled along the lines of the experiential, contrasted with the thought that goes beyond being, the thought of the infinite relation of proximity between human beings — is a central motif in Levinas's work. Levinas finds in Kant a basis for the distinction he makes, although the main thrust of the latter's noumenal/phenomenal distinction was inspired by his desire to overcome Humean skepticism, and to do so by declaring the noumenal world to be unknowable in principle, and therefore within the realm of the decisional, the "practical" or ethical.[8] Levinas then touches upon the Hegelian totality; it is no longer the completion of a perceptual whole, or representation, but the whole of being, with its organized parts, moving toward the concrete universal. Next, he introduces totality in the context of hermeneutics: the interdependence between the whole and the part. Finally, since Western thought has emerged out of a Greco-Judeo-Christian tradition, Levinas discusses the "troubling" element of transcendence, to which totality presents a negative aspect. Part 1, "The Whole in Intuition," decompresses this extremely condensed material.

In this part Levinas attends to the Gestalt notion of a perceptual whole and reviews the main distinctions between wholes drawn by the Ancients (natural wholes, i.e. wholes of *phusai*; wholes with no distinguishable parts, or *pan*; wholes with distinguishable parts and a specific ordering of them, or *holon*). This portion ends with a thumbnail description of Husserl's notion of the totality of the object, with its content and horizon.

In part 2, "Totality without Reality," Levinas takes up the distinction Kant makes between reason and understanding. Science can give conditions, but never gets to the ultimate condition, which reason requires. Totality remains a regulative idea, or an "idea in the Kantian sense." The section ends with a question. "Since the absolute does not lend itself to totalization, one may wonder whether intelligibility is reducible to comprehension, to an encompassing without remainder." We have here an intimation of Levinas's assertion that there is meaning (*il y a du sensé*) beyond comprehension, or beyond the sort of knowledge that has being as its object.

Part 3, "Truth Is the Totality," begins by denying truth to the Kantian tradition of knowledge, which remains too close to the immediacy of the given, or intuition, and is ultimately only a "view" of the truth. True thought is a breaking away from the immediacy of the given, a Platonic seeing of "the sun itself in its place of sojourn" and not its myriad reflections. Thus, the true function of totalizing thought is not to look at being but to determine it by organizing it. History is totalization. Levinas cites the Hegelian sense of history, putting it (provisionally) in its best light. The nineteenth century believed itself to be the dawn of a lucid and free humanity.

"The Hermeneutic Totality" (part 4) describes the sort of totality (*holon*) in which there is a circularity between the part and the whole, in which the meaning of the part is its relation to the whole, yet of a whole that only has meaning as the whole of the parts. This is Heidegger's hermeneutic circle, in which analysis and synthesis presuppose one another. It is contrasted with the habits of the Cartesian understanding, which moves from the simple to the complex, making the totality a simple summation of the parts. Levinas finds in this hermeneutic circle "a conception in which, in an incessant to-and-fro movement, totality validates the part, which would justify a religious or personalist conception of man at the heart of creation, of which he would be both part and end."

In part 5, "Beyond Totality," Levinas recalls the notion of a "totalized" universe that the pre-Socratics intuited in their assertions that "all" is this or that (water, fire, air, earth). Next he lists historic instances in which the concept of totality is seen as falling short: in the dualism of forces and values in Anaximander, in the good and the notion of a beyond Being in Plato and Plotinus; in the transcendence of the prime mover — a transcendent God that is not in the same totality as the creature. Levinas also lists Bergson's *durée*, and Rosenzweig's critique of the Western totality: God, human and the world are no longer a unity. "Do man and man form a totality any more than do these?" asks Levinas. The implication is clear: they do not.

In the last paragraph of this article Levinas points out that the failure of totality is not purely negative. It indicates a new relation, that of "diachronic time." The concrete accomplishment of such a relationship is the proximity between man and man, with no overarching synthesis possible. It is from this relationship that the State draws its meaning. "Humanity would not be, on this view, one domain among those of the real, but the modality in which rationality and its peace are articulated wholly otherwise than in the totality." It is this modality, this "wholly otherwise" that constitutes the most challenging and original part of Levinas's philosophy.

"Infinity"

This entry, a short essay, is divided into three parts and prefaced by two long and dense paragraphs that summarize the provenance of the concept of infinity. Its first use is to designate unlimited *quanta*, stretching either to absolute greatness or absolute exiguity. But it can also be used for superlative qualities, particularly superhuman ones, rising above specific qualitative excellences: in neo-Platonism, the Infinite One, which rejoins the perspective of Plato's Good beyond being; the one God of the Hebrew Bible, introduced by Christianity into European history. The Bible does not use the word infinite, but refers to a power beyond all powers, of unknowable ways — which, Levinas mentions in passing, poses an obvious epistemological problem, a problem thematized in his work, *Of God Who Comes to Mind* (1982). The God of Descartes is perfect and of unlimited, spontaneous will, as is, in a sense, the will of man. Free will and the infinite, without transcendence, characterize German idealism. The will to power (Nietzsche) is a transcendence of man himself, the super-man; and in a philosophy that considers transcendence beyond the reach of thinking by finite man (Kant, though not mentioned by name, is clearly intended), the infinite is a regulative idea, corresponding to nothing within being but guiding the science of the finite.

The second paragraph groups Spinoza and Hegel, for whom being has no "other": nonbeing does not qualify as other, as it is merely the negation of being. Transcendence is not the only way, Levinas says, of going beyond all limitations. A being that has no other would thereby be infinite. (This does not appear to be so for Heidegger, for whom being is finite and without "other.") For both Spinoza and Hegel, being is infinite, therefore, and its infinity discernible by means of intuition in the first case (different from imagination) and spirit in the second. Hegel's philosophy is qualified as totalizing, a philosophy in which all otherness is assimilated into the same. Indeed, there is considerable justification for the view that the other limits and threatens the same (e.g. in warfare). But the other person, *autrui*,[9] who is qualified as "the absolute other," is not just a threat. The face-to-face encounter with the other is credited with the potential of freeing the *moi* from itself. This departure of the subject from the limitation of itself — in the reflections of philosophers from Feuerbach and Kierkegaard to Buber and Gabriel Marcel — also deserves the adjective "infinite."

Part 1 of this entry is titled "The Problems of the Infinite." These problems arise from the problem of knowledge. Knowledge is the manifestation of what is, or the existent, to a conscious being. It is both the representation of the given and a going beyond the given. The given offers certain traits and withholds others. Its "essence" (being) is definite. If that limitation is construed as excluding only other "possibles," what shows itself does so against a background of a chaotic infinity, disturbing our knowing. In that case, essence or being would be finite, finished as a work of art is finished. But in fact, Levinas tells us, the knowledge that receives the given also refuses (presumably other) givens. The given not only excludes possible givens; it is an abstraction taken from the totality of the real that stretches beyond it on all sides. It is as if knowledge went beyond the given, without having to measure the height or degree of that beyond. This section furnishes a general background for various historical approaches, the last being the Hegelian unfolding of the infinite into manifestation.

Part 2, "The Historical Givens," begins with a section devoted to "the bad infinite." The negative view of the infinite as the indefinite or *apeiron* is the counterpart of the positive clarity and intelligibility of the "cosmos." The views of the Ancients on the question of the infinite are reviewed. Since only a few of these historical elements are relevant to Levinas's own philosophy, however, I shall be selective in my synopsis of them. Plato's "parricide" against Parmenides consists in asserting that nothingness in a certain sense is. He places the idea of the Good beyond being, thus founding the idea of an infinite that is not merely quantitative, and that will be taken up by the neo-Platonists. Thomas Aquinas identifies Aristotle's notion of pure form with the God of the Hebrew Bible, and Hegel recognizes, in Aristotle's actual infinity of the Absolute, the thought of thought. Nevertheless, this notion of the infinite seems to remain faithful to the older sense of the infinite as the endlessness of a *quantum*. Hence Levinas's second subtitle is "The Divine Infinite." Here the influence of the orient on patristic Christianity is adduced. In this new sense of infinity (Plotinus, but also the En-Sof of postbiblical Judaism) there is no longer an incompatibility between the infinite and the finite or definite forms, since the latter are contained within the former and emanate from it. Some thinkers, such as Origen, advise against the direction of those who, "for the simple love of beautiful language," deny any limitations in God, because that would render him unknowable. But after him there is no such restraint, and God consequently becomes inconceivable. Aquinas makes God infinite and the creation finite: the idea of a created infinity is absurd in his view. Finitude has become a sign of imperfection. It is not until the Renaissance that the finite world of Antiquity's astronomical system will become open to the infinite.

Only the human soul can receive the attribute of infinity. Nicolas of Cusa develops a notion of God as implicitly one and infinite, while at the same time (as world) explicitly multiple and finite — in a manner similar to that of the Kabbalists. Descartes, Leibniz, Newton and Kant (prior to the *Critique of Pure Reason*) affirm the infinity of the natural world, and connect it with the infinity of God and the excellence of the creation. Kant, in his *Critique of Practical Reason*, gives infinity a meaning for free or moral action, and this opens the way for the speculative philosophy of post-Kantian idealism.

The next subsection, "All is Infinite," presents Spinoza's doctrine of *natura naturans* and *natura naturata*, both of which are infinite, and then shows how Hegel introduces negativity into infinite being as the process of determination — the result of which is the concept. Levinas stresses the totalization of the Hegelian system, which absorbs the other. Individual consciousness is nothing more than the work of the infinite enclosing itself in the given. The totality is not a simple piling up of existents, but absolute thought asserting itself as absolute freedom, i.e. as act, efficient thought, actual infinity. The finite, asserts Hegel, is that which is posited with its immanent boundary as contradiction to itself, since its frontier necessarily alludes to what is beyond it, namely infinity. It is the very modality according to which the infinite reveals itself. This self-revelation is knowledge, and (self) knowledge is the event of the Absolute. From Hegel we move forward in time to "The Finite without Infinite."

In this subsection, Kant's critical philosophy posits the finite and the infinite in a new way. Finite nature is perceived as finite because of the finite nature of humans. Nature *qua* phenomenon is thus conditioned by the finitude of the perceiver, the human person. The infinite becomes a regulative idea, not constitutive of the given. Phenomenology carries forward the notion of the infinite as non-actual, as the horizon within which the finite given appears. In Heidegger the finitude of being is not the negation of the infinite. Finitude is described on the basis of certain positive notions, such as being-in-the-world, care, and being-toward-death. Heidegger begins with finite temporality, and through a process of leveling off the series of "nows," and of "publicity," derives infinite time.[10] Levinas quotes Heidegger's statement at the end of the latter's *Kant and the Problem of Metaphysics*, suggesting that nothing is more radically repugnant to ontology than the idea of infinite being. Time as *durée* (duration, as understood by Bergson and adopted by Heidegger) is interiority and the infinity of the possible. But is there not, hidden in the depths of this infinitude of the possible, the bad infinite, the endless repetition of Maurice Blanchot (which Levinas will call the *il y a* or the "there is")? In concluding this section, Levinas points out the new meaning Heidegger has given to the finite and the infinite: they should not be used as attributes of beings, i.e. entities (French, *des étants*, German, *die Seienden*) but of being (French, *l'être*, German *das Sein*), and understood on the ontological level.

The last part of the entry, "Infinity and Ethics," is the most directly pertinent to Levinas's own philosophy. As is usual with him, he introduces his own thesis in the form of a leading question. In the context of knowledge in which infinity appears in Western thought, the infinite absorbs the finite. But in its divinization of the infinite, has not the specifically religious divinity of the God who made it possible for the idea of the infinite to dominate Western rationalism been lost? The infinite has become so enmeshed in epistemological questions that any relation to the infinite that is not conceptual appears naïve. Is there not another route? Levinas suggests the Cartesian one, in which the presence of the idea of the infinite, too large for the soul of the creature, exalts rather than afflicts the latter. He further suggests that the alterity of the infinite is not to be reduced, but to become proximity and responsibility. Proximity is not a failed coincidence, but an incessant, infinite, and glorious increase of alterity. In conclusion, Levinas identifies a current within contemporary philosophy that denies the possibility (or appropriateness) of reducing the interpersonal to the objectification and thematization of knowledge, and identifies his own approach with the religious tradition of the idea of the infinite.

Philosophy and the Idea of Infinity

Earlier and more personal in tone than the two entries in the *Encyclopaedia Universalis*, the essay "Philosophy and the Idea of Infinity"[11] is an important prototext for *Totality and Infinity*, which was written four years later. In the introduction to the second edition of *En découvrant l'existence avec Husserl et Heidegger*,

(1965), Levinas alludes to the relation between the two texts. "The text Philosophy and the Idea of the Infinite has, since 1957, been expressed in the form of a book." The clarity and urgency of his original statement make it an invaluable document in its own right, as well as the best introduction to *Totality and Infinity*.

This short piece (14 pages in the original French) is composed of six parts, the last four of which deal specifically with infinity. The first two are devoted to the establishment, within Western philosophy, of the historic choice between autonomy and heteronomy, the penchant for autonomy, and the connection between autonomy,[12] freedom and atheism. Socrates' maieutic method of instruction limits the intrusiveness even of the master into the pupil's unfolding of an inner knowledge. But very rapidly this autonomy leads to the exclusion of the transcendent and to the primacy of the same. The other is the obstacle that must be overcome or assimilated if my freedom is to be maintained. Levinas next critiques idealism and — after the introduction of the idea that the same requires for its mediation the "neuter," an abstract essence "that is, and isn't," in which the other is "dissolved," as a preparatory step toward assimilation — directly critiques Heidegger. It is a critique of knowledge (*la connaissance*) first, which "consists in grasping the individual, which alone exists, not in its singularity which does not count, but in its generality, of which alone there is science;"[13] secondly it is the critique of the natural sequel or fulfillment of this modality of knowledge, which is power, mastery, ownership, riches. This critique reappears with little modification (though materialism is added to the charge) in part 7 of the "Conclusions" of *Totality and Infinity*.

If things cannot resist assimilation to the same through the "ruses of thought," what of human beings? Their resistance is war; but even to be overcome by the opponent does not destroy their freedom *de jure*. Here Levinas announces what will become axiomatic to all of his subsequent philosophy: "Freedom is put into question by the other, and is revealed as being unjustified only when it knows itself to be unjust."[14]

The precise nature of this new knowing, however, must be sharply differentiated from that of the acquisitive knowledge referred to earlier. Levinas will have to "clarify these formulations," but the result is that "if the same does not peaceably rest on itself, philosophy does not seem to be indissolubly bound up with the adventure that includes every other in the same."[15]

A difficult pass for philosophy: If it **includes** the other it thereby destroys it as unique other. But surely the recommendation is not to simply ignore the other. The rest of the piece elaborates on this paradoxical relationship between philosophy and the other.

Part 2, "The Idea of the Infinite," begins by announcing the intention of embracing an equally ancient tradition, and one that does not "read 'right' into 'might' and does not reduce *every other* to the same." Philosophy for Heidegger and the neo-Hegelians begins with atheism, but Levinas argues that the philosophy of the other is not necessarily religious: it, too, is philosophical. Again Plato is invoked, but this time in defense of the philosophy of the other, not the same. It is Plato who places the Good beyond being, and it is Descartes who expresses the idea of the Infinite in us. In thinking the infinite, thought thinks more than it thinks. The infinite does not fit into the "idea" of the infinite. It is not grasped. That idea is not a concept. It is the absolutely other. And it has been put into us; hence the passivity that is associated with that heteronomy.

One may be tempted to ask at this point when this idea of the infinite was put into us. Was it at the moment of creation? If that is the case, there is a premise of creation here. And if it was put in us at that moment, when did we lose the realization, which has to be activated through the encounter with the other? Now it may be that these questions can be — not answered, but kept from coming up, by Levinas's distinction between the diachronic and the synchronic, and his concept of an-archy. At this point, we can only say that the hypothesis of creation is no more or less justifiable than the Greek hypothesis that being always was. The notion of diachrony seems designed to avoid our placing creation within

the created universe and attempting to assign it a time and place
within that finitude. Levinas's philosophy is not an ontology. It
is a metaphysics of which, he says, there is no physics.

Part 4, "The Idea of the Infinite and the Face of the Other,"
opens with the thought that our experience of the infinite is in
the relation to the other. It is social. The face of the other "for-
bids me my conquest." But it is a forbidding that brings about a
change within me. "The structure of my freedom is, as we shall
see further, completely reversed." If the other simply resisted my
power with his or her power, my power might be overcome. But
this would not give access to an exterior being, which cannot be
enveloped or possessed, and in which our freedom renounces its
imperialism of self. The other is not just another freedom; in order
to give me the knowledge of injustice, its look must come to me
from a dimension of the ideal. The other must be closer to God
than I am. And that is "certainly not a philosopher's invention,"
but the first given of moral consciousness, which could be defined
as consciousness of the privilege that the other has relative to me.
Justice, no more than charity, begins at home, but with the other.

Part 5, "The Idea of Infinity as Desire," takes up themes that
will be fully developed in *Totality and Infinity*. But already here
Levinas introduces his idea of infinity as desire, distancing himself from Descartes. While espousing Descartes' view that the
infinite must have been put into us, Levinas rejects the notion of
the infinite as a possible object of contemplation. Our relation to
the infinite, without being merely subjective, is that of a thought
that thinks more than it thinks. That formulation leads to the notion
of the thought of the infinite as desire, since the intentional object
of desire has the characteristics of being both "greater than" what
we possess, and of "lacking." Desire is differentiated from need;
the former undermines or "hollows out" the desirer, and is not to
be satisfied by the possession of its object.

In part 6, "The Idea of Infinity and Conscience," it is suggested
that the idea of infinity is the demise of the good conscience of

the same. "For everything comes to pass as though the presence
of the face, the idea of infinity in the I, were the putting of my
freedom into question."[16] It is this recognition by the self (the
autonomous I) of its injustice that is the experience of the infinite.
And that realization is the other in the same, unsettling, causing
the downfall of my "good conscience." One of the important
corollaries of this idea makes itself felt in the political realm.
"In particular, modern political theories since Hobbes deduce
the social order from the legitimacy, the incontestable right, of
freedom."[17]

"Consciousness of my injustice is produced when I incline
myself not before the facts, but before the other. In his face the
other appears to me not as an obstacle, nor as a menace for me
to evaluate, but as that which measures me. For me to feel myself
to be unjust, I must measure myself against infinity."[18] This is
not a theoretical consideration, against which freedom might spontaneously take up its rights again. "It is a *shame* freedom has of
itself, discovering itself to be murderous and usurpatory in its
very exercise."[19] Freedom is not gratuitous, but invested. This
investiture of freedom constitutes moral life itself, which is through
and through a heteronomy. It is taking on the fate of the other or
responsibility for the other. God's commands, writes Levinas,
come to me only through the mouths of the needy, or those who
need my help.

The last paragraph of this important essay contrasts consciousness (*la conscience*) with conscience (*la conscience morale*). The
latter is normally considered an elaboration, an add-on, having a
more specialized preoccupation with values and norms. But Levinas
questions this. He asks: "Can the self present itself to itself with
so much natural complacency? Can it appear shamelessly, in its
own eyes? Is narcissism possible?"[20] One may wonder in exactly
what sense the words "can" and "possible" are being used here.
Is it "physical" or "ethical" responsibility? Levinas addresses the
question in a footnote to *Otherwise than Being*: "A purely ethical

impossibility is expressed in expressions such as 'impossible without shirking one's obligations,' 'without fault,' 'without sin.' If there were real impossibility, responsibility would be only an ontological necessity. But a 'purely ethical' impossibility is not a simple relaxation of an ontological impossibility. Being wanting, fault, sin, or as it can be put in a way more acceptable today, 'a complex' — that is not just a reality for the sheltered scions of upperclass families."[21]

The essay ends with the thought that the situation in which one is not alone (i.e. the real world) is "not reducible to the fortunate meeting of fraternal souls that greet one another and converse. This situation is the moral conscience, the exposedness of my freedom to the judgment of the other. It is the disalignment (*dénivellement*) which has authorized us to catch sight of the dimension of height and the ideal in the gaze of him to whom justice is due." This asymmetrical relationship with the "face" of the other person is the point at which Levinas's thinking departs from any system of thought that would attempt to generate an ethics from within being, i.e. within the ontological order of "essence." Levinas uses the French term *essence* in the sense of being.[22] There is no question here of developing a sense of mutuality, which has been widely considered to be the basis of morality,[23] out of an extrapolation from one's own case, whether in a rational, deontological manner, as in Kant (and Sartre), or as an empathetic transfer resembling that of identification with self through a Husserlian *Einfühlung*. As we shall see, the presence of the third party will mitigate the unbounded exigency of this morality of self and sole other. One might well ask the question, then: Why not introduce the principle of equality from the start? The answer lies, I think, in the fact that this "disalignment" (*dénivellement*) has "authorized" Levinas to glimpse "the dimension of height and the ideal in the gaze of him to whom justice is due."[24]

Definitions and Peculiarities of Usage in Levinas

For Levinas, the essential element of the notion of "totality" is closure. It is contrasted with the openness of infinity. The totality, in Levinasian usage, does not succeed in assimilating the goodness that is beyond being, and is limited to the ontological.

The term totality when used in its absolute sense would seem, by its very meaning, to include everything there is. This sense of all-inclusiveness is what is foremost in Levinas's use of the term. It is equated with being, or essence.

Much is at stake in the distinction that Levinas draws between totality and infinity. We are to think of an "outside" of the totality (which is intuited as closed) which constitutes an absolute break with both the totality and being. The aggressive agglutination of being, the modality of which is the insuperable Hegelian dialectic, necessitates this absolute break. The pertinent trait of that dialectic is its inexorable annexation of the negation to the affirmation. Hence Levinas insists that the otherwise than being is not non-being, which is a moment of Hegelian being, in the same way that "the man who flees is not yet free: in fleeing he is still conditioned by that from which he flees."[25]

But why is there a need for such a break? The very nature of reason would seem to militate against it. If our goal is coherence — a rational and systematic account of what is — the very idea of an absolute would seem undesirable, and highly questionable if not impossible. Is not all thinking a relating of some sort? Do not the prefixes, the in- (and its variants) and the non- and the a-, all indicate a relation to what they negate that belies their independence from the sway of their positive counterparts? Despite these considerable inconveniences, Levinas casts his philosophical lot with this "rupture," which runs through his entire work. Like any conceptual schema, its validity can only be assessed on the basis of what it makes possible. How does such a repartition reconfigure the landscape of philosophical thought?

My own view is that this mode of thought sheds new light on the nature of ethics, religion and humanism, to a degree that of itself justifies a serious attempt to understand Levinas's philosophy.

While the concept of the "infinite" as openness and transcendence is developed in the prototext summarized in the preceding section, along with the notion of the face and the ethics it mediates, the term "totality," which will enter so prominently into the thesis of *Totality and Infinity*, does not appear. It does appear, in great detail and repeatedly, in the talk Levinas gave at the second *Colloque des intellectuals juifs de langue française* in Versailles on September 27, 1959.[26] Levinas expressed his indebtedness to Franz Rosenzweig for his critique of the Hegelian totality. Levinas also attributes another important technical procedure of *Totality and Infinity* to Rosenzweig, that of reemploying theological concepts in philosophy: "Rosenzweig takes up theological concepts, then, and introduces them into philosophy as ontological categories."[27] The same has also been said of Levinas.

Of the two elements that make up this binary, totality is the negative one. It is derived from a combination of two critiques of Hegel: that of Kierkegaard in the early nineteenth century, and Rosenzweig's in the twentieth.[28] Kierkegaard's critique, as interpreted by Levinas, is essentially the one that grounds the new sense of "existence" to which the existentialists were later to turn, in securing a lineage. Levinas begins this essay with a paradox: Although idealism deserves the credit for having set the active subject at the center of our world, its development by Hegel into objective idealism seems to pass its essence over to the very world it was credited with discovering, if not originating. "It was as if a painter, upon completing his work, were to find himself caught up in the very painting beneath his brush, and transported to a world of his own creation."[29]

But Levinas's reading of Kierkegaard is not a full endorsement. Kierkegaard has wrongly described ethics as a generality.[30] "The singularity of the *I* would be lost under the rule that is valid for all."[31] But the relation of I to the other (and here Levinas addresses his critique to both Kierkegaard and Hegel) is not the disappearance of the former into generality; it is precisely the shattering of the totality through the relation to the face. Clearly the I represents a relative separation *qua* enjoyment and will, but in *Totality and Infinity* the other is credited with shattering the totality: "It is not I who resist the system, as Kierkegaard thought; it is the other."[32] This point will be taken up in chapter 14, below, in more detail, as it relates to Jacques Derrida's critique of Levinas.

Levinas's opposition to the totality and the neuter, which he associated with it, is at the basis of much of his critique of Heidegger, as well as his strenuous rejection of structuralism.[33]

From Infinity to Proximity

Levinas distinguishes the "bad" infinity, which represents an infinite repetition of the same, from the good infinity, which is associated with perfection, transcendence and God. Levinas's version of the bad infinity, the *il y a*, has nothing of the generosity of the Heideggerian *es gibt*, and is rather a menacing and impersonal world of chaotic being, devoid of (human) beings. It is out of this inhospitable chaos that, through the separation that is life, the self is formed. Within the "good infinity," we have seen the distinction drawn between the infinity of rationalism and that of the Hebrew Bible, which is described as a relation of a noncognitive variety. It is this latter notion that is at the basis of Levinas's understanding of proximity, which he will describe at considerable length in *Otherwise than Being*.

The concept of the "face," which indicates the presence of alterity, is the mediating concept by which the infinite is manifested in and to the finite. But the term "manifested" is not the proper term for any effect or action on the part of the infinite, since the latter is characterized by lack of manifestation. A demotion to the status of being would alter its quality of infinity. This is perhaps why Levinas develops the idea of "the trace," a more discreet form of evidence of the presence of the infinite within the finite.

But the face plays a somewhat diminished role in *Otherwise than Being*, the term itself appearing only a few times. It is dwarfed by "proximity." The approach to the other in proximity is infinite, in the sense that the closer we are the farther we are, and the more responsible we are the more inadequate, the more "accused" or "persecuted" by the other. This can only be meant — and understood — if there is a positive sense given to this accusation, or this existence in the accusative case, and this persecution. The same must be awakened or troubled by the other. Hence the goal of the *moi* cannot be serene tranquility. The dimension of proximity (proximity as the general name for the closeness/remoteness axis of experience) spans the next dichotomy that we will consider: that of same/other.

2. SAME/OTHER

The concepts of "same" and "other" are treated in Plato's dialogue, the *Sophist*, and they play a prominent role in the metaphysics of Hegel. What is new in Levinas's use of them is that he associates same with the "I" of subjectivity, and other with the other person and, in the form of illeity, with God.

From a purely logical point of view, same and other are diametrically opposed — and therefore interchangeable in the sense that same can be defined as the other of the other. Levinas uses the concept of same (often though not consistently capitalized in his work) to define the confinement of self within itself and its tendency, through knowledge, to annex otherness to itself by knowledge, possession, mastery. This "I," or naturally egotistical self, is designated as the *moi* in Levinas, a term I will transpose unchanged in this work, in order to preserve an important distinction that often becomes somewhat obscured in translation. Vital to Levinas's analysis of the relation between self and other is an undoing or emptying out of the self (*dénucléation*), as it is ethically solicited by the other. The self does not simply merge with the other in these circumstances, but is transformed into what Levinas calls the *soi*. The term *soi* means self in French, but not specifically myself, as does *moi*. It would be a mistake to try to draw too much from the normal usage of the word *soi*, however, in our attempt to grasp Levinas's usage, since *soi* is impersonal, and the transformation from *moi* to *soi* is described as one of not less but more "uniqueness." More precisely, the difference is really not of degrees of uniqueness but of the sort of uniqueness concerned.

The importance of the association of self with same in Levinas's thought can hardly be overestimated. In *Totality and Infinity*, more clearly than in *Otherwise than Being*, it is the self's confinement within itself that dramatizes the movement of transcendence; first the lower-level transcendence of perception and our dealings with the world of objects, and then the transcendence driven by "metaphysical" desire, which increases with the approach and "feeds, so to speak, on its hunger."[1]

It is the ineradicable anchoring of *moi* in same that introduces all the drama into Levinas's philosophy. The *corps propre* or "lived body" of phenomenology plays a similarly vivifying role in the philosophies of Husserl and Merleau-Ponty, but that implantation or incarnation of self is interpreted in the direction of a commonality or conaturality of self and world. Levinas's identification of knowledge and power with an imperialism of the self/same includes philosophy itself in this assimilative drive. Ultimately, only metaphysical otherness and transcendence, "exteriority" and infinity, can break through the advancing imperialism of same. It is not surprising that at the conclusion of *Totality and Infinity*, therefore, we should find embedded a quote from Baudelaire's "Fleurs du Mal," with its spiritual quest fueled by a *soif d'absolu*, a thirst for the absolute, for something new that would lead us out of our boredom, our *ennui*. Here Levinas is describing the false — tragic-heroic — solution of the Hegelian hero, but also of the Heideggerian one, who meets death with resolve. It is the solution of any salvific doctrine that seeks preservation of a self not previously "unselved" ("denucleated," in *Otherwise than Being*) by the "infinite time of fecundity."

> Heroic existence, the isolated soul, may make its peace in seeking an eternal life for itself as if its subjectivity could somehow not turn against itself in returning to a continuous time; as if, in this continuous time, identity itself did not affirm itself like an obsession, as if, in the identity that remains at the heart of the most extravagant metamorphoses, there did not triumph "ennui,

fruit of mournful incuriosity, which takes on the proportions of immortality.[2]

Description of the Moi in "The I and the Totality"

One might expect that, as in certain religious traditions, the self (the *moi* or selfish self) would be depicted negatively in Levinas. On the contrary, there is a marvelous vigor and freshness in Levinas's description of the *ipseity*, or unique identity of the self. The self is essentially separation and interiority. It sets itself up, an organism that thinks it is the world, in its own "economy," and is as it were the realization of a secret. Its egotism is not a vice, but its manner of being everything by being unaware of the outer world. Charlie Chaplin in *The Gold Rush* is unaware of the outside conditions except to the degree that they affect his balance inside his cabin as it plummets down a mountainside during a blizzard. He must, qua self, translate his inner experiences into hypotheses, since he has no direct opening onto the outer world. "If, stretched out on the floor, already a physicist, he gropes about, studying the elementary laws of those disorderly ups and downs and rejoins the world, it is precisely because he thinks."[3] This thinking has at its origin, however, a self-centered unconsciousness of exteriority, and this is what constitutes its freedom. It is never directly affected by the outer world: it lives beneath the sign of "liberty or death." Death is in fact a radical transcendence, but the end of thought. The deep affinity between metaphysics and death is that in the former case thought establishes a relation with the exterior, a consciousness that is both aware of its own particularity and of an exteriority beyond its nature: the infinite. In the latter case, when the instinctive system encounters the exterior as that which cannot be assimilated, the system dies.

The I-Thou relationship within the Same/Other

Levinas acknowledges (in *Proper Names*, and *Outside the Subject*) his indebtedness to Martin Buber, a pioneer (along with Gabriel Marcel) in the development of a philosophical interpretation of the significance of dialog. Buber's *I-Thou* describes two radically different ways in which the *I* relates to the other (person) and to things. Of course this is reflected in the formal, grammatical differences between the verb forms in the second and third "persons," but in fact the difference is that the subject-object model of knowledge is revealed to be fundamentally different than the I-Thou relationship. The latter is a listening, and the foundation of the ethical relationship of reciprocity upon which justice is based.

Levinas incorporates this relationship but denies its reciprocity or reversibility. Further, he sees it as the expression rather than the foundation of the self (or same)/other relationship. My responsibility for the other precedes anything explicitly said to the other, and there is less emphasis placed on the development of a friendship or spiritual affinity with the other through dialogue and more on a unilateral helping of him or her.

Beyond the Same/Other

There *is* a way in which something like a reversal or reciprocal relation between me and the other becomes possible ("by the grace of God," says Levinas), and that is when the "I" is recognized as another by the third. To give a rough summary, Levinas distinguishes two moments in the relation of self to other: first that of the couple, then that of sociality in a broader sense, since the third party — or "all the others" — is taken into account. That is the moment of justice, of law courts and a host of other institutions. All of these institutions are justified and even necessitated by love, which is in the I-Thou relation. Levinas admits that this is an analysis in the realm of timeless theory, and that in fact the others are always already present. I, too, can ultimately be seen as equal to the other; but this cannot be my concern. It is "thanks to God."

Discussions of this entry of the Third abound in Levinas's essays prior to the publication of *Totality and Infinity*. Perhaps the most detailed of them is in "The *I* and the Totality."[4] The entry of the third party modifies the structure of the I/Thou couple, but does not negate it or even weaken it. Yet there is, in the further evolution of Levinas's thought, a modification of that dichotomy, as is apparent in the later works.

This modification is the result of a transfer of emphasis from the same to the other. In *Totality and Infinity*, the other is presented as secondary to the same. "The *I* is thus the mode in which the breakup of totality, **which leads to the presence of the absolutely other**, is concretely established."[5]

Modifications of the Same/Other Dichotomy

Readers of *Otherwise than Being* will probably have noticed that the same/other dichotomy does not disappear altogether but is far less prevalent in than in *Totality and Infinity*. In fact, it could hardly be termed a dichotomy anymore. The dichotomy in the later work is the "saying" versus the "said" (*le Dire, le Dit*). That is to say, the main problem in that work is that of expression. Has Levinas abandoned the same/other opposition, or does he perhaps consider that its work — its critique of philosophy — has been achieved, so that a new series of problems, involving the approach — not of the same to the other, but of the "one" to the "other" — can be taken up as a related but distinct problematics? Or has he (this is Jacques Rolland's hypothesis) taken to heart Derrida's criticism of the way in which the Same/Other analyais is carried out in *Totality and Infinity*? Whatever the case may be, the terms of the opposition have been modified. Rather than the same and the other, we read more about the "one" and the "other," and about the one-for-the-other substitution by which I sacrifice myself for the other. In the account of "the approach" and of "proximity," the *moi* does not threaten the other by an egotistical or "selfish" aggressiveness, but is rather unsettled, disturbed by the other. I am "hostage" to the powerful other.

Thus, the same versus other undergoes a transformation from *Existence & Existents* (1947) to *Otherwise than Being* (1974). In the former work, we were presented with "the world of the spirit, in which the implications of Eros are not reducible to the logic of genera," as they were in the Greek cosmos or the world of Plato. That is the world in which "the *I* is substituted for the *same* and the Other [*autrui*] for *the other.*"[6] The focus of the latter work, by contrast, is on the transformation brought about by the other's presence in, and disturbance of, the *moi*. The other, not the self, now has the leading role. And the self is transformed by this presence of the other within it.

As the *moi* is progressively emptied out or transformed by the other, the term *moi* is replaced by the term *soi*. But it would be quite misleading to speak of a growing selflessness, since the *soi* is the irreplaceable, the responsible party, dedifferentiated partially by the very responsibility it bears without ever having "incurred" it. The self is now hostage.

3. Saying/Said

Language becomes increasingly central to Levinas's philosophy as his career develops. As in the philosophy of Levinas's contemporary Merleau-Ponty (1908–1961), language is both a system of signs, a code, and a domain preceding all decibels or inscription. I will have more to say about the similarities and differences between Merleau-Ponty's *parole parlante/parole parlée* (speaking word/spoken word) distinction, and Levinas's *dire/dit* (saying/said) opposition. They have, at first blush, much in common. For both philosophers, the first member of the binary pair is the more vital, and is preverbal. But Merleau-Ponty's philosophy, which might be characterized as an ontological aesthetics, is concerned with the originary silence, germinating in creativity, from which the spoken language emerges; Levinas's philosophy of human subjectivity and proximity culminates in a philosophical treatise, *Otherwise than Being*, much of which is devoted to an exposition of the complex relation of "saying" (the ethical, otherwise-than-being) to the "said" (the philosophical, the cognitive, and the necessary but ultimately impossible disambiguation of transcendence in immanence).

It is possible to distinguish two developmental moments in Levinas's philosophy in this regard.[1] During the first period, from 1949 to 1964, language is viewed primarily as transcendence; this is the theme of Levinas's 1949 essay on Michel Leiris's "Biffures," titled "The Transcendence of Words."[2] Unlike the world of sight, which is always synoptic and tends to totalize and objectify, the world of sound reveals an overflowing of the sonorous source beyond the limits of its form. Thus sound is "symbol par excellence — a reaching beyond the given."[3] Levinasian ethics describes conscience as listening to a voice, the subject "put into question" by the other, the face issuing a command, the saying of "Here I am" as response and responsibility.

Levinas follows Heidegger in giving language the function of isolating objects in their identity, as signified in discourse. This identification takes the form of a this *qua* this, or *qua* that. The counterpart of this thematization is what Levinas calls "invocation," and which directs discourse to the other, who precisely is not contained within what is said. It is in "the face," as it becomes a philosophical concept in *Totality and Infinity*, that the thematizing and the communicative functions of language are joined.

The second period of Levinas's thought on language begins with the publication of the essay "Enigma and Phenomenon" in 1965.[4] There for the first time we find the distinction between the *Dire* (the saying, or more literally the "to say") and the *Dit* ("the said").

Description of the Distinction being Drawn

The distinction did not, of course, appear out of nowhere: it arose out of an earlier reflection on two uses of language: the communicative and the thematic. Simply put, Levinas becomes attentive to the distinction we make between speaking to (someone) and speaking about (someone or something). These functions usually occur simultaneously. I speak to someone about something. But limiting cases would be (a) the salutary "hello" (communicative without thematization) and (b) a document addressed to no one (more precisely, no one in particular — since all utterance is ultimately addressed to someone, be it the speaker himself) on a topic and stored in the form of writing in a library. It is the first case, the purely communicative mode, that is of particular interest to Levinas, because that is the mode that carries the ethical relation of other to self.

This whole question of how we move from the saying to the said is an aspect of the question of how we move from the couple to sociality, or the third party. Thus it is also a question of the movement from love (charity) to justice. Another later version of the relationship between responsibility for the other and justice, and the birth of the theoretical, is to be found in the 1982 interview "Philosophy, Justice and Love."[5]

In "Énigme et Phénomène," we find an early instance of Levinas's discussion of the saying/said distinction. Here, Levinas writes, "The enigma extends as far as the phenomenon that bears the trace of the *saying* which has already withdrawn from the *said*."[6] What is the enigma? The enigma, the mystery, is here located in the "**trace**," an important word that will become a key concept, as the indication left behind within presence, i.e. within being, of the infinite otherwise-than-being. The trace here is that of the saying, which thus is associated with that infinite otherness which has already withdrawn. It is worth noting that the past participle, the said, is grammatically more past than the present participle, even though, as adhering or remaining in being it is more recent than that saying of which it is the trace, just as the footprint is the trace of a prior passage.

A few sentences further in the same paragraph we have a clearer indication of what is meant by "phenomenon." "Significations which link up cover over the traces of the *saying* that left them, as the perfect crime artist inserts the traces of his violence in the natural folds of Order. Phenomena susceptible to being shaped by a disturbance, a disturbance letting itself be brought back to order: such is the ambiguity of the Enigma."[7] The natural world and its phenomena appear in an order that covers over, dissimulates the violence of a saying. The so-called "cosmological" argument for the existence of God is reversed, or at least

quite problematized here, for it is not the order of the universe
that indicates the ordering of a wise and orderly master and creator of the universe. The traces of God are artfully dissimulated
behind the phenomena. Skipping to the end of the paragraph, the
meanings discoverable in phenomena represent the "said," the
orderly world of Newtonian physics: the "saying" is their interpretation. "Expression, saying, is not added on to significations
that are 'visible' in the light of phenomena, to modify them or
confuse them and introduce into them 'poetic,' 'literary,' 'verbal'
enigmas; the significations said offer a hold to the *saying* which
'disturbs' them, like writings awaiting an interpretation."[8] A difficult text, that establishes a parallel between perceived meaning
in things, and the said of a text that awaits interpretation. The
saying, in the case of a written text awaiting commentary, would
seem to come later than, to be added onto the meaning that is
already in the text. But no, the interpretation troubles the text by
a return to the irreversible anteriority of the Word.

The relation between the saying and the said is here, in what
is possibly its first expression, quite theological. We are not discussing a linguistic phenomenon, but the relation between the
Word (*le Verbe*) and Being (*l'Être*), as is apparent from the two
sentences immediately following the one just quoted: "But therein
lies the irreversible, the initial anteriority of the Word in relation
to Being, the irretrievable lag of the Said behind the Saying. Of
this anteriority the significations — which meanwhile suffice unto
themselves — bear a trace, which they straightaway deny and
wipe away."

This early version of the saying/said opposition is instructive
in that it reveals a clearly metaphysical infrastructure. If it is the
relation between the creating Word of God and the Creation, or
Being, the *écart* must be between a pure, creative spontaneity
without beginning, and an order of law, logic, and constituted
being. The saying is to the said as "the anteriority of God relative to a world that cannot accommodate him." It is left for us to

consider how this relation (or lack of one, *écart*) is coordinated with the pure vocative of discourse, the addressing of one to the other, as distinct from the thematization carried out within it.

To clarify the first element, the saying, Levinas considers a case of a saying without said, or perhaps a saying that is its own said. The passage is taken from the beginning of his essay on the German Jewish poet Paul Celan, and was published in 1965, the same year as Levinas's *Énigme et Phénomène*.

> "I cannot see any basic difference," Paul Celan wrote to Hans Bender, "between a handshake and a poem." There is the poem, the height of language, reduced to the level of an interjection, a form of expression as undifferentiated as a wink, a sign to one's neighbor! A sign of what? Of life, of goodwill? Of complicity? Or a sign of nothing, or a complicity for no reason: a saying without a said. Or is it a sign that is its own signified: the subject signals that sign-giving to the point of becoming a sign through and through.[9]

Here saying and said are used in a more directly linguistic manner, with terms such as sign and signified. But Levinas finds a deep affinity between Celan's poetry and poetics and his own metaphysical insight into language. If a poem can be viewed as a saying without a said, we must remember that there is, after all, something said in the poem.

> Things will indeed appear [i.e. in the poem], the said of this poetic saying, but in the movement that carries them toward the other, as figures of this movement. "All things, all beings, as they journey toward the other, will be figures, for the poem, of that other. . . . Around me who calls out and gives it a name it can gather." The centrifugal movement of the *for the other* — might it be the mobile axis of being? Or its rupture? Or its meaning? The fact of speaking to the other — the poem — precedes all thematization; it is in that act that qualities gather themselves into things.[10]

The internal quotes are from Celan, whose voice intertwines very closely here with that of the philosopher. Just as the saying of the poem, its prior vocative gesture, is "for the other," so the burden of the poem, the "things" it carries, will be gathered by the poet's call, summoned to journey toward that other. What we have here then, in the poem, is not a saying without a said, or even a saying that is its own said, but a saying that transforms and carries the said, now metamorphosed into "figures of this movement."

In *Otherwise than Being*, the saying/said distinction is carried to its most rigorous philosophical consequences. The interrelation between the two terms is analyzed, with specific attention to philosophical or metaphysical discourse. As we shall see, the discursive practice that is used to elaborate the theory of this polarity will itself have to find its place within the theory it articulates.

Philosophy qua "Indiscretion with regard to the Ineffable"

Section 3 of the "Argument" of *Otherwise than Being*, entitled "Saying and the Said,"[11] immediately plunges into a problem of inherence. Transcendence is bogged down, caught up "in war and matter, the inevitable modalities of destiny that being, in its interestedness, spins out."[12] How is this domain, that of the Said, characterized? First we note that it is Greek, not just as in Greek philosophy, but as in Greek mythology as well. It is the Fates who spin out, weave and eventually cut the threads of human destinies: the tragic Moirai (or Roman Parcae), whom Levinas contrasted 40 years earlier with the Judeo-Christian message of regenerative repentance.[13] Such is the province of being, of interestedness (of being involved in being, *esse*), in which the utterance of being's other is immediately enclosed. This is the failure, Levinas suggests, of a theology that thematizes the act of transcendence within the (Greek) logos, assigning a **term** (a name, a substantive, but also a terminus, end point, stoppage) to this **passage**, immobilizing it in a (Nietzschean) *Hinterwelt*, the French equivalent of which, *arrière-monde*,[14] Levinas uses here. A "heaven," stalled transcendence, made of things from here.

But as the text progresses we become increasingly appreciative of this failed attempt of the said to express the otherwise than being, or being's other, that outside of being, that exception to being. Why? Because "[t]he correlation of the saying and the said, that is, the subordination of the saying to the said, to the linguistic system and to ontology, is the price that manifestation demands."[15] Let us note that this necessary treason, the unfaithfulness that is incurred in passing into being, is not limited to language, but includes all manifestation. Here, of course, expression is uppermost, but we must recognize the metaphysical basis of this linguistics.

> Language permits us to utter, be it by betrayal, this *outside of being*, this *ex-ception* to being, as though being's other were an event in being. Being, its cognition and the said in which it shows itself signify in a saying which, relative to being, forms an exception; but it is in the said that both this exception and the birth of cognition [*la naissance de la connaissance*] show themselves. But the fact that the ex-ception shows itself and becomes truth in the said cannot serve as a pretext to take as an absolute the apophantic variant of the saying, which is ancillary or angelic.[16]

We must appreciate but not idolize the logos of the said. It is ancillary, angelic, an intermediary, a messenger. By means of it, even that which cannot be said in it (the "ex-ception," the birth of cognition) can be suggested. Apophansis, formal logic, already presupposes the grave responsibility for the interlocutor who stands beyond what is said in language. We thus find ourselves at the brink of a methodological problem. Can the preoriginal element of saying (the an-archical, the non-original — non-original not because derived, but because removed from the domain of origins, which is that of being) be revealed thematically? And if so, can it be reduced, or unsaid (*dédit*), in order to remove the marks left by thematization, the inevitable ontological marks of being? Levinas's project here is only possible by the mediation of the very realm of language in which that mediate and ontologically compromised nature of the "said" is said. The sentence immediately preceding the passage quoted above expresses that awareness. "**At this very moment** language is serving research conducted in view of disengaging the *otherwise than being* or *being's other* outside of the themes in which they already show themselves."[17] The project of philosophy itself is thus a part of this betrayal, thanks to which it can carry out what is probably its task: "indiscretion with regard to the ineffable."[18]

The saying of the otherwise than being must be un-said, in order for it to be extricated from the said, which would otherwise transform it into a mere being otherwise. But what of this saying and unsaying? Can they be simultaneous? If they were, otherwise than being would be transformed into being and not being. This being and not being simultaneously is skepticism (not in the eighteenth century sense of atheism, but in the classical sense of putting all true utterance in doubt). It is the skepticism troubling all logical repose, with such paradoxes as the Liar's paradox, or the very enunciation of the skeptical position, "All statements are false." We can demonstrate that the skeptic's "position" is itself paradoxical, but the fact is that the skeptic has no position, nor does he need one. Using the word "essence," as in all his later texts, to mean being, in its verbal sense, Levinas suggests that

> If, after the innumerable "irrefutable" refutations which logical thought sets against it, skepticism has the gall to return (and it always returns as philosophy's legitimate child), it is because in the contradiction which logic sees in it the "at the same time" of the contradictions is missing, because a secret diachrony commands this ambiguous or enigmatic way of speaking, and because in general signification signifies beyond synchrony, beyond essence.[19]

Levinas sees the functioning of the paradox to be the result of an inherent diachrony in skepticism, which both conveys and betrays that diachrony. The assumed temporality of formal logic is the simultaneity of a now. Levinas will even go so far as to say that it is precisely the value and virtue of formal logic to bring out more sharply, the more rigorous it is, the precise points at which these beyond-being significations transgress it. Further, "the myth of the subordination of all thought to the comprehension of being" is probably based on the value of reality as a measure by which the *écart* between signification and being can appear.[20]

The Motivation of "Subreption"

"Subreption" is a legal term, indicating a calculated misrepresentation through concealment of the facts. Levinas applies it to the case of the said, which limits what is thought or thinkable to being and reminiscence: i.e. to synchronic time and representation (which brings other times into coordination with the present).

The term subreption occurs in only one section of *Otherwise than Being*: in chapter 5, section 3: "From Saying to the Said, or the Wisdom of Desire." In it, Levinas moves to the deepest level of questioning. Why would proximity (to the other person), pure signification of saying, fall into being, into "essence" showing itself in being? "Why," Levinas asks, "have we sought being on its (proximity's) Empyrean heights?"[21] He wishes to find, in the proximity to the other person, "the latent birth of cognition and essence, of the said." He seeks proximity as it becomes knowledge, and a way of understanding why this movement from saying to the said should take place at all. Why not just proximity, just love? Why philosophy? What is the necessity for and origin of wisdom?

The answer is in the third party. If there are but two, the couple, love is sufficient. The "wisdom of love" refers not to some wise motivation for loving, but the necessary transformation of love, in order that love may realize its desire under the conditions imposed by the (new) situation of sociality, into wisdom. The arrival of the third party is the beginning of objectivity, social institutions, and — this concerns us more specifically here — the Said, or language as part of the Order. When there is only one other, I can always know that the other has first place, passes ahead of me. But when the third party enters, I must compare incomparables, decide who shall have precedence. This is the founding, explanatory myth of the beginning of society, or "sociality" as Levinas calls it.

If I use the term "myth," it is to avoid the impression that the "entrance of the third party" is an empirical occurrence. I could use the term "theory" to avoid that misunderstanding, were it not that theory carries with it a sense of truth as synthetic and simultaneous: a mental vision of a totality. Levinas relates a metaphysical story. He speaks of the "intrigue de l'infini," infinity's plot. His book *Totality and Infinity* will "**recount** how infinity is produced in the relationship with the other. . . ."[22] War is "the **saga** or **drama** of the interestedness of being" ("la geste ou le drame de l'intéressement de l'être").[23]

Poetry and Prophetic Discourse: A Trojan Horse within the Walls of Being

Despite certain similarities, the distinction Merleau-Ponty makes between "speaking language" and "spoken language" (*parole parlante* and *parole parlée*) is less radical than Levinas's saying and said. First, Merleau-Ponty's speaking language was one of spontaneity and creativity, having more to do with the emergence of meaning out of form or matter; hence his interest in Marcel Proust's "musical ideas" and "ideas without equivalents," which seemed to provide the missing link between sensibilia and the idea. But while Merleau-Ponty is fascinated by the vinculum and eventually the reversibility of idea and thing, Levinas's philosophy is one of rupture, radical difference and *écart*. For Levinas, "The sounds and noises of nature are words that disappoint us. To really hear a sound is to hear a word. Pure sound is the word."[24] To Merleau-Ponty, "to understand a phrase is nothing else than to fully welcome it in its sonorous being, or, as we put it so well, to *hear what it says*" (*l'entendre*).[25] The speaking/spoken word distinction is the product of an aesthetic ontology, or an ontology of the senses — those points of contact between self and the world of things, those dimensions of being. The saying/said distinction emerges from a metaphysics of subjectivity, of proximity and discursive relations — of persons, of the face, of sociality.

Despite these differences, it is true that the first element in both binaries (the saying, the speaking word) seems to participate in the creativity of the creation, like Spinoza's *natura naturans* contrasted with his *natura naturata*. But we must not make the mistake of thinking of Levinas's "speaking" as a particular use of language. Indeed, the domain of the said, under the aegis of *essence*, is the only language that is recognizably language — with its conventions, its temporality, its explicitness. Levinas describes how the said says saying or, less tongue-twistingly, the disturbance saying visits upon the said.

> Language exceeds the limits of what is thought by suggesting, letting be understood without ever making understandable, an implication of a meaning distinct from that which comes to signs from the simultaneity of systems or the logical definition of concepts. This possibility is laid bare in the **poetic** said, and the interpretation it calls for *ad infinitum*. It is shown in the **prophetic** said, scorning its conditions in a sort of levitation. It is by the approach, the-one-for-the-other of **saying, related by the said**, that the said remains an insurmountable equivocation, in which meaning refuses simultaneity, does not enter into being, does not make up a whole.[26]

To the concept poetry prefers the conceit, those pseudo-concepts that are more open to allusion and implication than their stricter cousins. It is clear by the expression "the approach, the-one-for-the-other of saying, related by the said" that the saying/said distinction is not one of linguistic usage merely, since one usage is not "related" or said by another usage. What the saying "is" transcends language as the term is normally used at least, since language must, in order to be language, accept the "conditions" of linguistic expression, those very conditions that are "scorned" by prophetic discourse. Language is equivocation or failed simultaneity, not the steady light of truth but the twinkling light of what we think we might have seen but . . . well, perhaps not.

Characteristic of the saying in the said is the connection with the outside, the listener or listeners. The written word seems to become completely "said," since all of its words are rendered graphically simultaneous. It would seem that a book, as interrupted discourse, would be able to produce a separate totality. In fact it, too, is still open to the outside, to the reader or listener. But a book can "say" that, state that openness, thereby tying up that openness with its own language still. According to Levinas, "The interruptions of the discourse found again and recounted in the immanence of the said are conserved like knots in a thread tied again, the trace of a diachrony that does not enter into the present, that refuses simultaneity."[27]

These knots (which politics does not tie, but simply cuts through) are the recognition of the interlocutor. Levinas says that this is true of the discourse he is writing "at this very moment." A book can include in itself the very interruption of the discursive structure of speakers and listeners. But even in that case "books have their fate; they belong to a world they did not include, but recognize by being written and printed, and by being prefaced and having themselves preceded by forewords." Not only are they still caught up in the web of sociality in that way, but in this ongoing relationship with alterity, they are also open to otherness in that they "call for other books, and in the end are interpreted in a saying distinct from the said."[28]

Interpretation is thus a way of returning the said to saying: the said, which were it not for the forces of philosophy, poetry, and prophecy, would enclose itself in a totality of silence.

4. BEING/BEYOND BEING

The terms "being" and "beyond being" are ontological. But there is an underlying ambiguity in writing about Levinas's ontology. He considered his own thinking to differ from Heidegger's, mainly on the issue of ontology. It remains to be determined (see below, chapter 6, "Ontology/Metaphysics," and chapter 13, "Levinas's Critique of Heidegger") exactly what that difference entails, but it is clear that Levinas understands his own philosophy to be metaphysical rather than ontological. Perhaps we can clarify the situation by considering a word that Levinas uses in his early (1935) essay, "De l'évasion" ("On Escape"): ontologism.[1]

Like Husserl's use of the word "psychologism," Levinas's "ontologism" carries with it an implied critique. It is directed against those philosophers who would have the domains of the thinkable and of being coincide without remainder. Parmenides is the founding offender in this regard. Levinas's writings frequently point out that being has been equated with truth — since to lie is to say what is not — and with excellence — for God, in the Thomistic tradition, is the Supreme Being, who lacks no quality, and being, in the theology of the ontological proof of the existence of God, is treated as a quality.

Nevertheless, to speak of Levinas's ontology is inevitable to the extent that he had important things to say about being. I begin with a characterization of being in general, taken from his late period, then discuss the *il y a* and the otherwise than being or beyond being. Perhaps it is precisely Levinas's characterization of being that makes it possible for him to move beyond it. In any case, the existentialist notion of "existence," that specific modality of being peculiar to human being (*Dasein*, in Heidegger) does not seem to have been assigned any important role in Levinas's later period. In his early works, Levinas uses existence (*existence*) and existent (*existant*) to mean being (*être*) and entity (*étant*), respectively. By *étant*, Levinas nearly always means a human being.

Levinas does not "do" much with the notion of being/nonbeing. His main interest is in describing what is of moral significance (interestedness, synchrony, competitiveness, the *conatus essendi*, and warfare). His early pronouncement on being, from which it is necessary to escape, is: Every civilization that accepts being — with the tragic despair it contains and the crimes it justifies — deserves the name "barbarian."[2] In those years, being was characterized mainly as an overfullness, a heaviness. Being is a burden to itself, riveted to itself. In his later work the same adjectives and characteristics are more frequently attributed to the *moi*, which must eventually free itself from itself to become *soi*. Pleasure is the process of leaving being. But it turns out that pleasure does not keep its promises.[3] "On Escape" shows clearly the direction Levinas's subsequent philosophy will take. "The brutal fact of being" that constrains human freedom is what prompts the desire to escape. Bourgeois self-sufficiency is modeled on the physical object. Already the idea of the *moi* is presented in close parallel with being itself and its inescapability. The two existential analyses in the piece are of shame and nausea.

"On Escape" also contains an analysis of need — and it should be noted in passing that the analysis does not yet differentiate between need and desire, a distinction that, while never absolute, plays an important role in the opening pages of *Totality and Infinity*.[4] The satisfaction of need is pleasurable, and pleasure is affectivity. Affectivity, Levinas claims, "is foreign to notions that apply to that which is, and has never been reducible to categories of thought and activity."[5] This "affectivity" (*affectivité* is the French translation of Heidegger's *Befindlichkeit*) will reappear 40 years later as "sensibility" (*sensibilité*) in chapter 3 ("Sensibility and Proximity") of *Otherwise than Being.* Affectivity, sensibility — perhaps use of the more Anglo-Saxon "feeling" would help naturalize Levinas's thought in English — are, along with subjectivity in its entirety, what we should think about when trying to overcome our heritage of "ontologism" and convey a more concrete sense of "otherwise than being." (A fuller account of "On Escape" is given below in chapter 15.)

Levinas's Ontology; the Economy of Being

In his preface to *Entre Nous*, Levinas uses a classification system that has a *prima facie* familiarity: the traditional tripartite description of the "modes of being." There we find the

> [o]rigin of all violence, varying with the various modes of being: the life of the living, the existence of human beings, the reality of things. The life of the living in the struggle for life; the natural history of human beings in the blood and tears of wars between individuals, nations and classes; the matter of things, hard matter; solidity; the closed-in-upon-self, all the way down to the level of the subatomic particles of which physicists speak.[6]

The violence in question is "violence" in the guise of beings who affirm themselves "without regard" for one another in their concern to be. The *conatus essendi* is most obviously present in the form of the Darwinian struggle for survival, but Levinas extends the notion to the inanimate world as well. Hence it becomes more than a psychological drive (although that is one of its manifestations): it is an aspect of the metaphysical structure of all being. Levinas's preferred term for being, in all these senses, is "essence" (in the later writings sometimes spelled essance); it is an abstract noun designating the verbal sense of the Latin *esse*, to be. Since this verbal sense is quite evident in the present participle "being," there is probably no reason to produce a corresponding neologism in English (e.g. "beance," or "beancy").[7] Although "essance" is common to all three modes of beings, and it has as its characteristic the common, recognizable feature of *conatus essendi*, the manifestations of essence vary. In the classification of "living," the *conatus essendi* is manifested in the struggle for life, while at the level of the "natural history" of human beings it is visible in the form of blood, tears, and war, and at the inorganic level it appears as solidity, being-closed-in-upon-itself, down to the intra-atomic level. Less dramatic than "violence," "hardness" is what characterizes being. Being in-itself, resistant to change — these expressions are the transposition of a phenomenology of "hardness" to the metaphysical plane.

The term "existence" is, as in Heidegger, normally reserved for the way human beings are, as is indicated in the passage quoted above. On the other hand, Heidegger infused existence with features he considered to be more adequate in accommodating the human way of being (e.g. *vohaben, Zuhanden, Vorhanden*, potentiality, being-toward-death, etc.); from that perspective, it would not be difficult to construe Levinas's metaphysical ontology as a giant step backward. But Levinas specifies that he is referring to "the natural history of human beings in the blood and tears of wars. . . ." Is there any other kind of history? The paragraph immediately following the one quoted above explains

> But behold! The emergence, in the life lived by the human being (and it is here that the human, as such, begins — pure eventuality, but from the start an eventuality that is pure and holy), of the devoting-of-oneself-to-the-other. In the general economy of being in its inflection back upon itself, a preoccupation with the other, even to the point of sacrifice, even to the possibility of dying for him or her; a responsibility for the other. Otherwise than being! It is this shattering of indifference — even if indifference is statistically dominant — this possibility of one-for-the-other, that constitutes the ethical event.[8]

This devoting of oneself to the other is described rather paradoxically as a pure eventuality (something that might or might not come to be) yet an eventuality that is pure and holy. This seems not to be included in "the natural history of human being." Or is it? For this preoccupation with the other is "**in** the general economy of being in its inflection back upon itself." It seems clear that the notion of the "inflection back upon itself" is what typifies being — at all three levels mentioned earlier. What we have then is an exception, emerging or standing out from and breaking free of the order of being: otherwise than being. It is this otherwise than being, or being's other, that constitutes "the ethical event."

Otherwise-than-Being Versus Nothingness

The most controversial aspect of Levinas's philosophy is a category he calls "being's other," which is neither being nor non-being. Being and non-being taken together form a totality. Levinas argues that the simple negation of being is a derivative of being, too tributary to break away from being's ambit.

This notion of non-being as a part of being is well established. Levinas insists that otherwise than being is not non-being. Nor is otherwise-than-being death. "To be or not to be is not the question where transcendence is concerned," writes Levinas at the beginning of *Otherwise than Being*.[9]

In this "other" of being, Levinas includes subjectivity, God, and the face (of the other person), and these are only indicated indirectly or ambiguously by what he calls the trace. This order (or more precisely disorder, for if it were an order it would be annexed by being) is also associated with "a past that never was present," i.e. a temporality referred to as "diachronic."

From Being to Beyond Being

In *Totality and Infinity* the term "being" is ambiguous: it is used in a deficient mode when it refers to objectivity, the totality and "the same," and in a rich or extended sense when it is equated with exteriority or alterity.[10] This ambiguous use of the term being was already present in "On Escape," in which, as we have just observed, Levinas has some harsh words to say about being. The term "beyond being" appears even in this piece, but only as a destination, the direction toward which transcendence moves in "escaping" or "exiting" being.[11] And in the short section titled "Beyond Being" in *Totality and Infinity*[12] it is still as a destination of desire that beyond being is conceived. *Totality and Infinity* remains to some extent a phenomenology and a metaphysics of presence, with the special circumstance that the phenomenon of the face, the direct and meaningful appearance of the other *qua* face, is a meaning without context, a pure revelation of the infinite.[13]

If *Otherwise than Being* is able to go beyond a metaphysics of presence, it is because the category of temporalization is developed in a direction that allows for a fuller characterization of otherwise than being. The Good of Plato, which is situated beyond being, is also situated in the timeless realm of eternity. Levinas attributes to being a specific sense of temporality, simultaneity. It is this sense of time that he finds in both Hegel and Husserl: a future and a past that are aspects of the present, which dominates the real, in the sense that for something to fully be, it must be now. The past and the future are deficient modes of the present in this sense. In *Otherwise than Being* we find, as distinct from the synchrony of being, the diachrony of the otherwise than being. Diachronic in a very different sense than that of the linguist Ferdinand de Saussure, in which it designated a cross-section of past, present and future viewed at one time, a theoretical time of linguistic analysis. Levinas's diachrony is a temporality no longer connected to the present. It might be termed an essentialist view of time, in which the pastness of the past is not to be confused with a former state of the world. It is a pastness that "never was present," and, it is safe to assume, never will be. It is to this sort of temporality that Levinas refers when he speaks of the deformalization of time. It is the interpretation of time as meaning, the idea of which Levinas says he borrowed from Franz Rosenzweig, the author of *The Star of Redemption*, to whom the past is essentially creation, the present revelation, and the future redemption. To what extent does Levinas adopt these meanings of temporality? Only the meaning of the past *qua* "immemorial" an-archic plays a role in *Otherwise than Being*.[14]

Perhaps the greatest debt Levinas owes to Heidegger is that the latter brought out certain areas of vagueness in being and demonstrated that being can be described or qualified — which Levinas also does, albeit quite differently from Heidegger. The outcome of his characterization of being (*qua* totality, simultaneity, and *conatus essendi*) is precisely to make it possible for this more circumscribed meaning of being to have an other, an "otherwise than being."

5. PERSON/THING

"Person" and "thing" have become emblems for opposing systems of thought over the past century or so. The conflicting worldviews that have configured themselves around them — science and the humanities — are ontologically distinct. Keeping in mind this dichotomy, we can grasp what is at stake in the speculative enterprises that have attempted to reconcile the two ontological systems or "warring cultures." It is in this context that the work of Bergson unfolds, and Merleau-Ponty's work can be read as an attempt to reconcile the two worlds by reaching beneath them to a pretheoretical level at which the problem is not yet irresolvable. Rosenzweig and Buber, on the other hand, are mainly interested in validating the human (and divine) domain. Remarkably for many readers, the dichotomy is not present in Levinas's writings. Science is not viewed as an alternate worldview to set in opposition to a humanistic one, and the negative view of science and technology found in other phenomenologists (e.g. Heidegger and Merleau-Ponty) is simply not a part of Levinas's work. Perhaps the closest equivalent we find in his writings is a rejection of the impersonal mode of structuralism's analyses. Georges Hansel, Levinas's son-in-law, himself a well-known mathematician and talmudic scholar, writes in his as yet untranslated *Explorations talmudiques*

> In other words, the Torah is intended to answer the question: Who is Man? But not man as substance or as object, the properties of which are to be spelled out. It is not a question of answering the question What is Man, but Who is Man, as subject, as person. It

is as an immediate result of that definition that the Torah addresses itself both to the will of man and to his thought, that its content is presented from the start and indiscernibly as knowledge and as norm, since, in the answer to the question "Who is Man?" it is impossible to distinguish what is and what must or should be. The ideal and the future, the project to be carried out and the being that must be engendered are as much a part of the definition of man as his past and the already constituted identity. One cannot be content here with an "I think, therefore I am," or an "I think, I exist"; I do not yet exist.[1]

Certainly Levinas was not confused about the difference between the project of philosophy, that historically determined tradition of inquiry that traces its origin from Greek thought, and the intent of the Torah. But the background of talmudic studies that informed his thought throughout his career indicates at the very least that talmudic thought — with its focus on "Who is man?" — was consonant with his own interest and approach. This dedication to the human being in the sense of "the will of man and his thought" suggests that within the person/thing binary, the former constitutes the center of Levinas's preoccupations.

That said, the "thing" plays a very important role in Levinasian thought. Levinas quotes the well-known statement of Lithuanian-born Rabbi Israel Salanter: "A person should be more concerned with spiritual than with material matters, but another person's material welfare is his own spiritual concern." The transformation from material to spiritual is mediated by the other (person), through the needs of the other person (in the sense of a "who"), anchored as he or she is in an ontology that encompasses both persons and things. This mediation is most obvious in the analysis of what would seem to be a hybrid with respect to the person/thing binary: money.

Levinas is one of the few philosophers to have examined the meaning of money. Despite the anathema of Amos (Amos 2:6) and the critique of the *Communist Manifesto*, writes Levinas in the last section of "The *I* and the Totality,"[2] there is a positive aspect to money, for in it "the personal is maintained while being quantified." It provides the category for comparing incomparables — which is what justice requires of us in a world in which there are more than two people, i.e. in human society. Without it, we could not break "the infernal or vicious circle of vengeance or forgiveness." And Levinas ends on this balanced note: "It is certainly quite shocking to see in the quantification of man one of the essential conditions of justice. But can we conceive of a justice without quantity and without reparation?" These quotes are from 1954. Twenty years later, we read in the early pages of *Otherwise than Being*, "Commerce is better than war, for in peace the Good has already reigned."[3] Better than war, commerce nevertheless displays the same vying, the same "drama of the essence's interest" the same "extreme synchronism" or "extreme contemporaneousness or immanence." This immanence is the milieu of the *moi*. "Egotism is not an ugly vice on the part of the subject, but its ontology. . . ."[4] The human in the ethical sense is an exception to the *conatus essendi*.

6. Ontology/Metaphysics

This chapter sketches out the relation between ontology and meta-physics, then more specifically the way these terms have been understood by phenomenologists, and finally Levinas's specific understanding and use of them in his own work. The distinction may prove helpful in differentiating the projects of Heidegger and Levinas.

Generalities

I use "ontology" to mean the study of being and metaphysics as the study of that which does not fall within the realm of the physical. These are fairly standard definitions, though ontology is sometimes used in the sense of the set of kinds of things to be admitted as being in some sense. Thus, an ontology might comprise spatiotemporal entities such as tables, chairs and planets, and also numbers and angels. Moreover, there is some controversy among Greek specialists whether Aristotle's use of the term "metaphysics" really entailed an allusion to something beyond the physical (meta = beyond) or whether it just referred to the "next" book, which came after the one he called "Phusis" or physics. Ontology as a term is a seventeenth century coinage from neo-Latin; metaphysics a fourteenth century one, from Greek through the Latin of the scholastics.

But what of the relation between the two terms? My use of the slash mark between the two words in this chapter might suggest that there is a strong contrast or "bar" between. But in fact ontology has been traditionally looked upon as a branch (in Descartes, the "root") of metaphysics. That situation may be said to have changed since Kant's First Critique, which cast doubt upon the possibility of the sort of knowledge to which metaphysics was thought to aspire. Heidegger accepts the critique of the metaphysical mansion, but leaves one room standing: ontology.

Phenomenology and Ontology

It may seem odd that Heidegger, who stands well within the phenomenological tradition, should develop a philosophy that has often been referred to as an ontology. The founder of phenomenology, Heidegger's teacher Edmund Husserl, was emphatic in his refusal to make any particular commitments with respect to ontological claims. In fact, his goal was to describe "phenomena" as they appeared, prior to any particular theory about their ontological status. The phenomenological reduction was intended to remove (by making them explicit) the traces of any "Einstellung" or ontological "standpoint" that prejudge the meaning of what is observed, either in thought or the "real" world. All the data of consciousness were to have equal status! But the "existential" turn taken by Heidegger's phenomenology resulted in further attention to the modality of being. Previously there was only one way for something to "be," whether rock, flower or human being. Husserl had refrained from asserting whether or not something was, in favor of saying what it was: its essence. But these essences were not construed as additional ontological elements. If Heidegger's philosophy is ontological, it is because it begins by a thorough critique of traditional ontology (the "thing" ontology that tends to treat all beings as variants of the physical object), and introduces a fundamental division between being itself (its verbal sense) and the concrete entity, substance. The "ontological difference" between being (*das Sein*) and beings or entities (*die Seienden*) is perhaps Heidegger's most original contribution.

Being is not an entity and has a different mode of being than entities. We should not be misled into thinking that Heidegger is simply drawing attention to the difference between abstract and concrete nouns, so that being indicates the abstraction of a quality that all entities have. Such a view would posit beings or entities first and make being an abstraction. In fact, the opposite is closer to the truth. It is the verbal sense of being that is primary; the "participial" form, *das Seiende* or the individual, substantial entity, only participates in this verbal being.

This is the essential trait of *Being and Time* that Levinas retained, and this distinction is basic to his own work. It was Heidegger, he claims, who taught us to hear the sound of being: "My admiration for Heidegger is above all an admiration for *Sein und Zeit*. I always try to relive the ambiance of those readings when 1933 was still unthinkable. One speaks habitually of the word being as if it were a substantive, even though it is a verb par exellence. . . . Heidegger accustomed us to this verbal sonority. This reeducation of our ear is unforgettable, even if banal today."[1] It is after this first "move" that the two philosophies go their separate ways. The sound of being heard by the two philosophers is very different. Heidegger hears the *es gibt*, which according to Levinas has a certain generosity about it (probably because *es gibt* is a form of the German verb "to give"); Levinas hears the monotonous, frightening inanity of insomnia. When asked by the interviewer François Poirié whether his "there is" (*il y a*) had affinities with Heidegger's "there is" (*es gibt*), he replied, "Oh no, it isn't Heidegger's 'es gibt.' His 'es gibt' is a generosity. It is the great theme of the last Heidegger; being gives itself anonymously, but as an abundance, a diffuse goodness. On the contrary, the 'il y a' is unbearable in its indifference, not anxiety but the horror of a ceaselessness, a monotony devoid of meaning."[2]

The fact that Levinas begins with an essentially negative qualification of being as opposed to Heidegger's more positive one is probably what was to supply the basis and set the direction of Levinas's future philosophical course toward what has been called an ethical metaphysics.[3] The appeal to "get out of being," launched in 1935 with "De l'évasion" and renewed in 1947 with *Existence & Existents*, is in fact what gives unity to Levinas's entire philosophical effort.

Levinas's Conversion of Ontology to Ethical Significance

Ethics was always for Levinas the relation between human beings. In order for such an ethics to get underway, the existent must emerge from existence (or beings from being). Out of the nightmarish neutrality of the *il y a* there will slowly emerge beings, substantive or nominal forms within the verbality of being, by "hypostasis." Later the *il y a* will become a milieu of *essence*, of being as an ongoing event, as simultaneity, warfare, and competition. The *moi* or "I" that emerges from such being contains, in eminent fashion, those same qualities that characterized being: egotism, usurpation, imperial aggressiveness. This *moi* is selfish, acquisitive, spontaneously or naively atheistic, unthinking (without regard for the other), and immoral. The self annexes the world. It is separate — a secret. It brings things home to enjoy. It extends, through ownership but also knowledge, its self, or selfsameness, onto the low-level otherness of the ambient world.

The self can never truly be reformed: it is its nature to be selfish. This is why Levinas says "No one is good voluntarily," and "Responsibility for the other is the good. It isn't agreeable, it's good."[4] But if this is the case, it is clear that Levinas's ethics must be heteronymous, since the good must come from elsewhere. Thus man, to the extent that he is good, is not free. Whence, then, goodness? It imposes itself upon the self by the other. (Such a view of humans cannot lead to an ethics of virtues.) It is this relationship with the other that will slowly convert Levinas's ontological language (still prevalent in *Totality and Infinity*) to that of ethics: proximity, responsibility, love, justice and peace. But this transformation is neither sudden nor complete, as an examination of the commentaries (part 3, below) will demonstrate. While *Totality and Infinity* is largely concerned with the phenomenology of life (life as separation, etc.) — work, eroticism, the face, the home, femininity — *Otherwise than Being or Beyond Essence* will thematize the problem of transcendence, alterity, and language. The problem of language and of "the expression of the ineffable" by an abuse of language in philosophy seems to move closer both to the outside (the world of which little can be said, without smuggling it into the realm of the said, which is that of being) and the inside (subjectivity, which is, in a sense, also outside — of being). We are, in the ethical relation of proximity to the other, both beyond (*au-delà*) and on the near side or the hither side (*en deçà*) of being or essance.

Can we still be said to be within the realm of ontology, when so much of the discussion concerns the beyond being or otherwise than being? It may be that, to take a Heideggerian point of view, ontology remained modeled on "thing-ontology" for Levinas. If that is the case, perhaps Levinas's view of ontology as too limited to contain or account for subjectivity is what led him to adopt, rather than just an "ontological difference," a difference or departure from ontology — a beyond or otherwise than being that is metaphysical, not ontological. Even the ontological difference was for Levinas too "totalizable," too attached to being, to accommodate true transcendence.

In the following passage, taken from the early pages of *Totality and Infinity*, Levinas argues that "The transcendence with which the metaphysician designates it [the transcendent movement] is distinctive in that the distance it expresses, unlike all distances, enters into the *way of existing* of the exterior being. Its formal characteristic, to be other, makes up its content. Thus the metaphysician and the other cannot be *totalized*. The metaphysician is absolutely separated."[5] The first thing that is remarkable about this text is that it refers to the metaphysician himself or herself as being a part of the world described by metaphysics. He or she is an ethical subject, perhaps **the** ethical subject. Secondly, the distance involved is what I termed in my introduction "essentialist," or in Levinasian terms, such that its way of being is its content. Third, there is an absolute disjunction between being and the subjectivity of the metaphysician, a necessary *écart*, in order for transcendence to be what it purports to be. It is because of this necessity for transcendence to leave the field of being entirely that Levinas's philosophy must be described as a metaphysics rather than an ontology.

7. SACRED/HOLY

In 1987, close to the end of Levinas's long philosophical career, François Poirié asked the philosopher what his project was at the beginning of his research. Levinas responded:

> I don't know whether it was my initial project or whether it is my final project; I have no idea, I can't tell you. I have never thought of those things in terms of well-written biographical pathos. But the idea that after all the true, unquestionable value, and the one that it is not ridiculous to conceive of, is the value of holiness. It has nothing whatsoever to do with doing without things. It is in the certainty that the other must be given the first place in all respects; from the "after you" before the open door to the disposition — hardly possible but holiness demands it — to die for the other.[1]

There are indications that this theme in fact dominated toward the end of his career. In the course of the same interview, Poirié asks, still in reference to the main theme of Levinas's philosophy:

> **Poirié**: So it's ethics, primarily?
>
> **Levinas**: The word ethics is Greek. I think much more, especially now, about holiness; the holiness of the face of the other, or the holiness of my obligation as such. Granted, there is a holiness in the face, but especially there is holiness or ethics toward oneself in a behavior that approaches the face as a face, in which the obligation with respect to the other is imposed before all obligation. To respect the other is to take the other into account, to put him before oneself. And courtesy! Ah, it is very good: to have him or her pass before me, that little courteous incentive is also

access to the face. Why should you pass before me? It is very difficult because you, too, approach my face. But courtesy or ethics consists in not thinking of that reciprocity.[2]

The idea of not considering reciprocity, not requiring the same behavior of others, is repeated constantly throughout the later writings and interviews. In saying that "it is very difficult, because you, too, approach my face," I don't think Levinas is referring to the practical difficulty of getting through doorways when each person is deferring to the other, but to a conceptual difficulty for objective thought. Ethics has, in the philosophical tradition, usually been viewed as a matter of arriving at principles that could be applied evenly and across the board to all human beings. Here ethics is only to be thought of in the first person. It is always only I who have responsibilities, I who am obligated, I who must yield to the other. The relation between self and other appears, at least for the purposes of ethical behavior, to resist any synoptic view.

Levinas's increasing interest in the idea of holiness is again attested, this time by Jacques Derrida: "One day, on the rue Michel-Ange, during one of those conversations whose memory I hold so dear, one of those conversations illuminated by the radiance of his thought, the goodness of his smile, the gracious humor of his ellipses, he said to me: 'You know, one often speaks of ethics to describe what I do, but what really interests me in the end is not ethics, not ethics alone, but the holy, the holiness of the holy.'"[3]

The uniqueness of the first person is already thematized in the work of the founder of phenomenology, Edmund Husserl; but there the uniqueness was of the epistemological subject rather than of the ethical one. The moral specificity of the I/thou relation doubtless owes everything to Martin Buber; but what is different from Buber's dialogical philosophy here is the asymmetry of the relationship. In Levinas, the other is always greater, always "closer to God" than I am.

Holiness would seem to be more at home in a religious, or perhaps theological, context, than in a strictly philosophical one. Yet the way Levinas proceeds to discuss the term is in fact philosophical. First, there is the gesture of the *distinguo*. One of Levinas's most persistent and systematic distinctions, which becomes particularly important in his critique of Heidegger, is between the "sacred" and the "holy" (*le sacré/le saint*).[4] He associates the sacred with something akin to magic or sorcery. His second anthology of talmudic readings is titled *Du sacré au saint*, or *From the Sacred to the Holy*.[5] In it, he explains why he rejects the concept of the sacred.

> We wished in these readings to bring out the catharsis or demythification of the religious that Jewish wisdom performs. It does this in opposition to the interpretation of myths — ancient or modern — through recourse to other myths, often more obscure and more cruel, albeit more widespread, and which, by this fact, pass for being more profound, sacred, or universal. The oral Torah[6] speaks "in spirit and in truth," even when it seems to do violence to the verses and letters of the written Torah. From the Torah it extracts ethical meanings as the ultimate intelligibility of the human and even of the cosmic. That is why we have entitled the present book *From the Sacred to the Holy*, even though these words pertain, strictly speaking, only to the theme of the third reading of the series.[7]

Cruelty and obscurity are contrasted with reason and ethics. It is important to note that Levinas's vindication of talmudic studies is meaningful within Judaism, taking its stand with the Mitnagdim or intellectualist tradition (an important center of which was in Lithuania, in the person and teachings of Rabbi Elijah, the Gaon of Vilna (1720–1797) and those of his disciple, Rabbi Hayyim of Volozhin (1749–1821) in opposition to the eighteenth century Hassidim movement, in which study was less emphasized and a more demonstrative fideism prevailed. It is also meaningful outside Judaism because medieval Christians considered the study of the Talmud a form of black magic, the epitome of irrationality. The pious Jew of the Psalms was less offensive than the Talmudist.

Levinas rejects the notion of the sacred that is tied to a place, to enrootedness. In Levinas's characterization of being and of "same," the "I" is riveted to itself, or to its sameness, until "troubled" or "awakened" by the other.

Another motif clearly set in opposition to enrootedness (and immanence) is Judaism itself. The diaspora of Judaism is probably emblematic of the condition of humankind. We are strangers on earth. Despite a propensity for anti-Semites to exploit it as a curse visited upon "the Jew," and despite the founding of the State of Israel, the motif of the wandering Jew has a metaphysical significance. We remain "strangers in a strange land."

For Levinas, the sacred represents a violent past that cannot be transcended by negativity, "which conserves what it negates, in its history." Goodness, however, "[d]estroys without leaving souvenirs, without transporting into museums the altars raised to the idols of the past for blood sacrifices, it burns the sacred groves in which the echoes of the past reverberate."[8]

PART TWO

Themes

A topical approach, though less strictly philosophical, has the advantage of offering the freedom necessary to enter into an intertextual domain — Levinas and Husserl, Levinas and Heidegger, and finally Derrida's reading of Levinas — and to pursue certain themes. Some are themes within Levinas's own writings (e.g. Judaism), while others, such as the metaphysical interpretation of grammatical terminology, are ad hoc headings I have developed to draw attention to a certain motif that runs through much of Levinas's work, though it is not specifically referred to by its author.

I felt it important to include the Holocaust among the themes discussed here both because of Levinas's direct references to it and because of the ways in which it has influenced the intellectual and spiritual life of all its survivors, using survivors in the broadest sense.

I do not pretend in the chapters that deal with Husserl, Heidegger and Derrida to present anything more than an overview of these philosophical encounters. There are, in fact, many studies available that can lead the reader into more nuanced discussion.

8. JUDAISM

It is generally assumed that the two works for which Levinas will be remembered are his two major philosophical contributions, *Totality and Infinity* (1961) and *Otherwise than Being* (1974). It is indeed true that it is in those works that Levinas has presented us with the fullest, most sustained and best "coordinated" presentation of his philosophical thought. Nevertheless, his writings on Judaic themes, as well as the talmudic lessons or readings, are intimately interrelated to his formal philosophical texts. This chapter will explore those writings and that relationship.

Levinas's Judaism

When asked, in the course of an interview with François Poirié, whether the fact that he was often presented as a Jewish thinker was meaningful to him, Levinas replied in a nuanced manner that he accepted it, as long as it was not intended to imply that he dared make certain rapprochements between concepts solely on the basis of religious texts, without philosophical analysis. He went on to explain his particular method of approaching biblical texts, a question that we shall consider in its place, then concluded by expressing some irritation at the suggestion that he used biblical verses to prove anything. He said that he sometimes might "seek by using the ancient wisdom," but he did not "prove by means of the [biblical] verse."[1]

The essential contours of Levinas's writings on Judaism are found conveniently gathered by the author himself in the collection of essays on Jewish themes, *Difficult Freedom*, originally published in 1963,[2] and containing pieces ranging from the Liberation on. There we find very personal yet philosophically profound expressions of the significance of Judaism, polemical texts, anchored in current events, short monographs devoted to specific figures (e.g. Rosenzweig, Gordin, Spinoza, Claudel), and a lengthy talmudic commentary on the theme of Messianism.

Perhaps the most important trait of Levinas's Judaism is expressed in the author's brief preface. "The other's hunger — earthly hunger, hunger for bread — is holy; only the hunger of the third party limits its rights; the only bad materialism is our own."[3] This is by no means a new idea in Judaism. One of Levinas's criticisms of Martin Buber was that the latter's I-thou relationship appeared to be too much on the order of a friendship, more of a spiritual affinity than Levinas's ethical and earthy coming to the aid of the other, regardless of whether there might be any psychological or emotive rapport involved.[4]

There is a perceptible and fecund interchange between Levinas's writings in *Difficile Liberté* and his philosophical works of the same period. The crossings are particularly discernible in the writings of the early 1950s: between "L'ontologie est-elle fondamentale?" (1951) and the first piece in *Difficile Liberté*, "Éthique et esprit" (1952); or between "Liberté et commandement" (1953) and "Le Moi et la Totalité" (1954). The institutional vessel in which Jewish and philosophical themes were able to coincide was the annual meeting of the Colloquium of Jewish Intellectuals, the first meeting of which took place in May, 1957.[5] There are many places in Levinas's texts in which the idea that religious and philosophical thought will eventually converge is noticeable. One clear example of this is the author's preface to *Entre nous: On Thinking-of-the-Other*, in which we read,

The main intent here is to try to see ethics in relation to the rationality of the knowledge that is immanent in being, and that is primordial in the philosophical tradition of the West; even if ethics — ultimately going beyond the forms and determinations of ontology, but without rejecting the peace of reason — could achieve a different form of intelligibility and a different way of loving wisdom, and perhaps even — but I will not go that far — the way of Psalm 111:10.[6]

Due for the most part, no doubt, to the fortuitous circumstances of his birth in Kovno, Lithuania, Levinas was, as mentioned earlier in passing, of the Mitnaged (meaning, in Hebrew, "opposed") tradition. This group, formed after the Gaon of Vilna placed a ban on the emerging Hasidic movement, was known for its emphasis on study and a generally intellectual approach, which set them at odds with the more mystically inclined Hassidim. The Gaon of Vilna's renowned student, Rabbi Hayim of Volozhin, author of *Nefesh HaHayim,* or *The Soul of Life*, was greatly admired by Levinas, who wrote an introduction to that work on the occasion of its translation into French.[7] In his brief, four-page preface, Levinas connects the view of the human interpreted by Volozhin at the end of verse 7 of Genesis 2 not as a "living being," but more literally as "a living soul" or "the soul of life," with his philosophical view of human beings as having unlimited responsibility, on whose actions the fate of the universe depends.

Levinas's Method of Exegesis in the Talmudic Readings

Levinas's technique of reading the talmudic texts avoids both the unquestioning acceptance of biblical verses on scriptural authority and their immediate, preemptive philosophical invalidation. He describes his approach as follows.

There are two ways to read a Biblical verse. There is the one that consists in relying on tradition, which grants it the value of a premise in its conclusions, without mistrust and without even realizing the presuppositions of that tradition and without even adapting its form of expression, with all the local particularities to which that language is subject. And there is the second way of reading, which consists not at all in an intellectual challenge at the initial stage, but in translating and accepting the suggestions of a way of thinking that, once translated, can be justified by what is manifested in it. For me, my relation to phenomenology was very important: to say, for every suggestive meaning, what the context of that meaning is, what intellectual acts and spiritual milieu it takes for granted.[8]

Levinas's phenomenological background is particularly well suited to a hermeneutics that has so many contingencies and so much history to transcend. The existential rapprochement between "Athens and Jerusalem," (or in Levinas's own shorthand, between Hebrew and Greek) that was Levinas's life was greatly facilitated by a philosophy of a particular kind, and a particular kind of Judaism. The philosophy was Husserlian phenomenology, with a progressively metaphysical orientation; the Judaism was, as we have seen, influenced by the Lithuanian Mitnagdim, distinct from and in opposition to Hasidism and known for its intellectual rigor and suspicion of the more emotive or charismatic tendencies of this latter movement.

But if these circumstances lend themselves to a diminishing of the distance between philosophy and Judaism, the point of coincidence or overlap is less contingency than choice. In Levinas's philosophical thinking, ethics replaces ontology to become "first philosophy,"[9] and in his view it is ethics that is at the very core of Judaism.[10]

In a remarkable passage from the last talmudic reading in the 1977 collection, *Du sacré au saint*, Levinas expresses the relationship between the terms of this polarity in a way that may at first appear perplexing, since it subordinates philosophy to religion. He is commenting on a Halakhic text, that is, one that concerns practical conduct or rabbinic law, a rare occurrence for Levinas, who normally restricted his commentary to Aggadic texts[11] because he considered himself insufficiently knowledgeable to take on questions of Halakhah. He notes that

> [t]he Halakhah, *without calling into play the interpretation of the reader*, is transformed into an Aggadah, into a homiletic text, which, as you perhaps know, is the way philosophical views, that is to say, the properly religious thought of Israel, appear in Talmudic thought. (I do not regret having brought together philosophy and religion in my preceding sentence. Philosophy, for me, derives from religion. It is called into being by a religion adrift, and probably religion is always adrift.)[12]

The rapprochement between religion and philosophy is brought about in the course of a discussion of a talmudic text. Considering the two categories of the Halakhic (legal) and the Aggadic (moral and philosophical), Levinas is able to place "religion" in the latter category, and to view moral and philosophical elaborations as two modalities of the "religious thought of Israel." We must of course not confuse this sense of the philosophical with Levinas's much more specific use of the term philosophy as "Greek," and as representing the intellectual effort to attain a synchronic grasp of the "totality." But if religion is probably "always adrift," and philosophy called into being by it, we may infer that philosophy represents at least to some degree the desire to cast an anchor.

Despite the value of his own talmudic readings and the general approach they suggest, perhaps Levinas's way of "blowing on the embers" of the talmudic texts is so personal as to prevent its engendering a method. The introduction to *Explorations talmudiques*[13] leaves open the question of "the precise relationship between Levinas's thought and Judaism," considering that the problem remains "essentially unresolved." Nevertheless, his sparse introductory pages are informative with respect to the reception of Levinas's work in the United States, Israel and elsewhere.

Further particulars concerning Levinas's view of the nature of the talmudic "dialogue" will be taken up in chapter 20, "And God Created Woman."

9. Hypostasis, Grammar, and Thematization

A Metaphysical Grammar

The philosophical significance of grammar has long been apparent to linguists, linguistic philosophers, and philosophers in general. Levinas does not explore this topic directly, but his approach appeals at key moments to cases and parts of speech which play specific roles in philosophical expression, and in the "trace" of transcendence, carried over from the saying (*le Dire*) to the said (*le Dit*). Our first observation is that Levinas has chosen the infinitive form (*le Dire* is literally the "to say"), which is particularly appropriate in that, as the vessel of infinity, it is indefinite, lacking — or unimpeded by — the specifications of person and number. The said, by contrast, is both past and passive, having traded off its transcendent life and indeterminacy for the advantages of manifestation, the delineations of immanence. "Language has done its work and the Saying that bore this Said — but was going further — was absorbed and died in the said: it inscribed itself."[1] Some of the more specific ways in which the saying and the said are articulated have already been discussed in chapter 3, above.

The Accusative

The accusative is the modality in which a subjectivity encounters otherness. In the most dramatic case, that of the first person, the "me" is an "I" as seen by another. Levinas translates the Hebrew הנני (here I am), as *me voici* in which *me* is the accusative, since it is embedded in the expression *voi[s]*, or "see" and *[i]ci*, or "here." It is myself standing in the presence of, and at the service of, the other. I stand "accused," persecuted eventually, incorporated with unlimited liability.

Levinas notes that the reflexive pronoun *se* in French has no nominative form. This is in fact the case, since it represents the same entity as the subject but taken as its own object (whether direct or indirect). One of the frequent uses of the reflexive is to give a passive meaning to the verb.

The importance of the change of case from nominative to accusative as applied to the *moi* or selfish self is admirably expressed in the following commentary by Guy Petitdemange:

> Exposure designates the absolutely initial status of the *moi* as a *soi*, the very first non-allergic nature of the self to the other and the priority of the other in this disposition. Exposure is the result of this letting-be of the other within the citadel of the *moi*, the letting-be of recurrence, of the return or coming of the other into the same. At that moment the *moi* becomes *soi* — identity in the accusative, not rid of the *moi*, but on the contrary summoned to appear, constrained from within to leave the shadowy refuge of interiority to answer, before all else, for this extraterritorialized outside that is never my object — the other.[2]

This existential explication of the grammatical category of the accusative is a subdivision of a broader category: that of the noun, the "substantive," that which is posited or thematized.

Hypostasis, thematization and the *il y a* ("there is")

The noun, or substantive, is an achievement. It is the emergence from "existence" (which in the early work *De l'existence à l'existent*, translated with some loss as *Existence & Existents*, is termed the *il y a*, or the anonymous "there is") into an existent, that is, into a separate entity or being. The verbal aspect of being is therefore "older" than the substantive. Tied to and paralleling this promotion from the anonymous *il y a* to the participial form of being (an existent = *existant*, the French present participle of the verb *exister*) is the progression from wakefulness or insomnia to consciousness. Paradoxically, one of the characteristics of consciousness is the ability to fall asleep, to shut out the *il y a* in this way. Levinas's use of the word "hypostasis" is derived from the Enneads of Plotinus, particularly the fifth.[3] Levinas uses the term to designate the emergence of beings from the *il y a* into a substantive state of "existents." An existent is "master of its existence, as a subject is master of its attribute."[4]

The *il y a* may well be compared to the state of the world before creation, the *tohu uvohu*, of Genesis 1:2. In order to escape from this state of impersonal and threatening chaos, Levinas develops the notion of the "hypostasis" of existents, that is, the passage going from being to a something, from the state of verb to that of thing. Whence the formation of distinct "things" and of the subject as well: the *moi*. Clarity replaces darkness, and consciousness the autonomous wakefulness or insomnia of the *il y a*. This was Levinas's first solution for escaping from the *il y a*. But later he became aware that the subject was not freed but remained riveted to itself. Rather than dominating "things" the *moi* was preoccupied with them, bound up with them, pulled downwards into the immanence of being. Hence the second solution, which Levinas attempts to work out for the remainder of his philosophical career: the hollowing out of the *moi*, which empties itself, or turns itself inside out, becoming a "for-the-other."[5]

Thematization and God

It may be said that in a general sense Levinas's metaphysical interpretation of the grammatical functions and parts of speech reflect the way in which meaning has a foothold in being. Signification does not constitute a separate ontological domain, but disturbs or interferes with the immanence of being in the realm of the said. Of particular importance is the word God. The title of one of Levinas's later works, *Of God Who Comes to Mind*, highlights the *mise en scène* in which "the word God comes to the tip of the tongue."[6] In this regard, neither noun nor verb — both too suffused with being — are appropriate. And in the final sentence of Levinas's last major philosophical work, *Otherwise than Being*, we learn that it is neither a noun nor a verb, but the "*Pro-nom*" (pronoun, or stand-in for a name), and **in the third person**, "an unpronounceable inscription" of that which is "always already past" that remains, marking with its seal "all that can bear a name."[7]

God cannot be a noun because a noun, a name, would thematize God, and to thematize is to place within the realm of being. In fact, as we have just seen, it is the thematization called hypostasis that forms entities from the *il y a*. In countless passages, Levinas points out that God, Aquinas notwithstanding, is not a being at all, let alone a supreme one. Hence all "proofs of the existence of God" are very far from the problematics of Levinas. It may also be the case that Levinas's refusal to "preach" morality or to address theological matters thematically is to be understood as the result of his understanding of the self-defeating nature of thematization in such matters. He does have quite a lot to say about many aspects of Judaism, as is clear to readers of his *Difficult Freedom*. But these are aspects of the way Judaism is lived. Religious significance is attributed to atheism, and in some texts Levinas goes so far as to use the term atheism to describe our inescapable state, which is "without God."

Illeity

The most direct route to an understanding of the role of this new concept in Levinas is through its functional necessity, an outgrowth the latter's critique of Martin Buber's I-Thou relation. That critique centers on the symmetry and reversibility of that dialogical relation. Buber emphasizes quite justly the importance of the I-Thou over the I-It relation, with respect to our rapport with other people.

It is the concept of "the face" (*visage*) that requires a move beyond this sort of reciprocity. The face of the other (person) is the basis of all morality, being in the "trace" of that "beyond being" the trace of the passage of a "past that was never present" or of God.

Why is God in the third person? Levinas remarks that Jewish prayers often begin in the second person and then switch to the third. The relevance of this observation to his own philosophy is that there is an important distinction to be made between the relation to God and the dialogical relation to the other person. The necessity of this was prompted by Levinas's rejection of the reciprocity of the Buberian "thou." It is certainly related to Levinas's forming of the term "illeity" in discussing the necessary distance (respect, separation) between human and God. Illeity is coined on the Latin demonstrative pronoun *ille, illa, illud*, which, as opposed to *hic, haec, hoc* designates something present but at a distance, such as "that great man over there" or anything to which one refers with respect. The term illeity appears — perhaps for the first time — in a piece published in 1963, "La trace de l'autre."[8]

The dialogical relationship brings with it elements that make it an inadequate structure for transcendence because of the reciprocity and eventual play of gratitude and psychological interplay to which both parties of the dialogue are open. The otherness of the other person is preserved and his or her stature as "greater than myself" safeguarded only if the face of the other is "in the trace" of illeity. "The *illeity* of the third person is the condition of irreversibility."[9]

The Secret of a Semantics

Levinas's critique of Buber's dialogical relation with the other (in the form of an I-Thou relation) is, as is so often the case with

Levinas, less a critique than an assimilation, coupled with a subtle but important reorientation. "What seems to me to be suggested by the 'philosophy of dialogue,'" he writes, "is that the encounter with the other man takes place neither on a side-street nor a detour, nor some parallel track of transcendence, and that the face of the other bears the trace of its straightest, shortest and most direct movement."[10] Only such a relation of transcendence (transcending the ontological realm, the hallmark of which is war, commerce, or some reasonable "balance of power") makes morality possible. Only thus does the word God cease "orienting life by expressing the unconditional foundation of the world and cosmology, and reveals, in the face of the other man, the secret of his semantics."

10. Proximity and Temporality

"Proximity" and "temporality" are both aspects of the relation between the same and the other. Proximity, the "non-indifference" of one person to the other, is deployed as temporality, which Levinas understands as a continuity across disjuncture.

The Centrality of Proximity

Proximity is the field that Levinas opens between the same (or the subject) and the other, in which the "intrigue of the infinite" unfolds. It evokes a spatiality of a rather abstract nature since it is the distance between the poles of a relation. The relation between subject and other was central to Levinas's philosophy long before the term proximity itself emerged in his writing. Proximity appears only seven times (of which six are relevant) in *Totality and Infinity* (1961), compared to a whopping 259 times in *Otherwise than Being* (1974). Of particular interest, therefore, will be the examination of the shorter pieces published in the interval between these two major works. What are the inner dynamics of Levinas's evolving thought over those years that move the concept of proximity to such prominence?

The Development of the Concept

As Robert Bernasconi notes,[1] there is a link between Levinas's decision to use the word neighbor (*prochain*) alongside the earlier word Stranger (*Étranger*) and the ascendancy of the notion of proximity (*proximité*). Bernasconi draws our attention to an interesting footnote to the essay "Enigma and Phenomenon" (1965) where Levinas writes, "Formerly we refused this term [*prochain*], which seemed to suggest a community by neighborhood. Now we retain in it the abruptness of the disturbance, which characterizes a neighbor inasmuch as he is the first one to come along."[2] Is there really any "abruptness" in the term neighbor, or any implication that the neighbor is "the first to come along"? In any case, Levinas intends to bestow such a meaning upon the term.

French has two words that correspond to the English word neighbor. Levinas is not discussing the term *voisin*, which is the normal term for the person who lives close by, but the term *prochain*, which is used in the Bible to indicate one's neighbor in the sense of one's fellow man (or woman). A relevant passage from "Transcendence and Height," which is from Levinas's response to a question in the ensuing discussion of that lecture, will help us understand the reasons for his initial rejection of the term. A certain Minkowski has just pointed out, in opposition to Levinas's notion of the absolute difference between self and other, that there is a lot of similarity between human beings, and that the notion of solidarity with one's fellow human being arises naturally out of this similarity. Levinas responds:

> In my opinion, transcendence is only possible when the Other (*Autrui*) is not initially the fellow human being (*semblable*) or the neighbor (*prochain*); but when it is the very distant, when it is Other, when it is the one with whom initially I have nothing in common, when it is an abstraction. In all this affirmation of the concrete from which philosophy today lives, one fails to recognize that the relation with the other (*autrui*) is an element of abstraction which pierces the continuity of the concrete, a relation with the Other *qua* Other, denuded, in every sense of the term. Consequently, it is necessary to avoid the words *neighbor* (*prochain*) and *fellow human being* (*semblable*), which establish so many things in common with my neighbor (*voisin*) and so many similarities

with my fellow human being. Transcendence seemed to me to be the point of departure for our concrete relations with the Other (*Autrui*); all the rest is grafted on top of it. That is why the transcendent is a notion which seems to me primary.[3]

This "element of abstraction which pierces the continuity of the concrete" is certainly a remarkable sort of abstraction. It is not an abstraction in the etymological sense of that term (*abstrahere*, to drag out of), which tacitly assumes a prior, fuller empirical context from which certain formal elements are removed and isolated for thematization. If my relations with the other are "grafted on top of it" it would be closer in spirit to those transcendent realities Plato called "ideas." Metaphysical, it is beyond (or on the hither side) of the physical. In this intervention it is not difficult to perceive (a) Levinas's opposition to an anti-Platonism of his time (as in Bergson, and as attested in Jean Wahl's *Vers le Concret*) and (b) an ethics that, as in Kant and in Judaism, rejects inclination (the sentimental concrete) as the principle of moral behavior. This use of neighbor (*prochain*) that Levinas has now accepted as a philosopheme is to be brought into the semantic family of proximity: *approcher*, to approach, *prochain*, neighbor, and *proximité*.

In the essay "Language and Proximity," first published in the second edition of *En decouvrant l'existence avec Husserl et Heidegger* in 1967, proximity is used to describe the relation "between me and the interlocutor,"[4] and it is distinguished in its singularity from the two speakers' participation in the universality of what is said. Is this a variant of speech act theory, as in J. L. Austin's illocutionary acts? The difference is — and it is a major one — that ordinary language philosophers situated language within the broader field of behavior, while Levinas's speculative metaphysics placed the relation between interlocutors in a space radically separated from the realm of being in which acts of any sort may be said to be performed: the domain of the

Dire — an-archical, meaningful without context, and unrepresentable. Proximity, in this one of several prototexts to *Otherwise than Being*, is also referred to as contact, as "tenderness and responsibility."

The term "work," or *œuvre*, was taken up by Levinas for a short time to designate what was later referred to as the "approach," i.e. the approach of the same to the absolute other. As far has I can determine, that term only appears in the essay "La trace de l'autre" which appeared in *Tijdschrift voor Filosofie*, no. 3, in 1963, was included in the second (1967) edition of *En découvrant l'existence avec Husserl et Heidegger*, and was reworked and incorporated into part 6 of *La sens et la signification* in *Humanisme de l'autre homme* (1972). Although the term "approach" seems to replace "work," it might be a Hegelian mistake to think that the later term sublates that former. There may be differences that need to be preserved. The term *œuvre* is, first of all, more closely allied with religious terminology, since it is associated by Levinas with the Greek term liturgy, which, we are told "in its primary meaning, indicates the exercise of an office not only totally without recompense, but requiring on the part of the officiate a monetary loss."[5] Levinas explicitly states that this term, work, is not to be taken as one of the "good works," described in the "positive religions." Although not "one of those works," it may be that it participates in the same transcendental source as the Jewish *mitzvah*, which, like my responsibility for the other, is in response to a heteronymous command.

It is now time to enquire more specifically into the precise nature of this proximity. But in order to do so, we must first examine a theory of meaning without which the idea of proximity would not have any claim to primacy.

An Essentialist Theory of Meaning

Levinas's initial objection to the use of the term "neighbor" (*prochain*) was now overcome, but it was really part of larger problem. The problem concerns the relationship between the figurative (or metaphorical) use of language and its "literal" meaning. More precisely, the question is not just of the "use" one may make of language, but of language itself. Here, another essay written during the time period we are interested in (1961–1974) will be of help. In the first section of "Meaning and Sense" (1964), subtitled "Meaning and Receptivity," Levinas challenges the notion that words have a literal meaning that underlies their figurative or metaphorical meaning. "[T]he experience of spring," he says, "remains authentic and autochthonous over and beyond the seasons and human ages." When Homer compares an attack by an enemy phalanx to the resistance of a rock to the waves, there is no anthropomorphism involved, since "[R]esistance is neither a human privilege nor a rock's, just as radiance does not characterize a day of the month of May more authentically than it does the face of a woman. The meaning precedes the data and illuminates them."[6] The "immediate" given is always a this *qua* this or that; experience is not intuition but hermeneutics. It becomes unclear whether we are speaking of the world or of language because objects "become meaningful on the basis of language and not language on the basis of objects given to thought and designated by words that would function as simple signs."[7] Meaning is therefore *a priori*. To make this doctrine somewhat more palatable it should be borne in mind that Levinas distinguishes between "significations" and "sense." The *a priori* meanings are those that derive from sense. *Sens* in French has the meaning of both sense and of direction, and Levinas plays off both meanings at once here because he is distinguishing the individual word meanings and cultural meanings from the meaning that is oriented within the unidirectional field (*sens unique*, unidirectional movement as well as unique meaning) of proximity (the direction going from self to other). More will be said presently about sense versus meaning.

Levinas is aware that this theory of meaning is in some ways a return to Platonism. With this theory of meaning in mind, we are now in a better position to understand what Levinas means and does not mean by proximity.

The "Absolute" or "Human" Sense of Proximity

Chapter 3 of *Otherwise than Being*, titled "Sensibility and Proximity," contains a sixth and last section called "Proximity." This text represents the final stage in the elaboration of a cluster of concepts connected with proximity. It is a slightly modified version of "La proximité," an essay published in 1971.[8] The latter was, Levinas tells us,[9] delivered as a lecture at the Faculté Universitaire Saint-Louis in Brussels in 1967, and remained faithful to the study entitled "Language and Proximity."

The section "Proximity" begins by distinguishing between the spatial or geometrical and the "absolute" or "human" use of the word proximity. The geometrical meaning is "relative" and "borrowed" (*emprunté*) or "derivative."[10] What does this mean? First, the geometrical meaning is described as "the interval diminishing between two points." One difference between Levinas's use of proximity and the geometrical one is that in the latter case both points are situated simultaneously and in relation to an observer. The observer is situated at neither of the proximate points being considered. In Levinas's usage, the two points are the other and the same: i.e. there is no outside observer, since the observer, *qua* subjectivity, is one of the poles in the relation of proximity.

Expanding upon the thought that geometric proximity is derivative, Levinas suggests that contiguity may not be thinkable without proximity, i.e. approach, neighborhood (*voisinage*), and contact. The absolute and proper sense of proximity, Levinas asserts, presupposes "humanity." Even the homogeneity of space is to be reduced to the notion of justice. On a purely formal level, we may say that here Levinas is beginning to replace the language of objectivity with one more suitable to the spatiality of proximity; a language I will designate as axiologico-ethico-affective.

If the language of Levinasian subjectivity is at once and perhaps indistinguishably affective and ethical, it is because the ethical subject is a sensible, not a conscious, subject.[11] Hence the terms vulnerability, wound, sensitivity, passivity, exposure; and also words that convey trauma, obsession, and the desire for the other of transcendence. For proximity is not serene repose or rest, but disquietude, always insufficiently close, like an embrace. In what sense always insufficiently close? This opens up the question of the relation between proximity and contact.

Proximity and Contact

In a curious footnote early on in *Otherwise than Being*, Levinas makes the point that it is exaggeration or emphasis rather than negation of the category that interrupts the system of logic or of the order of being. "In subjectivity the superlative is the exorbitance of a null-site, in caresses and in sexuality the 'excess' of tangency — as though tangency admitted a gradation — up to contact with the entrails, a skin going under another skin."[12] This seems to be the continuation of a thought first developed in *Totality and Infinity*, in the section "The Subjectivity in Eros," namely, "The structure of the subjectivity's identity that is produced in Eros takes us outside the categories of classical logic."[13] Contact would seem to represent the end point of proximity, yet already symbolized in the form of sexual intercourse we have something like an exaggeration of tangency, to the degree that the topology of "essence" or being makes that possible. The caress is also analyzed in its restless searching, its *marche à l'invisible*.[14] But it is frustrated in its transcendental *élan* beyond the *étant*, the entity within being. "In a certain sense it *expresses* love, but suffers from an inability to say it."[15]

The primacy of sound over sight, of auditory over visible form, is a constant in Levinas's philosophy. "The sounds and noises of nature are words that disappoint us. To really hear a sound is to hear a word. Pure sound is the word."[16] Just as the proximity of which Levinas speaks is not a measure of distance in space, it is not contact in any corporeal sense either. The more transcendental nature of sound, or perhaps we should say of the voice — the biblical Hebrew word for sound and voice are the same, *qol* — seems to attain a proximity that goes beyond surface topology, and to escape the immanence of presence and the present.

There is clearly a movement away from the visible and the tangible in the interval that separates *Totality and Infinity* from *Otherwise than Being*. Evidence of this is in the relative deemphasizing of the face and the body (the frequency of these words drops from 344 to 69, and from 98 to 33, respectively),[17] as well as in a stylistic evolution in the direction of aridity. Guy Petitdemange describes it as a "livre âpre [. . .] dur et sec à la peau comme tempête de sable" (an acrid book, hard and dry against the skin like a sandstorm).[18] It is in that work that we find a vocabulary that takes on the task of parsing the infinite field of proximity: obsession, hostage, recurrence, alterity, one-for-the-other, approach, substitution, glory, dia-chrony, an-archy, rupture, responsibility, trace. They are all interwoven in such a way that one could start anywhere. I have chosen to set out from recurrence, because I find its meaning to be the most elusive and therefore the most in need of elucidation.

Recurrence

This term does not appear at all in *Totality and Infinity* but is frequent in *Otherwise than Being*. It is possible to deduce from textual evidence given in Levinas's footnotes that the term was adopted after the completion of *Totality and Infinity* (1961) and not later than 1968.[19] In *Otherwise than Being*, it is the subtitle of section 2 of chapter 4, "Substitution." Its first appearance[20] is in reference to the recurrence of the reflexive pronouns, in the passive meaning (*les choses se montrent, les bagages se plient et les idées se comprennent*: things are shown, the luggage is packed, ideas are understood). There is a grammatical connection between this use of the reflexive pronoun (as passivity) and the accusative case. The grammatical oddity of the pronoun *se* in French is that it only occurs in the accusative, or object case. It is as if the subject turns back upon itself and takes itself as its own object.

Section 2 of the 1968 essay, "Substitution" is titled "Recurrence and the Hither Side" [i.e. the side closest to us].[21] There, recurrence is the "knot" in the thread spun by the mythological Parcae. This node is said to be an ipseity older than consciousness and more passive; it is the basis for both the *soi* and the *moi*, a crucial distinction not easily made in English, and that has resulted in a variety of translations. In order to avoid ambiguity here, I will naturalize *soi* and *moi*.[22]

Subjectivity is not substance but, by prolepsis, the hypostatization of a term generated from a relationship with the other. It is incessant recurrence, that is, "the identity of the Hegelian concept, in which, under the apparent naturalness of expressions such as 'for oneself,' 'for itself,' and 'by oneself' is concealed all the singularity of the recurrence to oneself, a recurrence without rest — the genuine problem of the subject."[23] Recurrence is related to election, but to an election that comes with an ineluctable responsibility that makes me unique. "Here uniqueness means the impossibility of slipping away and being replaced, an impossibility in which is knotted the very recurrence of the I (*je*)."[24] Uniqueness is, in French, more obviously related to oneness (*un, unique*). Just as the unique is what is one in an emphatic way, so recurrence is described as "but an 'outdoing' [*surenchère*] of unity."[25] It is important to note that the uniqueness of the *soi* is quite different from the uniqueness of the *moi* in Romanticism. The former is selfless, impersonal, abstract and inescapable, while the latter is a quaint concoction of memories, idiosyncrasies, intimacy, secrecy.

A Thematics of Recurrence

Recurrence is to be understood in its etymological sense of a "running back," but it is not exactly a return to the same, as is the act of knowing (recognition) in Levinas's view. Although some passages indicate that this recurrence of the *soi* underlies consciousness and recognition or knowledge, making those operations possible, there are indications that recurrence is not repetition. The first is that the return does not stop at the initial point of departure, but keeps going, to a point even closer to me than my *moi* or selfish self. This interpretation receives indirect support from Levinas's remark that in this case the recurrence returns to a place on the hither side of the point of departure.[26] The expression on the hither or near side (*en deçà*) is essential to Levinas's depiction of subjectivity, at least as important as that transcendence that goes in the opposite direction, the *au-delà* or beyond.

This inward bound movement of recurrence is **withdrawal**. Withdrawal is, of course, a venerable theme both as the gesture that leads to wisdom (Know thyself) and to spiritual enlightenment (the hermet or anchorite, the retreat). But in Levinas we cannot, of course, think of this movement as an act, since it is prior to the world of decision-making. Perhaps it is in order to sidestep these venerable terms that have so many familiar associations and edifying doctrines built into them that Levinas adopts a more fundamental language. I have grouped them thematically by motifs.

Digging, or hollowing out. There may be a trace of this motif in *Totality and Infinity*, where it is said of metaphysical desire that "the Desired does not fulfill it, but deepens it."[27] The motif is much more prominent in the original: *le Désiré ne le comble* *pas, mais le creuse*. Literally we have "the Desired does not fill it in, but digs it out."

Eating away, biting (the nonfigurative form of remorse), **gnawing** (*manger, mordre, le remords, ronger*). It is the *soi* that eats away at itself; "[G]nawing away at this very identity — identity gnawing away at itself — in a remorse" (*rongeant cette identité même — identité se rongeant — dans un remords*).[28] Here again, the etymological "mordre" restores to remorse its original bite. Or "The self is out of phase with itself, forgetful of itself, forgetful in biting in upon itself, in the reference to itself which is the gnawing away at oneself of remorse" (*Soi déphasé par soi, oubli de soi, oubli dans la morsure sur soi, dans la référence à soi par le se ronger du remords*).[29]

Contraction, crispation, anguish, anxiety. Another aspect of recurrence is a shrinking, in that "absolute passivity of a *soi* . . . whose recurrence is my contraction" (*la passivité absolue d'un soi [. . .] dont la récurrence est ma contraction*).[30] But this reduction leads to a non-Heideggerian anguish, specifically distinguished from the latter in a lengthy footnote, in which Heidegger's anguish is declared to be over the limitation of being.[31] For being *qua* being-toward-death, death is the hope of reaching the open sea of non-being. Levinasian anxiety, again in the etymological sense of a narrowing, a tightening, is not unrelated to contraction, but in this case it is a narrowing of the *moi* to the *soi* of the embodiment of the human being. Embodiment is distinguished from the enclosure of matter in form, in the world of things. "The ego is not in itself like matter which, perfectly espoused by its form, is what it is; it is in itself like one is in one's skin, that is, already cramped, ill at ease in one's own skin" (*Le moi est en soi non pas comme la matière qui, parfaitement épousée par sa forme, est ce qu'elle est, parfaitement; le moi est en soi comme dans sa peau, c'est-à-dire déjà à l'étroit, mal dans sa peau*).[32]

Maternal, material. It is "as though" recurrence, says Levinas — and the precise nature of that "as though" will have to be determined by examining the relations between the *dire* and the *dit*, no doubt — it is as though recurrence, that movement into itself, reached a dimension in which a retreat to the near side of immediate coincidence were possible, "a materiality more material than all matter." What turns out to be more material than matter is the body, which qualifies for this "more" because of its exaggerated passivity. More passive than the inertia of the physical thing is vulnerability, susceptibility, exposure to wounds. "Maternity in the complete being 'for the other' which characterizes it, which is the very signifyingness of signification, is the ultimate sense of this vulnerability" (*Vulnérabilité dont la maternité dans son integral 'pour l'autre' est l'ultime sens et qui est la signifiance même de la signification*).[33] The etymological link between mother and matter, which discreetly dominates this rapprochement, beckons toward the human *a priori* of the essentialist theory of meaning.

The "allée dans le plein" (going into fullness) and pneumatology. This movement ever closer, or on the hither side, this plunge into interiority, encounters itself as a fullness. It is a movement not toward some available empty space, but an inversion of materiality into itself, a going into fullness. "It is not a flight into the void, but a fullness, the anguish of contraction and breakup" (*Non pas une fuite dans le vide, mais une allée dans le plein, l'anxiété de la contraction et de l'éclatement*).[34] Suggested is a contraction and an explosion or a contraction that at the point of its fullness of consolidation then expands. "It is as though the atomic unity of the subject were exposed to the outside by breathing, by divesting its ultimate substance even to the mucous membrane of the lungs, continually splitting up" (*Comme si l'unité atomique du sujet s'exposait au dehors en respirant, en dépouillant sa substance ultime jusqu'aux muqueuses du poumon, ne cessait de se fendre*).[35] It is a return to a familiar reality, that of the living, breathing, and exhaling human body. But is this a return to something familiar, or is what is familiar but an empirical reflection of this metaphysical pneumatology?

The Meaning of Proximity

In the essay "Meaning and Sense" (1964),[36] Levinas makes a distinction between "meaning" and "sense" (*la signification, le sens*). Sense is what underlies all the other meanings in a culture or language, and meaning (e.g. word meanings) is only possible in a world that is structured by sense. I suspect that this distinction, adumbrated in *Totality and Infinity*,[37] eventually became the all-important *dire/dit* (saying/said) distinction. In the discursive logos, the *dit* of this essay, we must now ask: What is the meaning of proximity?

Using sense in the way Levinas does, we may say that proximity **is** sense. It is an underlying directionality (the asymmetrical, one-way movement from self to other) from which meanings emerge, in a manner analogous to that of objectivity emerging from the Kantian transcendental. At the end of chapter 4 ("Substitution"), this directionality gives a meaning to death. This is not exactly the same thing as saying that it gives meaning to life, but it is very close to doing so since for Levinas death is what threatens to make life nonsensical. Summarizing the concluding paragraphs of chapter 4, the self, as it divests itself of the egotism of perseverance in being, which is "the imperialism of the Moi," introduces sense into being. Mortality makes humans either tragic or comic, but in either case absurd, to the degree that their struggle against death is hopeless. Pleasure, which can be defined as the short-term forgetfulness of the tragi-comedy, is belied by death, but the latter, despite its adversity, is not opposed to the "for the other" of the approach.

One might object that Levinas has taken a long route to arrive at such a conventional moral. The task of leaving our egotistical for our better selves is common to most salvific doctrines, and altruism may be a universally recognized spiritual goal or value. Is Levinas the inventor of a new noble risk in the form of a myth, or, to speak in terms of social psychology, the originator of forms for a new sensibility, in the manner of Teresa of Avila's Inner Castle, offering imagery for the religious sensibility? "No one," he says, "is so hypocritical as to claim to have taken the sting out of death — not even those who make religious promises — but [if] we can have responsibilities and attachments by which death takes on meaning — it is because, from the start, the Other affects us despite ourselves."[38]

There is in that "from the start" (for the reader who has been attentive to the pages that precede it) both the hint that for Levinas "the start" (*dès le départ*) is really before any beginning in synchronic time, and in the "despite ourselves" the ever unwelcome and against-the-grain unselving or transselving, being awakened and bothered by the other, and the infinite trek or exercise of patience, bringing to pass a reversal in which being no longer regulates sense, but vice versa.

Temporality

Temporality in Levinas is an aspect of the relation to the other, the infinite, or the beyond being. We shall begin our discussion of time by distinguishing two very different notions of time developed by Levinas, one that typifies time within being, the other that attempts to get at our way of relating to the beyond-being, or radical otherness.

Consciousness, in conformity with the law of being, of immanence, and of the said, is synthetic. Here Levinas follows Husserl's conception of time as developed in his *The Phenomenology of Internal Time Consciousness*. Future and past are anticipation and retention and thus drawn into the synthesis of the present. This sort of time is designated by Levinas as "synchronic time." Its opposite is "diachronic time,"[39] a time that does not allow itself to be drawn into the present, and to which I have referred in my introduction (in an approximate, preliminary way) as essentialist. The first descriptions of this latter notion of temporality are from Levinas's early work *Time and the Other* (1947), in which the future is radically divorced from the "immanent" account of it which would make the future an anticipation in the present. The future is more than "creativity" (here Levinas is incorporating and going beyond a Bergsonian view) which is a renewal too bound up with the present.

In one sense these two sorts of temporality are contradictory, and philosophies that exclude the notions of transcendence and/or infinity would reject the idea of "diachronic" time altogether. But within the thinking of Levinas, "diachronic" versus "synchronic" time may be said to be only relatively contradictory; they both clearly have a role within his thinking — the former obtaining within being, the latter disrupting or leaving a "trace" of its passage within being, but testifying to a beyond-being. Synchronic time is disturbed or disrupted by the time of the other (that of the other person, whose temporality is neither a province of my own temporality nor the province of another me, an "alter ego").

One approach to clarifying this distinction is to consider the well-known problem of the origin of time. Levinas avoids placing the beginning of temporality within time itself. The origin of temporality cannot be an event in time but neither can it be, or so it would seem, an event outside of time, since the very notion of beginning is a temporal one. Of course one solution would be to posit time as infinite, along the lines of Plato's notion of time as the moving image of an unmoving eternity. Levinas rejects this solution, however, in favor of a notion of "an-archic" time: a time without beginning. Yet this time retains the notions of pastness and futurity, because Levinas maintains that these notions are not really abstractions derived from our experience with and within time (synchronic time, within being) but rather prior to experience — somewhat in the same sense in which the Kantian transcendental *a priori* (of time and space) precedes and make possible experience. There is one major difference between the Kantian a priori of time and Levinas's, however. For Kant, the temporal a priori is a necessary precondition for experience, whereas in Levinas this cannot be the case since Levinas does not admit any causal connection between being and beyond-being. Causality is restricted to the ontological domain. (This raises some doubts about how the beyond-being can disrupt and even leave a "trace" within being. To explore this difficulty would take us too far afield, but it is a problem Levinas himself addresses.)[40]

Another useful bias by means of which we may approach the Levinasian conception of temporality is through the position of Martin Heidegger, one of Levinas's early teachers and an ever-present counterpoint to his work. Of particular interest to Levinas was Heidegger's notion of existence as "ecstasis," a being-ahead-of-oneself, a being-toward-death. This anticipation leads to a specifically human way of being, characterized by anxiety. Rightly or wrongly (as some Heideggerians would maintain), Levinas assimilates being-toward-death (one's own, that is) to the Spinozan *conatus essendi* or self-preserving principles of being. (He connects Heidegger's preliminary description of Dasein as "ontically distinguished by the fact that, in its very Being, that Being is an issue for it"[41] with this same idea of self-concernedness.) For Levinas the key issue is the death of the other. His considerations on death involve the injunction not to leave the other to die alone, even if there is nothing we can do to prevent the outcome, and the vulnerability/inviolability of the face of the other.

In understanding the development of Levinas's treatment of time, it is well to remember that Levinas comes to philosophy through Husserl, as a phenomenologist. The phenomenological approach is to inquire into the **meaning** of time. In order to find the meaning of time, that abstraction, we must find its concrete meaning, or "deformalize" it. Hence Levinas's repeated references to *longueur de temps* (the length of time, i.e. its "dura-tion"), to patience, to aging, and so on. Patience is also impa-tience, aging the "passive synthesis." But these analyses are far more important to Levinas in *Totality and Infinity* (1961) than in *Otherwise than Being* (1974) because the latter work is devoted to breaking new ground. It takes on the description of the rela-tion (if that which holds between an absolute and the relative can be called a relation) between the saying and the said. The "diachronic" time of beyond being, with its beginninglessness (an-archy) and its "past that never was present" is startlingly unfa-miliar, and not readily intuitable. But there is also an implication that the clarity of logic and light of reason are in any case inap-propriate modalities here. Knowledge, in fact, as a form of appro-priation is limited to being.

Because time is the temporalization or work of the subject and because subjectivity undergoes a radical change of heart in Levinas as the same is invested by the other, it is hardly surprising that temporality, too, will undergo a transformation.

"Synthetic time" is that of the said, not of the saying. The say-ing is the face-to-face, the relation (if it can be called a relation) with the absolutely other. But we should not imagine that the other, in order to comply with the conditions of expression of the said, changes: the other enters the same illicitly, "like a thief." The other disturbs or distorts the conditions of speech — and is thus testimony, speaking **through** the same prophetically. This speech is not heard and tabulated afterward; it is the hearing of its own voice and an obedience before understanding.

Proximity is normally intuited in spatial terms, and it is reci-procal. Both spatial proximity and time are used figuratively, metaphorically, or — as I prefer to say — essentially by Levinas. It is because (spatial) proximity is reciprocal or reversible that Levinas augments that way of speaking, when attempting to describe the "non-indifference" between one person and another, with temporal language. At a colloquium held at the Centre-Sèvres in Paris in 1986, Levinas makes the following comment about time in his work:

> I think that the problems of time, which begin in our astonishment at diachrony — closeness or proximity without space or reversibility, that "together, but not yet," as Blanchot says, a series without simultaneity — lose their vividness in all the reductions of diachrony to spatial figures, which Bergson lamented. The image of a straight line, in which the instants are past when they are no longer there, or future when they are not there yet, is a definition of time in terms of time, a tautology.[42]

Levinas then cites approvingly Heidegger's temporal "ecstases," in which the tenses are thought of in terms of concrete human circumstances: his "thrownness" is the "already," the present is "being-next-to-things," and the future is "being-toward-death." Similarly, Rosenzweig deformalizes time by means of biblical references to creation (past), revelation (present), and redemption (future). Levinas points out that it is the general notion of finding the concrete meaning of these temporal dimensions that he approves — though he may not espouse the precise interpretations of Heidegger or Rosenzweig. He concludes his remark by a leading, speculative question. "Is the *future* not an openness expressing the permanent delay of justice in relation to the requirements of love?"

Thus philosophical speculation on being, time, space, and justice are renewed, brought back to the concrete human circumstances that are the wellsprings, in Levinas's view, of meaning.

11. The Holocaust

The rise of anti-Semitism in the 1930s, the threat of totalitarian-ism, and the Holocaust itself not only "mark" Levinas's work, they set in motion a complex intertwining of his philosophical reflection with the state of the world in which it unfolded. I have taken care in this chapter to present Levinas's writings that have a direct bearing on the Holocaust in chronological order because, whether they are of a philosophical, a political, or a purely per-sonal nature, these utterances should be considered in their rela-tion to the event of the Holocaust itself. Further, important developments in Levinas's thinking in this respect would other-wise be obscured.[1]

1934: "Reflections on the Philosophy of Hitlerism"

Already in 1934 Levinas published (in the progressive, avant-garde French Catholic journal *Esprit*, founded by Emmanuel Mounier two years earlier) "*Quelques reflections sur la philoso-phie de l'hitlérisme.*" The essay appeared in *Critical Inquiry* in 1990 as "Reflections on the Philosophy of Hitlerism." In a short prefatory note to the editors of that journal, Levinas sums up the intent of his startlingly prescient piece:

> The article stems from the conviction that the source of the bloody barbarism of National Socialism lies not in some contingent anom-aly within human reasoning, nor in some accidental ideological misunderstanding. This article expresses the conviction that this source stems from the essential possibility of *elemental Evil* into

which we can be led by logic and against which Western philosophy has not sufficiently insured itself.[2]

The note then makes a clear connection with "the ontology of a being concerned with being," a formula that is then identified as "a being, to use the Heideggerian expression, *'dem es in seinem Sein um dieses Sein selbst geht.'*"[3] Levinas takes the being thus described by Heidegger as still essentially the subject of transcendental idealism, "that before all else wishes to be free." This freedom is in turn associated with a "liberalism" that Levinas certainly does not disdain — but he questions whether it is sufficient "to achieve an authentic dignity for the human subject." In fact he judges it as being insufficient, as is clear from his closing question, "Does the subject arrive at the human condition prior to assuming responsibility for the other man in the act of election that raises him to this height? This election comes from a god — or from God — who beholds him in the face of the other person, his neighbor, the original 'site' of the Revelation."[4] This short essay begins with a brief justification for even speaking of a "philosophy" of Hitlerism. Journalists, Levinas says, may be content with contrasting the universalism of Judaism and Christianity with the particularism of race; in language that evokes an existentialist analysis, he proposes rather to return to "the original decision" and to examine "the secret nostalgia" within the German soul.

The West has always had a notion of the radical freedom of human beings. History limits that freedom, but both Judaism and Christianity find within the present something that can lift us out of the destiny inscribed in the past. That something is the painful recognition of our powerlessness to repair the irreparable. It announces "the repentance that generates the forgiveness that redeems."[5] Whence the defeat of the tyranny of the irreversibility of time and human freedom. In contrast with the tragic view of life reflected in Greek mythology (e.g., the curse of the house of Atreus), Christianity presents a "mystic drama." The Cross liberates, and the Eucharist is a daily new beginning. This new order triumphs by "tearing up the bedrock of natural existence." The soul's detachment is "not an abstract state" but rather "the positive power to become detached and abstract." Liberalism has retained from this spiritual revolution one of its essential elements, "the sovereign freedom of reason." This is a very direct assertion of the Judeo-Christian origin of liberalism. Already we see an ominous portent, however, for the world of liberalism seems oblivious of the determinative forces of history and the psychological, irrational drives within human beings.

Marxism is accredited as the first challenge to this view, with its now familiar questioning of the sovereign individual will which surmounts the material conditions of its being. Hence Marxism is opposed not just to Christianity but to idealist liberalism in its entirety, in which being does not determine consciousness but consciousness and reason determine being.

Still, the Marxist opposition is not absolute, since even for the Marxist it is possible, by becoming conscious of one's social determinations, to rise above them. This is possible because our situation, even if we are born into it, does not completely determine our being. It is the notion of the body and its determinism, conceived not as having been added to us but as constitutive of our very being, that is the true antithesis of the Judeo-Christian rationalist-enlightenment tradition of European liberalism.

The body has been viewed, in that tradition, as a prison-house of the spirit, an obstacle to be overcome, or an instrumentality. But the feeling of identification with the body, the idea of biological determinism, and the acceptance of being chained to the body constitute a new conception of humanity. This new conception is not just a private notion, but a universal message to be propagated to all humankind, and in this sense is comparable to the realization of Nietzsche's will to power and Zarathustra's descent from the mountaintop to preach to the crowd.

What makes this new philosophy of humanity attractive is a failure of liberalism, which has transformed its radical freedom into gratuitous play (or a game: *un jeu*), preferring to retain its freedom by not choosing anything rather than considering it the prelude to a commitment. This critique of liberalism is an indi-cation that Levinas intends that his own philosophical specula-tion should eventually lead to something other than a continuation of this game. Just as Descartes decided at the beginning of the First Meditation to "once for all seriously undertake to rid [him]self of all the opinions which [he] had formerly accepted," does not Levinas use the freedom of philosophy to arrive at a defensible philosophical and ethical position?

Levinas's analysis distances him from his contemporary Merleau-Ponty with respect to the body — the "lived body" that, accord-ing to the latter, I do not possess any more than it possesses me, and that I "am" more than merely "have." It also explains why one does not find in Merleau-Ponty, as one clearly does in Levinas, a necessary articulation between the political writings (which are ultimately a defense of parliamentary, liberal governments, despite the credit granted to Marxism as a critique of liberalism's failure to realize its spiritual values in the concrete world of economics) and the ontological ones.[6]

Levinas later expresses regret at having graced National Socialism with the term "philosophy." But there is a constant propensity in Levinas not to make a sharp distinction between the theoretical and concrete practitioner, noticeable also in *Totality and Infinity* in such statements as "[t]hus the metaphysician and the other can not be *totalized*" (TI 35), where clearly what is being referred to is not a philosophical specialist in that branch but the self as a polarity of transcendence, and where the term ontology is used not merely as the study of being but as a par-ticular way in which the self experiences itself in relation to being. Levinas said that his analysis is not that of a journalist. If one were to attempt to find a name for the genre of this essay it might be metaphysical sociology; the conflation of the theoretical and the concrete collapses these two perspectives into an unaccustomed synthesis.

1961: Totality and Infinity

There is no specific mention of the Holocaust in this, Levinas's first major philosophical work. Nevertheless, the preface sets the philosophical treatise within a context of reality *qua* war, from the very first sentence. "Everyone will readily agree that it is of the highest importance to know whether we are not duped by morality." The challenge to Levinas's ethics — perhaps it would be more accurate to say the conditions, the heat, and pressure, in which it was formed — is the everpresent sense of imminent catastrophe. That atmosphere will exert a determining influence on all aspects of his thought: the question of religious faith after the Holocaust, the meaning of Judaism, and the relation between being (hard reality, the struggle for survival) and beyond being.

The trial by force, says Levinas, is the test of the real. And that reality is characterized by the totality. Is there a possible relationship between that sense of totality and totalitarianism? Levinas's description of war is of a phenomenon that leaves nothing exterior to it, and that changes every other to the same. Is this not another way of expressing the Hitlerian directive, the *Gleichschaltung*, a command that the entire Reich was to think and act in unison? The description of war is taken up again and augmented, in the opening pages of the next great thesis, *Otherwise than Being*, with a temporal aspect: "War is the deed or the drama of the essence's interest. No entity can await its hour. They all clash, despite the difference of the regions to which the terms in conflict may belong. Essence thus is the extreme sychronism of war."[7]

1966: "Nameless"

The last essay in *Proper Names* is titled "Nameless."[8] It contains a moving and profound statement that combines personal experience with an attempt to find meaning even in the horrifying catastrophe of the Shoah.

> When one has that tumor in the memory, twenty years can do nothing to change it. Soon death will no doubt cancel the unjustified privilege of having survived six million deaths. But if, during that stay of grace, life's occupations and diversions are filling life once more . . . nothing has been able to fill, or even cover over, the gaping pit. We still turn back to it from our daily occupations almost as frequently, and the vertigo that grips us at the edge is always the same.[9]

This brief essay recommends that three truths derived from the experience of the concentration camps be passed on to the new generation. The first is that "to live humanly, people need infinitely fewer things than they dispose of in the magnificent civilizations in which they live." It was as if during the Holocaust the Jews returned to the desert, or to a "space-receptacle." The second is that in crucial times, when it seems that all human values are swept away, "all human dignity consists in believing in their return." One should not embrace the warlike virtues, but live dangerously "only in order to remove dangers and to return to the shade of one's own vine and fig tree" (an echo of Micah 4:4). The third and final truth is that the new generation must be taught "the strength necessary to be strong in isolation," that is, when there are no institutions left to count on, and one has only one's own inner certainty left. "We must, through such memories [as those of the *maquis* and other resistance groups], open up a new access to Jewish texts and give new priority to the inner life. The *inner life*: one is almost ashamed to pronounce this pathetic expression in the face of so many realisms and objectivisms."

Levinas expands on the last point, the inner space of conscience, with the thought that morality, during the time of the
Shoah, returned to the private space of conscience as to its womb.
The section bears the subtitle "The Jewish Condition." Returning
to the guiding motif of the essay (those times when the "objective" institutions that safeguard ethics are burned, destroyed, over-
turned), Levinas asserts that the risk upon which the honor of
humanity depends is "the dangerous situation of its morality resid-
ing entirely in its 'heart of hearts.'" "Judaism," he proposes, "is
humanity on the brink of morality without institutions." Not that
the Jews are not "a people like all other peoples" who would like
"to know that the voice of their conscience is recorded in an
imperishable civilization." But the Jews are a people so situated
among the nations that they may be herded into ghettos, and
reduced to "an inner morality that is belied by the universe." Their
election consists in their having been chosen to hear anti-Semitic
language, "[an] exterminating language, causing the Good, which
gloried in Being, to return to unreality and crouch at the bottom
of a subjectivity, chilled to the bone and trembling. . . . That election is indeed a hardship."

The essay concludes with a reference to the "four cubits of the
Halakhah," a term referring to the space necessary for the study
of the law. It is used here by Levinas metaphorically to refer to
"the fragility of the conscience . . . that precarious, divine abode."

1973: "Poetry and Resurrection: Notes on Agnon"

In another essay in the same collection (*Proper Names*) devoted
to Shmuel Agnon, Levinas quotes that Nobel Prize-winning Israeli
novelist.

> Six million Jews murdered by the Gentiles among us. A third of
> Israel has been killed, and the other two-thirds orphaned. There
> is no one in Israel who does not have several dozen dead among

his or her close relatives. . . . It was a great thought that He who lives eternally had, to have chosen us from among all the peoples, to give us the Torah of Life, although it is a little difficult to understand why he created, facing us, a kind of human beings that would take our lives because we observe the Torah.[10]

Levinas comments with a question. Why the reservation? Why the surprise that murderers should kill those who keep the Torah of Life? He answers his own question: to recognize Evil in evil and Death in death. That is, the surprise is in order not to accept in a blasé or hardened manner the way of the world — to see in life a version, muffled at times no doubt, of a metaphysical drama. In order not to lose our innate (or an-archic) requirement for justice; and to "avoid comfortable theodicies, consolations that cost us nothing and compassion without suffering."

Levinas took particular pleasure in evoking the names of those who were close to him or who influenced his philosophy. Thus the title of this collection, *Proper Names* (1976), which uses names as the structural principle (in alphabetical order of last names) of the essays: from Agnon to Wahl, by way of Buber, Celan, Derrida, Jabès, Kierkegaard, Proust, and Father Herman Leo van Breda, among others. Names evoked to stem the tide of oblivion and the leveling of death. One aspect of Levinas's anti-Hegelianism is this insistence on the importance of preserving the uniqueness of each individual life, protesting death and history's alienating metamorphosis.

1974: Otherwise than Being or Beyond Essence

There are two facets to Levinas's perception of the Holocaust: the universal and the particular. They are both reflected in the inscriptions at the beginning of *Otherwise than Being* (v). The first is in French:

To the memory of those who were closest among the six million murdered by the National Socialists, and the millions upon millions of all confessions and all nations, victims of the same hatred of the other man, the same anti-Semitism.

The testimony is at once specific (those who were closest, six million, National Socialists, anti-Semitism) and general (millions upon millions, all confessions, all nations, hatred of the other man). It is probably assumed by most readers of *Otherwise than Being* that the Hebrew text at the bottom of the same page says the same thing in Hebrew. In fact it is a much more personal testimony, and reads as follows.

> To remember the soul of my father, my teacher, Rabbi Yechiel, the son of Rabbi Abraham Halévi; my mother, my teacher, Deborah, the daughter of Rabbi Mosche; my brothers, Dov, the son of Rabbi Yechiel Halévi, Aminadab, the son of Rabbi Yechiel Halévi; and my father-in-law, Rabbi Shmuel, the son of Rabbi Gerschon Halévi, and my mother-in-law, Malcha, the daughter of Rabbi Haim.
> May their souls be bound.

1982: "Useless Suffering"

The theme of theodicy — the attempt to "justify the ways of God to man," in Milton's celebrated phrase — and the impossibility of creating a new theodicy or subscribing to an existing one is central to Levinas's important essay (1982), "Useless Suffering."[11] In it, the author's thesis of the asymmetry of the relation between self and other is applied to the specific circumstance of suffering, with the result that the latter is "meaningful in me, useless in the Other." This piece moves from a phenomenological analysis of suffering to "the suffering of suffering, the suffering for the useless suffering of the other, the just suffering in me for the unjustifiable suffering of the other," which "opens suffering to the ethical perspective of the inter-human." The attention and the action the suffering of the other requires imposes itself with an immediacy that makes it impossible for us to await the intervention of an omnipotent God "without lowering ourselves." "The consciousness of this inescapable obligation brings us close to God in a more difficult, but also in a more spiritual way than does the confidence in any kind of theodicy." The theodicy of divine intervention, with its punishments and rewards and according to which the Diaspora reflects the sins of Israel, is implicit to some degree in the Old Testament. Levinas joins Emil Fackenheim in viewing theodicy after Auschwitz as an impossibility.[12] The essay ends with an informal presentation of the theses elaborated in *Otherwise than Being*, in which the interhuman is prior to and underlying the "coexistence of a multiplicity of consciousnesses." The interhuman is not objectifiable, it "does not consist in adopting a point of view relative to it, but in restoring it to the dimensions of meaning outside of which the immanent and savage concreteness of evil in a consciousness is but an abstraction." It is prior to the reciprocity of rights and responsibilities such as are reflected in impersonal laws. The latter are "superimposed on the pure altruism of this responsibility inscribed in the ethical position of the *I qua I*."[13]

1986: The Poirié Interview

In an extended interview with François Poirié in 1986,[14] Levinas is led to differentiate his thought from that of Martin Buber. Buber was asked by an elderly, pious Jew how Samuel was able to act with such cruelty toward King Agag, whom he slays while he is in chains, after having been taken captive by Saul (I Samuel 15:33). Buber responds that the prophet did not understand what God was asking of him. Levinas objects strongly to that interpretation. He quotes Deuteronomy 25:17, in which God reminds his people that the people of Amalek (of whom Agag is later king) are evil incarnate and that they treacherously attacked the Israelites as they were leaving Egypt. He then quotes I Samuel 15:33: "As thy sword hath made women childless, so shall thy mother be childless among women." He then comments: "I do not always agree with Buber, as I said. I continue to think that without extreme attention to the Book of books, one cannot listen to one's conscience. Buber, in this case, did not think about Auschwitz."[15] Levinas's interpretation is clearly that Saul's sin was not to have destroyed Agog when he had the chance. "It is the duty of man, when he is free from evil, to strike the ultimate blow against evil." The injunction of Deuterononomy 25:19, "thou shalt blot out the remembrance of Amalek for under heaven; thou shalt not forget" means that Amalek is to be slain and not just forgotten. The lesson here? Although Levinas does not spell it out any more explicitly, the lesson is that in time of peace attention should be paid to the elimination of evil before it becomes the Third Reich. And that is why the evil of Auschwitz is to be remembered. Levinas's critique of Buber is that Buber has not sufficiently appreciated the unity of the voice of conscience and that of Scripture. Or perhaps it would be more accurate to say that Levinas expresses his hearing of the voice of conscience through his interpretation of Scripture.[16] The transcendent voice connects conscience, to which one "listens," and the commandments received by Moses. The voice of conscience is rendered audible by the example of, or along the same lines as, the voice of a divine command, or the face of the other (person).

In the same interview, Levinas makes a much more direct comment on the Holocaust. "As for myself, I was not at Auschwitz, but after all I lost my whole family there. I ask myself still today whether there is not a strange teaching — may God pardon me for saying 'a teaching of Auschwitz' — a strange teaching, according to which the beginning of faith is not at all a promise, and faith is therefore not something one can preach, because it is hard to preach — i.e., to propose to someone else — something that is without promises."[17] First let us note, for the sake of accuracy, that Levinas is using Auschwitz as a symbol of the Holocaust. According to his biographer Anne-Marie Lescourret, Levinas's parents and brothers were taken out of their house one morning and shot by the Nazis.[18] Secondly, it is clear that Levinas feels that there is something irreligious, something "wrong" about deriving any lesson from the Holocaust. Nevertheless, unlike Laurence Langer, whose *Preempting the Holocaust* is devoted to the worthy task of defending the meaninglessness of that horror from any understanding that would make it less disturbing, less disruptive to the mind, Levinas does attempt to find a "teaching" there, albeit a "strange" one, about the nature of faith and of Judaism. But that teaching can never become a preaching, due to a principle that Levinas has already developed elsewhere: The relation between self and other, between I and Thou, is asymmetrical. The other is always greater than myself. The preceding quote continues,

> But one can teach it to oneself, one can require it of oneself; I am not saying that I always succeed in consenting to it. Let us recall everything I told you about symmetry and asymmetry: to bear Auschwitz without denying God — perhaps it is possible to ask that of oneself. But yet again, perhaps there would be, in doing so, an offense, in contradicting the despair of those who were going to their death. We may wonder whether even to ourselves we should allow ourselves to say that: a religion without promises.[19]

This extremely subtle text is of particular value in that it serves as a concrete "filling in" of the abstract parameters of proximity (see chapter 10, above), the relation between the other person and me. I cannot make the same requirements of others that I must make of myself. But in this case even the added requirement I make of myself is perhaps suspect, perhaps insensitive, a cruelty — because in **allowing** myself (no longer **requiring** myself) to continue to believe in God despite Auschwitz am I not being insensitive to the despair of those who went to their death without that consolation? Am I not "contradicting" their despair? Hence the final turn in this labyrinth of compassion (to the point of substitution for the other): Perhaps the formula was too easy, difficult though it sounds. To have faith in a religion without promises, is such a faith not too much of a strength? Does it not cut me off, put me at a distance from the suffering of those without this recourse? And therefore (admittedly prolonging Levinas's reflection here, albeit in a direction already clearly traced) is there not a duty to believe in the promises (the coming of the Messiah, a future judgment and justice) of religion — not as consolation but as an open wound, a longing that connects us to the despair of the other? If so, the quality of that belief would not be that of a natural inclination, a hunch about "the way things are," but of a duty: faith as duty, as piety.

12. LEVINAS'S EARLY WORK ON HUSSERL

Phenomenology stands at the beginning of Levinas's career as a philosopher, and it is therefore of some interest to consider what aspects of Husserlian phenomenology appealed to and affected the future development of his thought. He arrived in Strasburg (from Lithuania) in 1923 at the age of 18. He began by reading (in the original German, as a student at the University of Strasburg) Husserl's *Logical Investigations, Philosophy as a Rigorous Science* and *Ideas I*. In 1928–29, he went to Freiburg, Germany to study under Husserl and Heidegger. In 1929 he published *On Ideas*, a synthesis of Husserl's *Ideas I*, and he collaborated with a fellow student, Gabrielle Pfeiffer, to translate Husserl's *Cartesian Meditations*, a series of lectures on phenomenology given at the Sorbonne. Levinas translated (from German to French) the Fourth and Fifth Meditations. The Fifth (and last) Meditation is by far the longest, and contains the problem of how we perceive (or "apperceive," to use the Husserlian term) "someone else." The problems surrounding the perception of the other of course became central to Levinas's philosophy. The Pfeiffer/Levinas translation of *Cartesian Meditations* was published in 1931, some 20 years before Husserl's German original. Husserl was not satisfied with it.[1]

The Theory of Intuition in Husserl's Phenomenology (1930) was Levinas's thesis at the University of Strasbourg.[2] Levinas had studied under Husserl himself in Freiburg, been received in the Husserl household, and given French lessons to Husserl's wife in exchange for financial help. While clearly an eager and gifted student of the founder of phenomenology, his understanding of Husserl was strongly influenced by Heidegger's *Being and Time* (1927), as has been convincingly demonstrated in a recent study by Jean-François Lavigne.[3]

Levinas himself expresses what was new and had a lasting importance for him in his first master, Edmund Husserl:

> I read *Logical Investigations* very closely, and got the impression of having come upon — not another new speculative construct but new possibilities of thought, a new possibility of moving from one idea to another, other than deduction, induction and the dialectic: a new way of developing "concepts," beyond Bergson's call to inspiration in "intuition." I became aware that the gaze that focuses on a thing is also covered up by that thing, that the object is a blinding abstraction when taken in isolation, that it lets you see less than what it shows by engendering an ambiguous discourse; and that by turning back to consciousness — to the forgotten lived experience that is "intentional," i.e. that is enlivened by an intention intending something other than that mimicked lived experience, and that, always the idea of something, opens an horizon of meanings — one discovers the concreteness or the truth in which that abstract object is lodged. The movement from the object to the intention and from the intention to the whole horizon of intentions contained in that intention — that is true thought, and the thought of the true or, if you will, the world of what is given to you in purely objective knowledge. Sometimes I formulate this by saying that one must move from the object to its "mise en scène," from the object to all the phenomena implied in its appearing.[4]

The logic of this development may become clearer if we consider that the phenomenological movement from its inception was oriented toward "meaning." The "ambiguous discourse" alluded to by Levinas is that of meaning that presents itself as coming from the object, but is at the same time *Sinngebung*, to use Husserl's term: the giving of meaning. Intentionality originates in the subject or subjectivity. But in *Otherwise than Being* Levinas discovers a reversal of intentionality in its relation to the other person. "The intention toward another, when it has reached its peak, turns out to belie intentionality. Toward-another culminates in a for-another."[5]

Levinas found in phenomenology a new freedom, a way out of rationalism and the elements that would allow him, taking at least as much liberty with Husserlian phenomenology as Heidegger did, to develop first an ontology (this would be the stage at which "reality is exteriority," as in *Totality and Infinity*, which is subtitled *An Essay on Exteriority*), then an ethical metaphysics. Although he always maintained that he was a phenomenologist, his perception (auditory at least as much as visual) of the face of the other person, for example, goes beyond what any Husserlian phenomenologist would be willing to recognize as an *Abschattung* (profile). Levinas makes it abundantly clear that perception of the plasticity of the face has nothing to do with what he means by perception of the face of the other. The closest Husserlian methodology comes to this sort of perception is what Husserl called *Appräsentation*, the presentation of an object's invisible side by the one facing us, by implication so to speak. This mode of presentation is typical of cultural objects. But what was decisive for Levinas was not the proposed solutions to the problem of *Fremderfahrung Analyse* (the analysis of the experiencing of what is other), but the problem itself (as in paragraph 49 of the *Cartesian Meditations*). How do we perceive otherness?

Levinas (and thanks to his translation, Sartre and Merleau-Ponty as well, although the latter eventually consulted the original texts in Husserl's "Nachlass" in Louvain, Belgium) devoted much of his philosophical career to responding to this problem: What does it mean to perceive otherness? The experience of otherness, we now know, could not be a form of perception or even knowing in the traditional sense at least. It is, for Levinas, the transcendence toward alterity, toward the infinity of the unknowable other.

A Levinasian "Method" of Phenomenology?

Can there be a "method" involved in such an experience? Dutch phenomenologist Theodor de Boer questioned Levinas about his method in 1975. He answered, "What is said in the preface of *Totality and Infinity* remains true, all the same, to the end for me with respect to method. It is not the word 'transcendental' that I would retain, but the notion of intentional analysis. I think that, in spite of everything, what I do is phenomenology, even if there is no reduction, here, according to the rules required by Husserl; even if all of the Husserlian methodology is not respected."[6] He goes on to explain that the essential element that he and others (even those who no longer call themselves phenomenologists) have retained is the technique of "proceeding back from what is thought [*ce qui est pensé*] toward the fullness of the thought itself [*vers la plénitude de la pensée elle-même*, my emphasis]." The distinction Levinas is making is between what is thought about in thought, and the thought itself, respectively; in more technical phenomenological language, it corresponds to Husserl's intentional object (or "noema") and his act of thought ("noesis"). The latter expression is closer to the subject-pole or origin of the "intentional act," and it is in this that Levinas finds "dimensions of meaning, each time new."[7] "It is the fact that if, starting from a theme or an idea, I move toward the ways by which one accedes to it" they reveal "a whole landscape of horizons that have been forgotten and together with which, what shows itself no longer has the meaning it had when one considered it from a stance directly turned toward it." It is difficult not to be reminded here of the work of another phenomenologist who strayed from the strict application of Husserl's methodology, but who speaks in similar terms of this necessary obliqueness, Maurice Merleau-Ponty, who writes, "Personal life, expression, understanding, and history advance obliquely and not straight toward ends or concepts. What we strive for too reflectively eludes us, while values and ideas come forth abundantly to him who, in his meditative life, has learned to free their spontaneity."[8] Levinas concludes his answer with a more general observation about method. He does not believe "transparency" to be possible in this domain. "Those who have worked on methodology all their lives have written many books that replace the more interesting books that they could have written." One cannot help wondering whether it occurred to Levinas that Husserl himself might be considered among those methodologists.

Levinas often uses the word *mise en scène* to describe his manner of approaching lived experience: "Sometimes I formulate that by saying one must pass from the object to its 'mise en scène,' from the object to all the phenomena implicated in its appearing. To clarify objectivity through one's phenomenology like a stage manager ('metteur en scène') who moves from the text to the concrete event and is obliged to bring in all the fullness of appearance in which that event will, in the end, appear, or become truly visible."[9]

To summarize, Levinas begins as translator and introducer of Husserl, but early on emphasizes the theory of intuition and the subjective pole of experience and to see Husserl through Heideggerian eyes, giving priority to the *Seinsfrage*, the question of being. It is quite true that Levinas will move beyond ontology, but he specifies that it is Heideggerian ontology that he is moving beyond, not the Aristotelian ontology that Heidegger rejects. We now turn to the precise reasons for Levinas's initial enthusiasm and increasing disenchantment with respect to Husserl's brilliant student, Martin Heidegger.

13. Levinas's Critique of Heidegger

What Levinas Says about Heidegger

In 1932, Levinas published his first study on Heidegger, "Martin Heidegger and Ontology." In it, he expressed his unbridled enthusiasm for the German philosopher:

> For once, Fame has picked one who deserves it and, for that matter, one who is still living. Anyone who has studied philosophy cannot, when confronted by Heidegger's work, fail to recognize how the originality and force of his achievements, stemming from genius, are combined with an attentive, painstaking, and close working-out of the argument — with that craftsmanship of the patient artisan in which phenomenologists take such pride.[1]

This passage was omitted from the revision of the essay that Levinas published in 1949 in *En découvrant l'existence avec Husserl et Heidegger.* Both this text and numerous statements by Levinas in the course of interviews attest to his embarrassment at his youthful enthusiasm for that rising star among Husserlian phenomenologists. Levinas was at Davos and witnessed the famous debate between Heidegger and Cassirer — and admitted having been more taken with the former. This raises an obvious question. To what degree, if any, was Levinas's reading of Heidegger affected by the latter's unrepentant support of Hitler and his policies? It could be argued that this question has no philosophical significance, and that in any case there is no reliable way to answer it. Given the circumstances — that Heidegger became a member of the Nazi party, that Levinas was Jewish, that his Lithuanian family was murdered by Nazis and/or local collaborators, and that he himself spent the war years in a German prison camp — it would indeed be surprising if Levinas's reading of Heidegger's work were not colored by circumstances. There are numerous examples, especially in the interviews after the war, of Levinas's emotional reactions to Heidegger's Nazism. Levinas was familiar with Heidegger's manner of speaking, since he had been a student of his in Freiburg, Germany during the 1928–29 academic year. When asked about his personal impression of Heidegger and how he understood the latter's attitude toward National Socialism, he recalled: "He seemed very authoritarian to me. . . . His firm, categorical voice often came back to me when I listened to Hitler on the radio. His family might have had something to do with it, too: Frau Heidegger was a follower of Hitler early on."[2]

The possible relationship between Heidegger's philosophy and his support of the Nazis has received much attention. Frederick A. Olafson's essay "Heidegger's Thought and Nazism,"[3] the work of a well-established Heideggerian who is both convinced of the great importance of that philosopher's work and deeply distressed by his abysmal failure as a human being, takes up the question of whether there is anything in Heidegger's philosophy (as expressed in *Being and Time*) that would lead its proponents to have a pro-Nazi disposition. He concludes that there is not, but does establish credible links between Heidegger's social background (rural antimodern), his reaction to his early religious training for the priesthood (Nietzschean backlash), his failure to develop, on the basis of *Mitsein*, any limits to how other *Dasein*(s) are to be treated, and his delusional fantasy of becoming the Führer's own philosophical Führer.

Leaving aside the question of the degree to which he may have felt humiliated by his initial enthusiasm for Heidegger, it is a fact — difficult for some Levinasians to accept — that Levinas never wavered in his admiration for the phenomenological analyses of *Being and Time*. In a 1981 interview with Philippe Nemo, he says: "Very early I had a great admiration for this book. It is one of the finest books in the history of philosophy — I say this after years of reflection. One of the finest among four or five others."[4] He admits to having been less impressed with, and less versed in, Heidegger's later publications. We must bear in mind also that Levinas was a student of Heidegger's during the latter's early period, the winter semester of 1928–29.

The areas of research, being and time, are shared by these philosophers. The most important aspect of Heidegger's work, in Levinas's view, is the ontological difference, which Levinas tends to speak of as the difference between the verbal sense of being (*das Sein*) and the participial sense (*das Seiende*).

The general consensus by well-informed readers of both Heidegger and Levinas — for example Jacques Rolland and Marlène Zarader — is that Levinas's critique of Heidegger is based on either misunderstanding or misrepresentation. Jacques Rolland calls Levinas's concept of *amphibologie* a "*version déformée de la doctrine heideggerienne du Pli*," i.e. a "deformed" version of Heidegger's doctrine of the fold [*Zweifalt*].[5] Levinas's interpretation of Heidegger seems dubious in two further areas. He may be right in saying that for Heidegger the "existential" dominates the "existentiel," and that individual entities are understood within a horizon, but Heidegger states that one can only understand being through beings, and in particular a being that is somehow privileged, namely Dasein, the specific, in fact the origin of specificity, without which there would be no "there." Secondly, while Levinas's discussion of Heidegger does not distinguish between different sorts of *étants*, Heidegger makes a very marked distinction between Daseinish creatures and non-Daseinish ones. What needs to be considered is whether or not a critique of Heidegger that fails to make these distinctions can have any validity. The only way to save Levinas's critique would be to show that the distinctions he fails to make are not vital to his argument. In fact, I hesitate to use the word "argument" here.

Levinas perceives certain elements of Heidegger's work and makes judgments regarding their significance, particularly in relation to his (Levinas's) own work. In any case, I believe that what most readers of Levinas are looking for is not a balanced view of Heidegger's philosophy but a means of understanding exactly how Levinas's thought relates to it, which elements are rejected, which assimilated, and which transformed, be it by misunderstanding or design.   .

The Relationship Between Two Philosophies

"*On se pose en s'opposant.*" One posits oneself by opposition: the expression is eminently applicable to Levinas's relation to Heidegger, particularly in Levinas's early period. It has become clear to careful readers of *Existence & Existents* (the very title of which, more clearly in the original, *De l'existence à l'existant —* **from** existence **to** the existent — already suggests an inversion of the Heideggerian undertaking) that Levinas's thought is profoundly intertwined with that of Heidegger,[6] and that its turning away from it is comparable, *mutatis mutandis*, to Marx's inversion of Hegel.

In an early text devoted to Heidegger, "Martin Heidegger and Ontology," Levinas focuses on what he call the "ontologism" of *Being and Time*. This in contrast with the anthropological or existential readings that were more prevalent at that time. Heidegger's achievement is to have overcome both idealism and intellectualism in his analysis of Dasein. Jean Griesch's study on the Heidegger-Levinas relationship[7] reads the early texts of Levinas on Heidegger not only in light of *Being and Time*, but also in light of the course Heidegger gave in the winter of 1928–29, the one Levinas attended. That course, modestly titled "Introduction to Philosophy," was structured around the following three issues: the relationship of philosophy to science (philosophy cannot be a rigorous science, nor should it be; it is not by insufficiency but by excess that philosophy cannot be a science), to a worldview (*Weltanschauung*), and to history.[8]

How can we formulate the essential element of Levinas's critique of Heidegger? From the multiple points of divergence in the earlier works, a more general difference emerges, finding its clearest expression in the 1951 essay, "Is Ontology Fundamental?"[9] The essay begins by distinguishing between the older sense of ontology, which is "liberated from temporal contingencies," and the contemporary sense of the term, which "coincides with the facticity of temporal existence." The separation between philosophy and life is diminished, since "to understand being as being is to exist in the world." Contingency and facticity are not just possible objects of intellection, but themselves acts of intellection. This demonstrates "the transitivity of understanding." Of course part of this achievement is attributed to Husserl's "signifying intention," but Levinas credits Heidegger with the application of this possibility to the intellection of being in general.

There is, to be sure, a danger of "drowning ontology in existence." In any case, there seems to be a definitive break here between intellectualism, or the theoretical tradition of philosophy, and existentialism. Even though Heidegger rejects the latter term as a description of his philosophy, it is an inevitable consequence of his view of the relationship between knowing and being. "To understand a tool is not to see it, but to know how to use it; to understand our situation in reality is not to define it, but to be in an affective state. To understand being is to exist."[10] The act is no longer pure but mixed with the accidental, with facticity. As a result, we find ourselves "responsible beyond our intentions."

But then Levinas reverses the direction of this movement from ontology toward existence as "the philosophy of existence immediately fades away before ontology." Existence is not just understood, it is understanding. Those early readers who interpreted Heidegger's philosophy as contemptuous of intellect were entirely mistaken. The "openness" of being naturalizes intelligibility, so to speak. Intelligence is actualized in existence; even misunderstanding is but a deficient mode of understanding, and *haecceity*, the thisness of things incorporated into being by the *Da* of Dasein, is "the condition of the very intelligibility of being." An enlarged, unorthodox conception of knowledge has been elaborated in such a way as to preserve the theoretical tradition of philosophy after all, transposed to a higher register as it were.

From this point on, the essay articulates a break with Heidegger, i.e. with fundamental ontology. Heidegger understands the entity (*das Seiende*) within the horizon of being (*das Sein*). In so doing he rejoins the "the great tradition of Western philosophy," which is to understand "the particular, which alone exists," within the context of a knowledge of the universal. This question of whether Heidegger's way of understanding entities in relation to being is appropriately assimilated to the understanding of the particular existent by the universal is, as Jean Griesch judiciously observes, "the most litigious point in the debate opposing Levinas and Heidegger."

In Levinasian terminology, Heidegger does not leave the sphere of the same because his Dasein is not in dialogue with other Daseins. (Indeed it is not clear that Dasein really has a plural; Mitsein, or being-with, is a domain that Heidegger left largely undeveloped.) How does Levinas propose to deal with the other person, that troublesome other subjectivity that Husserl attempted to analyze his *Fremdanalyse*, an analysis of the meaning of alterity, in his Fifth Cartesian Meditation? The essence of that otherness, which is precisely irreducible to an essence or "eidos," is only to be approached by philosophy in the vocative, as the illocutionary other who stands forever outside any thematizing discourse-content that would reduce it (him, her) to an eidetic predication. It is with the introduction of "the face" as a metaphysical term that Levinas attempts to transcend the radical finitude of Heidegger's fundamental ontology.

Perhaps the most severe critical remarks directed against Heidegger's philosophy are to be found in *Otherwise than Being or Beyond Essence*. The following paragraph, taken from an early section of *Totality and Infinity* titled "Metaphysics Precedes Ontology," offers us a critique of Heidegger that has become an accusation, a condemnation even.

> A philosophy of power, ontology is, as first philosophy which does not call into question the same, a philosophy of injustice. Heideggerian ontology, even though it opposes the technological passion issued forth from the forgetting of Being hidden by existents, subordinates the relationship with the Other to the relation with Being in general, remains under obedience to the anonymous, and leads inevitably to another power, to imperialist domination, to tyranny. Tyranny is not the pure and simple extension of technology to reified men. Its origin lies back in the pagan "moods," in the enrootedness in the earth, in the adoration that enslaved men can devote to their masters. *Being* before the *existent*, ontology before metaphysics, is freedom (be it freedom of theory) before justice. It is a movement within the same before obligation to the other.[11]

The first point of criticism is that ontology is a philosophy of power. What is the basis for this accusation? But before we ask that question we should perhaps ask what is wrong with power.

From the perspective of Levinas's philosophy, power is closely associated with violence or misuse of power. But even before we get to the level of misuse of power, there is in Levinas's notion of the asymmetry of the relation of self to other the idea that I should yield to the other — a passivity, or at least the yielding of priority. It would be inaccurate to say that this is announced as a doctrine to be followed, but clearly there is a deep suspicion of power — not just on the human level. The humility or kenosis of God is also an aspect of Levinasian thought. This critique of power is connected with the very notion of ontology, in which being is conceived as a struggle. Hence any philosophy that remains ontology, i.e. does not move from the status quo of being to the ethics of a beyond being, is a philosophy of power, and hence potentially at least of injustice and tyranny. One of the consequences of this philosophy is to introduce an absolute separation between physical and moral necessity, and to make the moral being at least as strongly subject to the latter as to the former.

The ontology of power is said not to call into question the same. This is a failure to put oneself into question: to fail to question one's right to be, even though one's own being might stand in the way of or threaten the being of another.

Heidegger's aversion to technology (which, it has been suggested, may have more to do with a village background in Messkirch, a childhood to which the philosopher was nostalgically attached, and a distaste for modernity) seems out of step with the violence of his ontology. But even that (good) aversion is couched in ontological terms: the opposition to "technological passion" is the opposition to an ill that is derived from the "forgetting of Being." That forgetting, in turn, is attributable either to our inability to make a clear enough "ontological distinction" between existents and being, or to a fateful obfuscation of being by its manifestation in existents, which thereby "hide" it.

Thus, in Levinas's view, even the good trait of opposition to the technological passion is derived from the very same bad tendency contained within Heideggerian ontology — namely the preeminence of being, which "subordinates the relationship with the other to the relation with Being in general." That relationship with the other is precisely what is missing from Heidegger's philosophy, thereby rendering it incapable of generating a morality. Not only is that being in general responsible for the failure to recognize or be attentive to the relationship to the other: the preeminence of being in general puts the proponents of that philosophy "under obedience to the anonymous." This conducts one ineluctably to "imperialist domination, to tyranny."

At this point the meditation seems difficult to connect with any precision to the evils of ontology and its sequels. But it is clear that somehow paganism (which is attachment to nature as to a deity) is a result — or possibly a cause — of fundamental ontology. The culprit is not the "extension of technology to reified men" in any case, or at least not in any straightforward way. The source of the evil is pagan "moods," a dark brooding, and an "enrootedness in the earth." The adoration of power is not that of free men but of slaves who adore their master. It is as if awe of the powers of nature led to a sociological extension of the Stockholm syndrome. The underlying charge here is of a hidden connection between Heidegger and Hitler — a connection that we are to understand on the basis of a philosophically articulated vision.

The vision draws its strength from the ascendancy granted "being" over the "existent," which translates into the priority granted to ontology before metaphysics. But how are we to understand that this arrangement has led to the adoration of slaves for their master, when this ontology before metaphysics is precisely freedom before justice? In order for this progression to be assured, the freedom must be specified as "theoretical freedom." This theoretical freedom is the freedom of free inquiry and of knowledge, the freedom to think anything, and to be bound by nothing. This is the freedom (inherited from Judeo-Christian spirituality, passed down into political liberalism and philosophical skepticism) whose lineage and decadence Levinas traced in his 1934 piece, "Reflections on the Philosophy of Hitlerism":

> Thought becomes a game. Man revels in his freedom and does not definitively compromise himself with any truths. He transforms his power to doubt into a lack of conviction. Not to chain himself to a truth becomes for him not wishing to commit his own self to the creation of spiritual values. Sincerity becomes impossible and puts an end to all heroism. Civilization is invaded by everything that is not authentic, by a substitute that is put at the service of fashion and of various interests.[12]

It was this "end of all heroism" that led to the Germanic cult of the hero, and a longing to embrace the enchainment to the reassuring basis of *Blut und Boden* (blood and soil) under Hitler. This is the gratuitous freedom of theory that is capable of a sudden transformation into pagan slavery. And these are the long-term consequences of putting freedom (or at least a certain sort of freedom) before justice, and ontology before metaphysics. For ultimately this freedom is but a "movement within the same," which fails to develop into an "obligation to the other."

The preceding, which I have called a philosophically articulated vision, has an inner coherence that is important to bring out without muddling the distinct moments of exposition and critique. The question might well be asked: Was Levinas as circumspect with respect to the philosophically articulated vision of Heidegger?

The Dantesque view of Heidegger's philosophy we have just examined, from 1961, should not make us forget the 1932 treatment of that same philosophy, in which the greatest care is taken to follow with tact and sensitivity every nuance and intention of the German "genius." "In this study," writes the young Levinas, "it is important for us to understand, above all, the true intentions of our author, to illuminate what he thinks really needs to be said, and to surmise what is most critical for him . . . We have, thus, every chance of gaining access to his thought by the main door, so to speak. Once inside the system we will try to trace its outlines. . . ."[13]

The relationship between the philosophies of Heidegger and Levinas is very close, intimate in fact — although not mutual. To my knowledge there is no indication of Heidegger's ever having been aware of the existence of Levinas. It is important to have a clear sense of what Levinas's evolving view of Heidegger's philosophy was in order to understand his (Levinas's) own thought. At the time of writing *Totality and Infinity*, the ultimate meaning and possible consequences of Heidegger's way of philosophizing

were interpreted by Levinas in a very negative way. That interpretation was made along ethical lines. Even Heidegger enthusiasts, with perhaps a few exceptions, would probably not contend
that ethics was the area in which Heideggerian thought has made
its most impressive contributions; and even Levinasian enthusiasts would probably concede (again, with a few holdouts no doubt)
that Levinas's philosophy is heavily indebted to that of Heidegger.

It is not a balanced, fair assessment of Heidegger that we will
get from Levinas. One way to understand the dramatic reversals
in the latter's views in this regard would be to consider that
Levinas, having internalized several of the main Heideggerian
theses (the ontological difference, the interrelatedness of ontology and temporality, the self-affecting of *Befindlichkeit*), reacted
with the intensity typical of self-critique. Perhaps that is why one
is left with the sense that what we are able to find in Levinas's
critique of Heidegger is something far more instructive and engag-
ing than a fair-minded assessment. In a footnote to *Otherwise
than Being*, Levinas at last finds precisely the right words to
express his relation to Heidegger. "These lines, and the ones that
follow them, owe much to Heidegger. Deformed and misunder-
stood? Perhaps. At least the deformation is not a way of denying
the debt. Nor the debt a reason to forget."[14] That lapidary note
says most of what needs be said about the indebtedness, the
changes Levinas has made to Heidegger's thought, and the idea
that these changes may be interpreted as misunderstandings or
deformations, but that in any case they are based on Heidegger's
thought and as such attest to an indebtedness. But that debt
does not cancel the memory of Heidegger's approval — never
retracted — of Hitler and the Nazi Party.

The lines to which the note refers are those contained in the
section of chapter 2 of *Otherwise than Being*, titled "The Amphibology of Being and Entities." Heidegger's notion of "amphibology" in this sense is based on Heidegger's ontological difference,
and even more precisely on the latter's notion of the *Zweifalt*.

Levinas uses the term amphibology to designate the ambiguous relationship between being and entities (or beings), which
corresponds (as Levinas states expressly in an introductory note
at the beginning of *Otherwise than Being*) to Heidegger's distinction between *das Sein* and *das Seiende*. Levinas's French terms
are, for being, *essence* (occasionally written *essance*, a departure
from normal French usage), and a being or individual entity *étant*,
the present participle of the verb to be. Jacques Rolland has suggested that this amphibology not only designates the Heideggerian
ontological difference, but also and more specifically the twofold,
or *Zweifalt* of which Heidegger speaks in, e.g. the essay *Moira*.[15]
In *Moira*, eight lines of fragment 8 (34–41) are analyzed in detail,
along with the very short fragment 3 ("For thinking and Being
are the same."). After a rapid survey of the history of the theory
of knowledge, Heidegger turns away from Descartes, Berkeley,
Kant and Hegel to adopt a Platonic approach as being closer in
spirit to Parmenides. Since for Plato the ideas, which give being
to beings (entities), are to be seen purely only in *noein* (thinking), being must belong to the realm of the *noeta*, which are non-
and super-sensible.[16] Heidegger concludes from this that being is
something non-sensible. He then moves on to the verb form *eon*,
an Ionic form of "on," which is the present participle of the verb
"to be." The participial form, he concludes, is not simply the
expression of beings in themselves, or existents, nor is it "being
for itself," as if the nonsensible nature of being were set in opposition to and conceived in isolation from beings *qua* entities.
Neither is it the notion of being as the Being of beings, as in the
much earlier *Being and Time*. The *Zweifalt*, as Jacques Rolland
points out, is not the sort of reversibility suggested by Levinas's
amphibology.

> But Twofold that does not mean the prefect reversibility that, as
> we have seen, characterizes amphibology; Twofold in the fold of
> which there is rather a declivity — by virtue of which being gives
> itself as that which withdraws and pulls away ("zurückhält und

entzieht": cf. Heidegger's *Zur Sache des Denkens*, Tübingen: Niemeyer, 1969, p. 8), at the same time that it pro-duces the being ["étant"] or lets it be and, in this withdrawal itself offers itself to oblivion.[17]

This distinctively Heideggerian play of reciprocal hiding (of being) and showing (of beings) that Heidegger finds in the "participial" character of the Parmenidean notion of being, before being disambiguated by the wrong-headed history of Western metaphysics or perhaps the self-obfuscation of being itself, does indeed differ from Levinas's use of the concept of being's amphibology, most obviously so in that the Levinasian variety takes place entirely within the realm of "essence" (i.e. being) and of the said.

14. DERRIDA'S READINGS OF LEVINAS

"Violence and Metaphysics"

Jacques Derrida's essay on Levinas, *"Violence et métaphysique,"* is a defense on Derrida's part of other philosophers — namely Kierkegaard, Hegel, Husserl, and Heidegger — against what he considers to be Levinas's inaccurate interpretation of them. This approach, though negative in an obvious sense, has the advantage of moving us with great accuracy toward what is most properly Levinasian — since it is precisely the convergence of all these "biased" readings that points most directly to the heart of Levinas's own philosophy. At the same time, Derrida's text can be read less felicitously as reductive, overemphasizing the sites from which the stones of a new edifice have been constructed. This tendency is observable in the early criticisms of philosophers before their importance was firmly established. To understand the novelty of a work is, paradoxically, to cease perceiving it as a recombination of elements that already exist, and to apprehend it in the direction of its own teleology. The phenomenon may also be described in terms of an epistemological process with which Levinas himself has familiarized us: knowledge as the reduction of otherness to the same. And we must bear in mind that Derrida's critical essay — the first extensive analysis, bringing Levinas to the attention of the distinguished readership of *Revue de la métaphysique et de morale* — was published in 1964, a full decade and scores of publications before *Otherwise than Being or Beyond*

Essence,[1] which many consider Levinas's crowning philosophical achievement.

Derrida's substantial essay of over 100 pages undertakes a task that appears to its author such that the "brevity" of its pages will hardly suffice to its task. What is that task? To summarize Derrida's own statement of purpose (84),[2] it is to give a simultaneously genetic and thematic account of Levinas's philosophy, an enterprise condemned thereby to "incoherence," but prompted by Hegel's warning that the result is nothing without the becoming. He will maintain "the possibility of the impossible system" on the horizon to protect him from "empiricism." Since empiricism will be Derrida's main charge against Levinas, we should note this precaution he himself takes, and examine it for any clues it might contain concerning the precise nature of this pitfall. What Derrida reminds himself to beware of choosing between is "the history of Levinas's thought and works," i.e. their becoming, and "the order or aggregate of themes," i.e. the result. Neither will be chosen, which will result in incoherence, but Levinas will not "systematically" resign himself to incoherence.

The essay begins by setting the scene of the enquiry: It is an "archeology" of the Greeks, a "repetition" of sorts. It is made up of Husserl's phenomenology and of Heidegger's ontology.

1. The Greek origins, and the fraternal differences of interpretation of the Greeks, particularly Plato, by Husserl and Heidegger.

2. A subordination, transgression, or reduction of metaphysics (in different senses, for Husserl and Heidegger).

3. A disassociation, in this agreed upon dispensation, of ethics from metaphysics. (Clearly Derrida is setting up the philosophical situation in such a way that Levinas's arrival on the scene will appear in its most jarring aspect.)

Our philosophical tradition has thus become, according to Derrida, a dialogue between Husserlian phenomenology and Heideggerian "ontology," within a Greek context or background.

It is difficult not to be struck by the narrowness of the tradition Derrida is adducing here.

Having established this context, Levinas's thought is introduced as one that no longer wants to have as its foundation the thought of being and "phenomenality." Derrida then goes over the three "motifs" just mentioned.

1. Levinas's thought (which is "in Greek, but not Greek") summons us to a "dislocation" of the Greek logos, and toward an "exhalation" (French: "respiration"), a prophetic speech. A Jewish content within a Greek expression and tradition? Derrida finds a more agile metaphor: "A thought for which the entirety of the Greek logos has already erupted, and is now a quiet topsoil deposited not over bedrock, but around a more ancient volcano." This thought frees itself from Greek domination "solely by remaining faithful to the immediate, but buried nudity of experience itself" (82). This faithfulness to experience (or undue reliance on it, since here experience appears to be incorrigible in the technical sense) is what will become the target of the accusation of "empiricism."

2. Levinas seeks to resurrect metaphysics, though in opposition to a tradition as old as Aristotle.

3. He does so through an ethics of the other (person), who is infinite *qua* infinitely other.

Derrida terms this unprecedented enterprise a messianic eschatology. It "seeks to be understood from within a *recourse to experience itself*." (83)

The first section of the body of the essay is titled "The Violence of Light." It is a critical examination and assessment of Levinas's first study of Husserl, *The Theory of Intuition in Husserl's Phenomenology*. It begins with an examination of Levinas's modest protestations over Husserl's propensity for theory. (The original Greek meaning of *theorein* was to see, hence the relation to light; phenomenology, *phaino*, meaning "I shine forth," reinforces the relation to light.) They reflect the increasing influence of Heidegger, although the same critique, that of theory, knowledge, and power (all of which are connected with light) will become ever more violent.

The second section, "Phenomenology, Ontology, Metaphysics," shifts the focus away from the earlier essays and studies to the great work, *Totality and Infinity*. It is here that Levinas ceases to express his own certitude through the negations (critiques) of other philosophers; a certitude that structures "a powerful architecture" (92). Levinas reinstates metaphysics, at the heart of which is metaphysical transcendence: desire. This movement is the only one that does not violate the other by knowledge, possession, or appropriation of any sort. Remarking on the very anti-Hegelian character of Levinas's notion of desire (Hegel's notion is described as the negation of alterity required in becoming "self-consciousness"), which is metaphysical, respectful of the other and ethical, Derrida points out the difference between the Hegelian "natural necessity" and the violence I must forbid myself with respect to the other. Levinas distinguishes between enjoyment and desire (the latter ultimately endless, insatiable, and even increasing to the degree it is fulfilled), while Hegel apparently does not. Hegelian desire is only need in the Levinasian sense.

Desire is transcendent, seeking an absolute otherness: infinity. Derrida detects Kierkegaard in this desire that realizes itself without renouncing the object of desire. Derrida's breadth of reading is impressive; what may occasionally sound like criticism (a sense that Levinas is not revealing what he owes to other thinkers) is probably not that, but just Derrida yielding to the temptation of making rapprochements within a common theme (such as the comparison between the senses of sight and hearing in Levinas and Hegel, 98–100). And how should we calibrate the level of critique in the following comment, moderated somewhat perhaps by being placed in parentheses? "(It could no doubt be demonstrated that Levinas, uncomfortably situated in the difference between Husserl and Heidegger — and, indeed, by virtue of the history of his thought — always criticizes the one in the style and according to a scheme borrowed from the other, and finishes by sending them off into the wings together as partners in the 'play of the same' and as accomplices in the same historico-philosophical coup)" (97–98).

The adjective "uncomfortable" is often attributed to Levinas's position when Derrida wishes to suggest that there is some untenable configuration of ideas lurking in Levinas's thought. The allusion to "the history of his thought" refers to the fact that Levinas was first the student of Husserl, then of Heidegger. It is therefore not surprising that the movement of an honest thinker's mind should seek integrity by confronting each with the other, and moving (in a Hegelian way that should be pleasing to Derrida) to a higher synthetic level. If such mildly unflattering innuendos are inseparable from the nuanced, nearly always accurate and insightful commentary Derrida has contributed to Levinasian scholarship, it should not be too much for devotees to put up with — and it is hardly surprising that such a consummate ventriloquist as Derrida should find ventriloquism everywhere.

Derrida offers a marvelously alert account (104–06) of the untranslatable French *autrui*, which seems to rebel against any of the usual grammatical specifications (singular or plural, common or proper noun?) even before getting to what is specific about Levinas's use of it. His observations on what Levinas means and does not mean by "the face" are perfectly accurate and placed in relation to other thinkers (e.g. Feuerbach) on the same theme. It is this ability to contextualize Levinas's problematics with such philosophical ubiquity that makes him so valuable a commentator.

In a helpful discussion of asymmetry (of the I-Thou relation), non-light (Levinas's rejection of vision and its totalizing effect, as well as of light as a "neutral" element, leading inexorably to the ontology of the physical object as the benchmark of all being), and commandment (the commandment "Thou shalt not kill," issued from the Most-High, i.e. the face, and by analogy from God), Derrida points out that these very elements would be injustice, darkness and tyranny "if they established relations between finite beings, or if the other was but a negative determination of the (finite or infinite) same" (106–07). He proceeds to surmise that this is why God is necessary for Levinas; otherwise (but is it truly otherwise?) there would be terrible violence in the world. There ensues a discussion too nuanced to be summarized here, and one that Derrida does not carry beyond the paragraph, probably because he wishes to limit his essay to commentary. In the course of this short discussion, however, Derrida makes the observation that in Levinas there is a silent axiom: the totality is finite. Since it is an axiom, even silent, there should be no expectation that Levinas should attempt to establish it. The totality is violent, just as its opposite, infinity, cannot be violent. The theme of violence, which appears in the title of the essay, will pull together these strains in the last part of the essay.

The third and last part of the body of the essay is "Difference and Eschatology." It features the problem of language. That problem has already come up — indeed, as Derrida points out, there is a sense in which his entire philosophy involves this problem — in the discussion of the other (*autrui*), whose alterity is unassailable by language because the other can only be reached by the vocative, spoken **to**, and can never become (*qua autrui* at least) that which is spoken about **in** speech.

The first subdivision of part 3 is "Of the Original Polemic." It begins by noting an apparent inconsistency. In the late 1940s (in *Existence & Existents*, and *Time and the Other*), Levinas protests against the use of same and other as Plato does, as genera, and prefers "the I" and others (*autrui*), specific human beings who can function as illocutionary participants. But in *Totality and Infinity* Levinas identifies the two binaries: the *moi* is the same and *autrui* is the other. There is an implication of inconsistency here, but I do not find it particularly troubling.

Not only is it permissible for a philosopher to make serious modifications to his philosophy over a decade; the modification in this case is not as major as it might seem, since Levinas is not **substituting** the "same" for the subject and the "other" for the other person or other people, but identifying the first two and the last two terms with one another. I do not think Derrida's suggestion that Levinas thus fails to distinguish between the two concepts (the ego and the same, or the other person and the other) is apposite; more to the point is that he deliberately conflates the self with what was a logical abstraction in Greek philosophy — the same — and performs a similar operation on the other. In their new guises, as the acquisitiveness and competitiveness of being come to a head in the first instance, and the infinite object of transcendent desire and inviolable alterity in the second, the essential terms for the further development of an ethical metaphysics are established, although that metaphysics will not take on its most striking features for another ten years, in *Otherwise than Being*.

A related issue is raised by Levinas's statement to the effect that it is not the subject, or subjectivity, that challenges the Hegelian notion of the totality, but the other. "It is not I who do not accept the system, as Kierkegaard thought, it is the other."[3] Derrida protests in Kierkegaard's name that the latter would have been "deaf" to such a distinction, since the uniqueness of the other is derived from the fact that it is after all a transfer of subjectivity, an alter ego. Of course this would be unacceptable to Levinas, since it would invalidate the "asymmetrical" relation between same and other. Furthermore, the uniqueness of the subject (unlike the unique and solitary self of, say, J.-J. Rousseau) is not *sui generis* in Levinas but the result of an inescapable responsibility for the other. There may be a further problem with Derrida's suggestion of a putative genesis of the uniqueness of the other from the ego. Kierkegaard would probably have rejected Derrida's universalized concept of subjectivity. Can the specificity and uniqueness of subjectivity, specifically fragile, "existential" Kier-kegaardian subjectivity, be thus transported in the form of a concept, namely that of "a" subjectivity, from one self to another? Derrida argues that doing so involves no logical inconsistency (i.e. in prefacing uniqueness with the indefinite article, thus necessarily implying that there are more than one of them), but is that logic not very Hegelian for the father of existentialism?

This is a familiar philosophical problem, which is sometimes approached as one of language. All but proper nouns are subject to generalization — in fact there is a sense in which proper names are not part of the language, which is why they are normally not translated. Proper names seem to come closer to expressing the uniqueness of the person, but as Derrida points out, the name of the philosophical subject who says "I" is always in a sense a pseudonym. Derrida argues that Kierkegaard protested against the "possibilization" of individual existence, which "resists the concept." Since this individual existence must also be assumed to subtend the Levinasian other (whose uniqueness must be at least that of "a" subjectivity), Derrida claims that in order to be consistent Levinas would have to "eliminate even the notions of an *essence* and a *truth* of subjective existence," but that he does not do so and cannot "without renouncing philosophical discourse" (110). The fact is that Levinas does describe subjectivity, that he devotes many pages to characterizing it as being the principle of identification, with its traits of egotism, acquisitiveness and so on, and has no need to resort to nonphilosophical discourse to do so. When Levinas uses the expression *"cri égoïste de la subjectivité encore soucieuse de bonheur ou de salut, de Kierkegaard"* ("Kierkegaard's egotistical cry of subjectivity still concerned for its happiness or salvation"), he is not speaking, as Derrida suggests (by protesting that "[t]he philosopher Kierkegaard does not *only* plead for Søren Kierkegaard. . . ."), of any egotism on Kierkegaard's part personally, but in strictly philosophical terms of subjectivity itself, which is essentially, not accidentally, egotistical.[4]

It is not the possibility of the uniqueness of the I's becoming "a" subjectivity, a *Jemeinigkeit* ("each one's ownness," a Husserlian term) that Levinas denies. It is the absolute otherness of the other that he defends. Of course there is a logical reciprocity involved in these two subjectivities, that of the other and my own. This question has been discussed in greater detail in the chapter devoted to same/other (see chapter 2, above). The uniqueness of the I is an accomplishment, attained by the I in his or her relationship with the other.

Derrida then proceeds to describe what Levinas's project would have to be, in order to be successful.

> And, if you will, the attempt to achieve an opening toward the beyond of philosophical discourse, which can never be shaken off completely, cannot possibly succeed *within language* — and Levinas recognizes that there is no thought before language and outside of it — except by *formally* and *thematically* posing *the question of the relations between belonging and the opening*, the *question of closure*. Formally, that is by posing it in the most effective and most formal, the most formalized, way possible; not in a *logic*, in other words in a philosophy, but in an inscribed description, in an inscription of the relations between the philosophical and the non-philosophical, in a kind of unheard of *graphics*, within which philosophical conceptuality would be no more than a *function*. (110–11)

It is quite remarkable that Derrida was at least able to antici-pate some of the elements of *Otherwise than Being* on the basis of *Totality and Infinity*. Jacques Rolland goes so far as to assert that *Otherwise than Being* is a response to Derrida's critique, an interesting claim I see no way of establishing one way or the other.[5] A more likely hypothesis is that Levinas's thought already contained, for such an astute reader as Derrida, the exigencies that were not to be worked out until later, but so clearly inscribed *in potentia* that Derrida's essay was able to decipher some of them. Does Derrida himself not recognize this when he writes at the beginning of the third part of his essay (109), precisely the most critical one, "First, let it be said, for our own reassurance: the route followed by Levinas's thought is such that **all our questions already belong to his own interior dialogue,** are displaced into his discourse and only listen to it, from many vantage points and in many ways" [my emphasis]? This being the case, it would be both unnecessary and unlikely for Levinas to have shaped his future work on Derrida's critique.

But to return to Derrida's critique, let us examine the specific terms of what, in Derrida's eyes, still remains to be accomplished. Levinas will have to achieve "an inscription of the relations between the philosophical and the nonphilosophical, in a kind of unheard of *graphics*, within which philosophical conceptuality would be no more than a *function*." He will therefore have to somehow relativize "philosophical conceptuality." But that accomplishment, which is no less than "an opening toward the beyond of philosophical discourse" will have to be carried out in philosophical discourse to some extent, since that discourse "can never be shaken off completely." On the other hand it "cannot possibly succeed *within language*" unless it be "by *formally* and *thematically* posing *the question of the relations between belonging and the opening,* the *question of closure.*" These are precisely the questions taken up in *Otherwise than Being*: questions of expression, of language, and of the difference between the saying and the said, the "relations between the philosophical and the nonphilosophical," if we take the nonphilosophical as the prophetic (see *Otherwise than Being*, chapter four, part 2d, "Witness and Prophecy"). The "function" of philosophical conceptuality will be inscribed within the "opening" of the said, "described" in its relation to saying. (It is true that the saying/said analysis is already present in *Totality and Infinity*, but is not fully developed until *Otherwise than Being*.) This characterization does, admittedly, contain some approximations, but at least indicates an approach to *Otherwise than Being* as the response to a certain number of problems posed by the relationship between Levinas's earlier philosophy and the limits of philosophical conceptuality.

Continuing his defense of Kierkegaard, Derrida writes, "Let us add, in order to do him *justice*, that Kierkegaard had a sense of the relationship to the irreducibility of the totally-other, not in the egoistic and esthetic here and now, but in the religious beyond of the concept, in the direction of a certain Abraham" (111). It is difficult not to notice a taunting inflection in his italicized emphasis: "Let us add, in order to do him *justice*, that Kierkegaard. . . ." as well as in "a certain Abraham." But in fact in May of 1963 the *Schweizer Monatshefte* had published a piece by Levinas on Kierkegaard, "*Existenz und Ethik*" ("Existence and Ethics") in German. There is no indication that Derrida had read this piece, which appeared only 14 months before the first half of "Violence and Metaphysics" appeared in the pages of the *Revue de la métaphysique et de morale.*[6] In that piece, Levinas makes his very nuanced position vis-à-vis Kierkegaard quite clear. He admires the latter's defense of authentic subjectivity against idealism (which offered it a philosophical status, but altered its essence in "the generality of the concept"), on the basis of prephilosophical experience. What was that experience, that "secret of the self"? It was "a tension on itself" (*tension sur soi*) that was expressed in Spinoza as a *conatus essendi* and in Heidegger as existence existing in such a way that its being has this very being as an issue. It is in fact egotism — egotism which is not an ugly vice on the part of the subject, but the subject's very ontology. As for the allusion to Abraham, Levinas finds that the truly ethical moment in the episode of the sacrifice of Isaac is Abraham's ability to hear and heed the second, ethical voice forbidding him human sacrifice, rather than the first. Kierkegaard's interpretation is the opposite: the voice of God (religion) is above ethics. In Levinas's view (and it is surprising that this aspect of Levinas's philosophy, which is so often expressed in *Difficult Freedom*, should have eluded Derrida) religion **is** ethics, and the "Thou shalt not kill," experientially encountered in the face of the other, is nonetheless a law. Derrida asks, "And did he not, in turn — for we must let the other speak — see in Ethics, as a moment of Category and Law, the forgetting, in anonymity, of the subjectivity of religion? From this point of view, the ethical moment is Hegelianism itself, and he says so explicitly. Which does not prevent him from reaffirming ethics in repetition, and from reproaching Hegel for not having constituted a morality" (111).

The not so gentle sarcasm of "for we must let the other speak" (read "Levinas, whose philosophy makes so much of giving priority to the other, should at least let Kierkegaard speak out and defend himself . . .") is followed by an accurate description of Kierkegaard's dilemma. It may be to some extent the dilemma of Christianity in general and of Protestantism in particular, which tends to see in "the Law" not Hegelianism certainly, but a formalism that has lost its connection with the truth of religious subjectivity. But while Derrida has given an accurate representation of Kierkegaard's position, his description of Levinas's ethics is far less so. "It is true that Ethics, in Levinas's sense, is an ethics without law and without concept, which maintains its non-violent purity only before being determined as concepts and laws" (111). Of course if we read Levinas without taking his Judaism into account, if we refrain, by a scruple of philosophical method, from taking *Difficult Freedom* into account, and if we remember that it is not until *Otherwise than Being* (1974) that Levinas works out the relation between love and justice, and the relation between philosophy and prophetic inspiration, Derrida's view is more comprehensible. The difficulty is that the essence of religion is ethics, and the source of ethics is not philosophy. Since that source (or sources, for Levinas finds "traces" and hints of the ethical in a variety of places, including the Jewish Bible and Russian literature) is inadmissible in philosophy, Levinas can only refer to the concrete, prephilosophical experience (such as the perception of the commandment not to kill in the face of the other). But since

Derrida's main criticism of Levinas is precisely "empiricism," his requirement that ethics should emerge from the philosophical concept cannot, and perhaps should not, be met. But Derrida goes on to make a distinction that may be of some help, writing, "This is not an objection: let us not forget that Levinas does not seek to propose laws or moral rules, does not seek to determine *a* morality, but rather the essence of the ethical relation in general" (111). This is an important observation of the total lack on Levinas's part of any rules of behavior in the form of maxims or injunctions. It is true that there are moral implications in what he says, but they are almost always expressed in such a way that the reader must draw her or his conclusions and is not given the option of just "reading them off." In speaking of the essence of the ethical relation we may think of the relation between self and other — of an infinite and asymmetrical relation between them. Is it a "theory" of ethics, a manner of "metaethics" that we find in Levinas? Derrida argues, "But as this determination does not offer itself as a *theory* of Ethics, in question, then, is an Ethics of Ethics. In this case, it is perhaps serious that this Ethics of Ethics can occasion neither a determined ethics nor determined laws without negating and forgetting itself. Moreover, is this Ethics of Ethics beyond all laws? Is it not the Law of laws? A coherence which breaks down the coherence of the discourse against coherence — the infinite concept, hidden within the protest against the concept" (111).

Derrida is right in denying that Levinas gives us a *theory* of ethics, and in affirming that what he gives us is better described as an ethics of ethics. And part of that ethics of ethics concerns the modality of ethical truth. Here Levinas had very positive things to say about Kierkegaard, who described a suffering or humble truth, a faith/doubt modality that is not a deficient mode of truth, a mere lack of a more perfect certainty that would immediately impose its obviousness upon everyone's mind. This is yet another reason why Levinas often asserts the impossibility of "preaching."

While it is true that this ethics of ethics has a certain humility and discretion attached to it, that does not preclude the possibility of "determined ethics." In fact, these ethical or moral laws do not need to be invented so much as recognized. Their nature may be off-putting given the natural tendencies of the selfishness of the self — but there is no question in Levinas of discovering new and surprising moral principles that have somehow escaped the notice of the human race. If Derrida's description of Levinas's philosophy is indeed a convolution of discourses turned against one another (which is partially, I believe, the result of an attempted simplification, or schematization, of Levinas's actual work), then Derrida reads Levinas, on the first level, as essentially "against coherence." Here Derrida designates Levinas's introduction of a radical break, or *écart*, between ontology and ethics. But the fact that this break can take place within a philosophical discourse indicates that there is a level of coherence that makes the articulation of that first-level incoherence philosophically communicable.

The final twist of Derrida's dialectic is, as we have seen, his notion of a Levinasian ethics of ethics that would function as a "law of laws." But since in Derrida's view the second level of coherence is in fact a theorization of the radical break and a "protest against the concept," introducing a concept in the form of a "law of laws" would oppose that opposition to the concept. This ethic of ethics would be tantamount to the introduction into philosophy of a different kind of concept, an "infinite" concept (or a concept of the infinite and the transcendent, those philosophical outlaws), but a concept nonetheless. The dramatized oppositions involved in this semantic "nesting" of concept against counter concept, of difference and the expression of difference which overarches or transcends this difference, is evocative of what takes place within a system into which foreign elements have been introduced. Derrida's deciphering of Levinas's philosophy is moving toward a breakthrough that, like Champollion's deciphering of hieroglyphics, will be mediated by the realization that he is in the presence of a mixed system: partially iconographic and partially phonetic in the case of hieroglyphics, partially Greek/ philosophical and partially Hebraic/prophetic in that of Levinas.

Derrida concludes this part (part A) with an explanation of the motivation of his inquiry or critique. He is not denouncing "an incoherence of language or a contradiction in the system." He is wondering, he says, about "the meaning of a necessity," namely that of "lodging oneself within traditional conceptuality in order to destroy it." Finally, he wonders if this does not indicate some inescapable power of the Greek logos, some "unlimited power of envelopment, by which he who attempts to repel it would always already be *overtaken*" (111–12). These are ambitious and worthy questions. The goal of the present study, which does not dissimulate its favorable bias toward Levinas's project of an ethical metaphysics, seeks mainly to implement an accurate understanding of it. Derrida's observations about Levinas's merger of the notions of the same and ipseity or the subjective "I" interest me not because of what they may imply with respect to a conceptual transgression upon the inner telos of the Greco-European tradition of philosophy, but because of what they reveal about Levinas's project itself. From that point of view, the merger means the reemployment of the same/other binary in such a way that its elements become fixed, anchored so that the sameness becomes the burden of subjectivity and the principle of its closure or immanence. It sets the stage for the philosophical drama of the human situation, positing the other as not only not reversible (not the other of the same, an other same), but not adjacent, not limiting of the same, and not in a relation of symmetry. I do not mean to suggest that Levinas's use of this binary is pure fiat, for which an x would have done as well. As always in these cases, it is as if the new usage to which the term is put, if it is successful, revealed a hitherto unnoticed facet of its meaning. This is particularly true in this case, since sameness seems to add a psychological dimension to self that completes an intuitive feeling one has about oneself as already familiar. But I do not think that Levinas's enlisting of this term for a special mission is likely to eclipse the whirling mobility of the more classic couple. In any case, in terms of this study, the necessity of this stabilization of the same, inhabited by the inalienable identity of subjectivity, is to be understood as the establishment of the ethical self in need of renunciation of itself that should, in Levinas's words, "accompany that desire for salvation so underrated by systematic philosophy."[7]

Part B of "Of the Original Polemic" (113) begins with an inconsistency in Levinas's use of the word "exteriority." In *Time and the Other* (1948), Levinas writes: "It is the other's exteriority, or rather his alterity, for exteriority is a property of space, and brings the subject back to himself through the light which constitutes his entire being."[8] Exteriority is a property of space, hence of light and of the phenomenon. Yet in *Totality and Infinity*, which includes in its very subtitle *An Essay on Exteriority*, that outer realm is that of absolute alterity. Derrida wonders why this change is necessary. In the linguistic terminology that typifies his approach, he asks why it is necessary to "obliterate" this notion of exteriority without erasing it, and more generally why it is necessary to state "infinity's *excess* over totality *in* the language of totality," and the other in the language of the same (112). There is no need to go into the details of the discussion, since Derrida's view of the essential metaphoricity of language is consonant with Levinas's working out of the derivation of so-called literal meanings from their "metaphorical" meanings. (The relevant material is in the essay "La signification et le sens,"[9] published in 1964, which Derrida consulted, but to which he could only make "brief allusions," since his essay had already been written at that time. *Otherwise than Being* contains a fuller working out of this problem, both in the problematics of the "trace" of the infinite within the Said and in the priority of meaning in sensibility.) But while they agree on the essentially metaphorical nature of language, Levinas would probably not concur with Derrida's: "Language, son of earth and sun: writing" (112–13), which strikes a more

Heideggerian note. Levinas's notion of language and meaning as
a priori is in fact quite distinct from Derrida's, as revealed by the
latter's assurance that we could never "separate language and
space," or "snatch speech away from light," suggesting a naturalistic origin of language whose meanings are derived from our
perception of the world.

The shift in Levinas's use of the term "exteriority" — and this
does not appear in Derrida's account, which quickly broadens the
discussion to the relation between philosophical discourse and
language in general — should be understood in relation to his
shift in focus from the *il y a* to being (or "essence," to use his
later terminology). From the point of view of the hypostasis, i.e.
the formation of entities, including the subject *qua* "substance,"
exteriority is precisely spatiality and light, since it is the movement from a less-than-full being, a nocturnal, threatening "there
is," to "daytime" being or the being of the world. Exteriority is
being. But as Levinas's philosophy evolves, in its essential search
for "the Good" that is beyond being, exteriority takes on a more
essentialist meaning, divesting itself of the association with spatiality that is generally, though perhaps wrongly, thought of as
the original and literal sense of the term. The evolution of the
term exteriority thus shifts according to the being to which it is
exterior. The term "otherness" or "alterity," on the other hand,
covers a wide a range of phenomena, but no radical shift in usage
is noticeable since the same can accommodate a relative (or "only
formal") alterity which is to be distinguished from the absolutely
other (*autrui*).[10]

With the next section, "Of Transcendental Violence," we
approach the heart of Derrida's critique, the charge of violence
on the part of Levinas's philosophy. The theme prolongs the motif
of light, now in the more specific sense of the "phaino" of phenomenology. Levinas's metaphysics cannot escape phenomenology, even in its critique of phenomenology.

Part A of this section (118) again points out an inconsistency in Levinas, who rejects the majority of the literal results of Husserl's analyses, but claims, in *Totality and Infinity*, to be faithful to the phenomenological method. This would not be an inconsistency if method could be separated from content or findings, but Derrida finds a text written 30 years earlier in which Levinas denies that method can be thus sundered from content. Driving the wedge deeper, Derrida claims that it would be "too easy to show" that the phenomenological method refers to Western philosophy's decision since Plato to consider itself as science. Ergo, Levinas is in contradiction with himself in attempting to use the phenomenological method against that scientific pretension on the part of Western philosophy.

The fact is that, since his early writings, Levinas has not shown a strong or unambiguous affiliation with phenomenology, particularly with the phenomenological method, whatever that may be.[11]

The Derrida article "Violence and Metaphysics" raises interesting questions (many of which displace interest from Levinas's work to the broader, more abstract issues that go under the general rubric of postmodernism), and has brought Levinas to the attention of many readers who might not otherwise have read him. But it has had other results as well. Some of the younger Derridian followers summarily assumed it to be a successful "refutation" of Levinas (despite statements to the contrary in the essay itself). The length and difficulty of the essay, the blatant charge of "violence" directed against the metaphysician (Levinas), and the author's renown as a subtle deconstructionist of texts may lead the hurried or unprepared reader to make this assumption and move on to more ostensibly promising fields to prospect for truth.

On the other hand, Levinasian enthusiasts, in reaction to the misguided negativity generated in some readers by the insufficient reading of Derrida I have just described, are prompted to hear a call to arms. As Robert Bernasconi remarks: "Almost always Derrida's textual interlocutors construe themselves as victims and so try to resist or overturn the deconstructive reading."[12]

Levinas and Derrida

As an adjunct to these considerations on Derrida's critique of Levinas, a few words should be said about the interrelationship between the two philosophers. There is some controversy as to whether or not Levinas was in any way influenced by Derrida's critique of his work. Robert Bernasconi, who appears to have given considerable attention to the issue, thinks there probably was such an influence, but nuances his judgment. "Might not *Otherwise than Being* be seen as a re-reading of *Totality and Infinity* in the light of 'Violence and Metaphysics?' It is clear that Levinas read Derrida's essay, but because Levinas does not refer to 'Violence and Metaphysics' by name in any of his books or essays, all such arguments, however plausible, are for the most part based upon allusion and conjecture."[13] Jacques Rolland, in a recent study of Levinas, makes Derrida his most frequent interlocutor. In contrast with Bernasconi's more conciliatory view — that Derrida's deconstructive reading is essentially a dual and incompatible reading that leaves the reader in a position of deferred judgment — Rolland takes Derrida's essay as "in the final analysis nothing short of a vast enterprise of demolition, by de-legitimization, of the one [the discourse] risked by Levinas in 1961 [i.e. *Totality and Infinity*]."[14] It is a critique whose *mises au point* (clarifications) are "devastating."[15] Rolland follows approvingly the twists and turns of Derrida's arguments as the latter questions the possibility of speaking of the "Totally-Other," at least in the way in which Levinas does so. He compares Husserl's description of the alterity of the *alter ego* within the relationship of intersubjectivity with Levinas's description, which is lacking in any theoretical basis, and appears to appeal to empiricism. But empiricism, according to Derrida, is not a philosophy, unless it recognizes itself for what it really is, which is a metaphysics of presence.

Derrida ends on a note that is perhaps not as negative as Rolland seems to think. He calls empiricism "the philosophical pretention to nonphilosophy," which is the inability to justify oneself. Derrida here entertains the hypothesis that this "dream of a purely heterological thought" must end with the birth of language. I can only assume that this means that whatever is said in language (and thought in thought, since Levinas does not believe there can be thought without language) is relative in that it is linked with the speaker, and that no absolute otherness is possible in philosophy. This is not an unorthodox view. But why, Derrida wonders in conclusion, this need for philosophy, the residence of Greek thought, i.e. philosophy *tout court*? (This absolute association of Greek with philosophy is not a Derridian principle, but a Levinasian one.) "Such a site of encounter cannot only offer *occasional* hospitality to a thought which would remain foreign to it." "The Greek" who owns the house cannot stay away and let the Jew and the Christian meet there to discuss eschatology and the absolute. Greek thought has already welcomed alterity into its house, and therefore can never be totally taken by surprise.

Although Levinas may never refer to Derrida's essay in any of his writings, he does respond to a direct question concerning Derrida's essay, "Violence and Metaphysics," in an interview that Bernasconi includes in a volume he coedited. The question put to Levinas here concerns Husserl's position on the alterity question as Derrida presents it, as well as the latter's insistence that the other must appear as an alter ego, and therefore cannot be totally other, and that the dissymmetry of the ethical relation depends upon a prior symmetry. In his answer, Levinas does not mention Husserl, but speaks rather to the larger issue.

> Derrida has reproached me for my critique of Hegelianism by saying that in order to criticize Hegel, one begins to speak Hegel's language. That is the basis of his critique. To which I respond that for me, on the contrary, the Greek language is a language which does not imprint itself in what it says, and consequently that there is always the possibility of unsaying that to which you were obliged to have recourse in order to show something.[16]

There should be no surprise that Hegel is taken as the representative of "Greek," i.e. the academic language of philosophy. Levinas's response is effective, denying Derrida's premise that philosophy is not just a language and derived from the Greeks but has certain built-in philosophical commitments. Levinas then states the ethical importance of the dissymmetry of the self-other relation, and adduces the quotation with which all readers of Levinas are familiar, from Dostoyevsky: "Everyone is guilty in front of everyone else and me more than all the others." He points out that this situation is modified by the fact that there is justice, and that from that external point of view we are equal.

This interposition of the third party between the subject and the other introduces an element not present in *Totality and Infinity*. Earlier in the interview Levinas attempts to explain the main differences between *Totality and Infinity* and *Otherwise than Being*. He explains that the former uses ontological terminology, and that, although the later work avoids it, the use of ontological language in the earlier work was intended to create a distance from empirical observation and from psychology. Another important difference (and this concerns the introduction of the "third party" in ethical discussion in *Otherwise than Being*) is that the use of the word "justice," formerly applicable to the relation between two people (the archetypical couple, the only two people in the world so to speak), is later associated with knowledge and politics. Returning to the theme of dissymmetry, Levinas attempts to clarify the significance and status of what he has also alluded to as a "curvature of space":

> But, in the ethical act, in my relationship with the other, if one forgets that I am guiltier than the others, justice itself will not be able to last. But the idea of dissymmetry is another way of saying that in the perseverance of being we are all equal, but the idea that the death of the other is more important than my own is an affirmation that we are not being looked at from outside, but the essential difference between me and the other remains in my look.[17]

This statement, which may not immediately seem pertinent to Derrida's critique, does in fact answer some of the complaints. It says — without explaining why — that the justice of equality is dependent upon the subject's asymmetrical perspective vis-à-vis the other. This aspect of the final statement of Levinas's philosophy represents an addition to the earlier one, and is more fully presented in chapter 5 of *Otherwise than Being*, specifically in the third section, titled "From Saying to the Said, or The Wisdom of Desire." The dissymmetry of the relation of myself to the other is a structural way of expressing the meaning of love, which is the motivation for justice.

Levinas wrote one piece on Derrida, in 1973, after both his major works were published, which is included in *Proper Names*: "Jacques Derrida: Wholly Otherwise." It begins with a suggestion that Derrida's philosophy may be akin to the Kantian critiques, in taking us beyond yet another level of naiveté. Derrida the master of critique is evoked here. In a hallucinatory flashback comparison with the French rout, disarray, and mass retreat of 1939, Levinas sees Derrida sweeping through comfortable villages and changing everything overnight into a postmodern world! (He does not use the word postmodern.) Everything is torn down (*déconstruit*); the "difference" (deferral?) of the future is suddenly transformed into the present. One cannot help but wonder whether there is not, in this description of the panic flight before the relentless German advance, a glimpse into Levinas's subjective reaction to Derrida's critique. At the end of the piece, Levinas describes the crossing of their paths as "probably the very modality of the philosophical encounter." If so, it is brief and incisive, and does not seem to lead to any convergence. Nevertheless the short essay ends on a cordial note. "In emphasizing the primordial importance of the questions raised by Derrida, I have desired to express the pleasure of a contact at the heart of a chiasmus."[18]

But what does Levinas have to say specifically in this essay about Derrida's philosophy? Or perhaps I should refer to Derrida's manner of philosophizing, since it is a manner that does not seem to lead, beyond the accumulation of texts that may be said to constitute it, to anything resembling "a philosophy" in the traditional sense of a body of doctrine or a conceptual system? Most of Levinas's comments are on *Speech and Phenomena* (*La voix et le phénomène*, 1967), a critique of Husserl and a deconstruction of the present, which is denounced as "a simulacrum or an illusion,"[19] a deconstruction in which truth is no longer eternal or omni-temporal. It is "an exile or a casting adrift of Knowledge beyond skepticism, which remained enamored of the truth, even if it did not feel capable of embracing it, and truth is "not the main thing."[20] Levinas writes, "One might be tempted to draw an argument from this recourse to logocentric language in opposing that very language, in order to question the validity of the deconstruction thus produced. That is a course that has frequently been followed in refuting skepticism; but the latter, thrown to the ground and trampled on at first, would right itself and return as philosophy's legitimate child. It is a course Derrida himself, perhaps, has not always disdained to follow in his polemics."[21] I believe this last sentence is an allusion to Derrida's critique of Levinas in "Violence and Metaphysics."

Next Levinas seizes the opportunity for a rapid exposition of a key theme in *Otherwise than Being*, namely the way in which skepticism makes use of but at the same time makes manifest the lack of synchrony between the saying and the said. (This principle is also the secret of many of the Greek paradoxes, e.g. the Liar's paradox.) He notes a very slight temporal discrepancy, "but wide enough for the discourse of skepticism to creep into it without being choked off by the contradiction between what its *said* means and the meaning of the very fact of uttering a *said*."[22]

Levinas makes a sharp distinction between Derrida and his followers. "The path leading toward these pathless 'places,' the subsoil of our empirical places, does not, in any case, open out upon the dizziness caused by those who — frightfully well informed

and prodigiously intelligent and more Derridian than Derrida —
interpret the latter's extraordinary work with the help of all the
key words at once, though neither having, nor leaving to their
readers, the time to return to the thinking that was contemporary
with those words."[23]

Although "Violence and Metaphysics" remains the most substantial and important statement by Derrida on Levinas, two more
recent texts deserve comment.

"En ce moment même dans cet ouvrage me voici"

"At This Very Moment in This Work Here I Am," included in
a festschrift for Levinas in 1980,[24] begins with a statement that
haunts the author (Derrida): *il aura obligé* (he will have obligated). This highly impressionistic piece sets out with a free-asso-
ciation reverie about these three words — containing one, two,
and three syllables, respectively. We are in a poetic modality —
the "shore" of the phrase lost in the darkness of night. This is
"the poetry of Derrida," "a new frisson" to which Levinas alludes
in his essay "Wholly Otherwise."[25]

But if it is poetry it is also philosophy, though in an unaccustomed mode. The "he" who has obligated seems to be Levinas,
and the one obligated is that first one to come along (*premier
venu*), and in this case Derrida. Clearly the situation of writing
something "for" Levinas, to contribute to the festschrift in his
honor, is part of the "context" that borders the haunting phrase
without limiting it. In what I read as a reference to the formal
impersonality of "Violence and Metaphysics" (16 years separate
these texts), Derrida now wonders, "And why after so many
attempts, so many failures, here I am obligated to renounce the
anonymous neutrality of a discourse proposed, in its form at least,
to no matter whom, pretending self-mastery and mastery of its
object in a formalization without remainder? . . . when here I am
sending it to you like a letter."[26]

We now move on to what I will call the problematics of the gift in Levinas. It has as its origin a passage that, as Derrida points out, is identically worded in two essays written within a year of one another. The philosophical context is that of the *sens unique* or one-wayness of the ethical gesture. This can be viewed as part of the notion of the embeddedness of the self in the same. Put in its simplest terms, my act is not pure if it seeks recompense. It is an outward movement, pure loss in a sense, but not in a sense that should lend itself to any sort of tragic pathos. What I do for the other I must do within a timeframe that is "without me." I must be willing not to enter into the promised land. The meaning of the ethical gesture is not "economic," not calculable, but a movement of the same toward the other that does not return to the same. "The Work (*Œuvre*) thought through all the way requires a radical generosity of the movement which in the Same goes toward the Other. It consequently requires an *ingratitude* of the Other; gratitude would be the *return* of the movement to its origin."[27]

On the face of it, despite its logical consistency (given the premise of dissymmetry between self and other and the one-way movement of giving), there is something quite counterintuitive about this arrangement. The usual way of thinking about such things would be something like this: Although I am happy to give without any expression of recognition or gratitude on the part of the recipient, I would feel some satisfaction in seeing an expression of recognition for what I have done **for the sake of the other**. Indeed, since Levinas suggests elsewhere that I am responsible even for the actions of the other, even for the other's persecution of me, it would appear that Levinas is inconsistent with himself here. Should one not want the other to act in an ethically lofty manner, if indeed one is responsible for his or her actions?

Derrida gets beyond this paradox by construing the ingratitude to be on a different level. Neither the debt (which was never incurred, yet owed by me) nor the gift are situated within economic meaning. And just as the haunting phrase *il aura obligé* is linguistically adrift, without context, so Levinas's *Dire* (*le Dire* is an infinitive, which I have translated, not faultlessly, as saying) is without the usual parameters, having neither person nor number.

I will not attempt a full commentary on the entire text here, since Simon Critchley has done so in *Re-Reading Levinas*.[28] I will merely dwell for a moment on this impersonal aspect of Levinas's ethics. Personal or impersonal? I suggest that Levinas's ethics, in order to avoid ethics becoming what Heidegger would call "ontic," transcends the level (which is perhaps the level upon which Martin Buber's ethics is situated) of psychological attachment. This is not to say that there is a bifurcation between duty and inclination, as in Kant, but rather that there is an experience of transcendence or a Platonic spirituality of the abstract in Levinas. How is it, for example, that it is not the "neighbor," in the sense of the person living nearby whom I know well, that is the other: it is the *premier venu*, the first person who happens to come along, the stranger? It is this way of going beyond the system of magnanimity and gratitude, of seeing the other as a recognition of the Eternal, that constitutes the ethical for Levinas. Let us recall that one of the rare passages cited by Levinas from the New Testament is Matthew 25:35–40, the passage in which the Son of Man, having come in his glory, recognizes those who fed and clothed him and rebukes those who did not. He does not rebuke them for not having recognized him, but for the way they treated him in the form of the needy stranger.[29] It is in these terms, perhaps, that we can understand in what sense Levinas's ethics transcends the personal yet is not an abstract system of propositions based on reciprocity, not a deontology. (The kind treatment Zeus and Hermes disguised as mortals received at the hands of the elderly couple Philemon and Baucis may be read as a non Judeo-Christian kenosis of this kind.)

One must be cautious, however, in making general statements

about Levinas's "ethics." I am not thinking here so much of Jacques Rolland's distinction between ethics and *das Ethische*,[30] i.e. the ethical in general that would transcend any particular ethics, as about the distinction Levinas himself makes (not in *Totality and Infinity* but in *Otherwise than Being*) between love, already present in the primordial relation of self and singular other, and the justice motivated by it (the wisdom of love) that springs up in the form of the neverending development of institutions aimed at justice within "sociality."

It would be tempting, but I believe erroneous, to imagine the distinction as one of the concrete versus the abstract, or the particular versus the universal. One wonders how Levinas would have responded to Robert Bernasconi's observation that

> [W]hat usually tends to get omitted from Levinas's discussion of ethics is the importance of particularity in the sense of religion, race, nationhood, culture, gender and so on. Levinas tended to aim at respect for the singular *qua* human and nothing else, so that all of these other features of the discussion are treated as obstacles. But this means that the persecuted one is welcomed not in terms of what he or she has been persecuted for — as Jew, as African-American, as woman — but in his or her universality, which is not the welcome they seek.[31]

Should we see Levinas's ethics at least to some degree as response to a "nonphilosophical" experience, namely that of the Holocaust? Such an ethics would be less concerned with being "welcomed" or even recognized than being allowed to live. Levinas saw France as the country that upheld the universality of human rights. He himself wished to be read as a philosopher, not as a "Jewish" philosopher. But these biographical and contingent issues aside, Bernasconi's question is indeed an important one. I must provisionally close the question he raises by suggesting that although this matter may not be one Levinas dealt with explicitly, the philosophical problematics he has set up (the couple and love versus sociality and justice) may suggest a general line of argument. If the very generic traits or categories that engender prejudice are the same as those for which the persecuted seek recognition or even love — perhaps justice, despite its quasi-abstractness, would be a better thing to seek, at least on the societal level. Another direction in which one might elicit a response to Bernasconi's question is in the reservations Levinas addressed to the philosophy of Martin Buber, whose encounter with the other had too much of the personal, spiritual friendship and not enough of the impersonal or God-mediated charity of the mitzvah, the command.

Adieu

It remains for us to consider the text Derrida wrote on the occasion of Levinas's death in 1995. The publication contains two discourses: Derrida's funeral oration for Levinas (delivered on December 27, 1995, at the cemetery of Pantin, a suburb of Paris) and a longer introductory speech opening the conference "Visage et Sinaï" in Levinas's honor one year later at the Sorbonne. The funeral oration is a direct and moving "à-Dieu" to Levinas, with personal memories, thankfulness, the expression of sadness, and a few reflections on the meaning of death taken mainly from the course notes of "Death and Time" (1975).[32] The second piece, "A Word of Welcome," takes welcoming, or more particularly, hospitality as its theme, and begins with the rather surprising view of *Totality and Infinity* as "an immense treatise on hospitality."[33] It soon becomes clear that the title of his talk, "Le Mot d'Accueil," could be taken as either the word welcoming those attending a two-day colloquium in honor of Emmanuel Levinas, sponsored by the Collège International de Philosophie, or as the word "welcome," particularly in the thought of Levinas. It is both. Under hospitality Derrida subsumes the reception or welcome, and connects it to the theme of the colloquium, which is "Le Visage et Sinaï." The tone of this opening lecture is quite different from Derrida's earlier works on Levinas. It is as if now, for the first time, Derrida is willing to allow himself to explore a theme (of his own choosing, a central theme), hospitality, without thematizing his own misgivings. Of course this is partly because these themes (friendship, hospitality, welcome) were central to his work at the time (*Politiques de l'amitié*, 1994; *De l'hospitalité*, 1997). This is not to say that Derrida does not express doubts and reservations about some of Levinas's texts, particularly in his interpretation of certain aspects of Zionism, of which more will be said presently.

Derrida insists upon the importance in *Totality and Infinity* of the term "hospitality," but especially — since it is "more operational than thematic" — the welcoming movement in the direction of the other that it signifies. Derrida notes that Levinas extends this reception of the other to reason itself — thus overriding the traditional philosophical separation between the passive receptivity of sensibility, on one hand, and rationality on the other. How is this worked out in Levinas? "Reason," in Levinas, says Derrida, "*is* sensibility. Reason itself is a welcome inasmuch as it welcomes the idea of infinity — and the welcome is rational." What is interesting about this statement is that it is bordered by, as one can easily sense, a "reason" that does not welcome infinity, and would therefore be adjudged not welcoming of the other. One could easily imagine a variety of reason as well that may be welcoming enough of the "idea" of infinity (as a regulative idea) but not of "the infinite," specifically when attributed to the otherness of the other (person).

The "dwelling," which plays such an important role in the analyses of *Totality and Infinity*, is seen less in the Heideggerian sense of gathering than as the establishment of the possibility of welcome. It is as if the teleology of the dwelling were welcoming, along with the principle of "femininity," a theme taken up by Derrida later in the lecture. Derrida moves on to the notion of justice and of the third party, which modifies my relation to the singular other and necessitates the comparison of incomparable "uniquenesses" and the mediation of institutions of law. It is also the birth of knowledge and of the question. The third party (and here the chronology seems to be purely expository, as we are told that there was never a time when the third was not present — he or she being already present in the face of the other) is protection against the violence of the I-Thou relationship. But the third can also bring us institutions that cease to be the realization of love.

Derrida discerns a "double bind" (the term appears in his text in English) within Levinas's axioms — an irresolvable conflict between my loyalty to the other before the arrival of the third (but can the "before" be construed as strictly temporal?) and my duty within the context of justice after that arrival. Derrida thus connects justice with perjury since I must (eventually) violate my obligation (silent and passive, an-archic as Levinas would say) to the singular other for sake of justice to all the others. My own observation would be that this is doubtless a potential conflict on an empirical level, but that it only appears as a double bind in Levinas's "axioms" because Derrida has attempted to reduce Levinas's "ethical" (in Jacques Rolland's sense) to an unduly specific morality. Despite valid parallels that have been drawn between Levinas and Kant, nothing could be further from the spirit of Levinas's philosophy than a set of philosophical axioms from which moral behavior could be deductively determined.

The home (*la demeure*) is the locus of welcoming, the "interiority" of which seems to reflect that of the separation which is life, the "secret of a subjectivity." This brings us to the theme of "feminine alterity." The language of intimacy, the *tu*, or the thou is not yet the language of the other. It is understanding without words, the I-Thou of Buber. Derrida quotes Levinas's statement that "[t]he I-Thou in which Buber sees the category of interhuman relationship is the relation not with the interlocutor but with feminine alterity."[34]

In *Time and the Other* and *Existence & Existents* the phenomenology of the caress and Eros develops in the direction of
an ontological category: that which retires from the light. This
research is pushed much further in section 4 of *Totality and Infinity*.
Levinas attempts to forestall the objection that the woman is after
all a human being, an empirical, sexed individual, not an ontological principle. Levinas himself makes the distinction quite
explicitly, but it cannot be said that in doing so he has escaped
criticism from feminists, who see in his characterizations the return
of a number of old myths about women. In any case, the fact
remains that in Levinas's view the feminine and the home are at
the origin of hospitality, a hospitality prior to the economy of
ownership.

Section 2 of the lecture thematizes hospitality — which is paradoxical, or at least difficult, since hospitality has been declared
to "resist thematization" (48). Hospitality resists thematization by
being prior to thematization, which "already presupposes hospitality, welcoming, intentionality, the face" (all of these terms are
more or less equivalent, often joined by the copula "is"). This is
why Levinas says that of peace there can only be an eschatology.
This welcoming (and friendship) is also the essence of language.

There is a notable difference in the tone of Derrida's account
of the relationship between Husserl's and Levinas's notion of the
other in the earlier essay, "Violence and Metaphysics," and in his
"Adieu." Derrida is no longer defending the idea of the other as
alter ego (Husserl's view) before the dissymmetrical other of
Levinas. In this text, on the contrary, Derrida restates Husserl's
view that the other is distinctive in that it (he, she) cannot appear
in originary perception (*originaliter*) but only in a special mode,
that of "appresentation." This structure, says Derrida, "is not
insignificant for Husserlian phenomenology or Levinas's discourse
on the transcendence of the Other — **a discourse that has also
in its own way inherited this interruption**" (51–52, my emphasis). The relationship between Husserl and Levinas has clearly
become one of continuity rather than contradiction.

The approach to the other in proximity is not a knowing. Subjectivity is redefined as hospitality. "The subject is a host."[35] This formulation, from the conclusion of *Totality and Infinity*, finds its logical extension — via substitution — in a formulation that occurs in *Otherwise than Being*: "The subject is hostage."[36] Derrida sees the connection between these two in openness. Not the Heideggerian *Erschlossenheit* or *Offenheit*, which is a spatial figure, but the ethical meaning of openness that is welcoming, an opening of the door, a vulnerability, a being put in question. Derrida refers us to Émile Benveniste's *Indo-European Language and Society* for the etymology of hospitality and its complex relationship with hostility as both a clarification and a vindication of Levinas's philosophical host-hostage constellation.

Section 3 translates these observations into "three types of questions." The questions have more to do with the internal significance of certain features of Levinas's philosophy than with comparisons with other philosophical systems. The first type of question is about the meaning of the transformation from subject *qua* host to subject *qua* hostage. Does this movement represent shift or continuity? More specifically, is it a logical and historical shift (over the years between *Totality and Infinity* and *Otherwise than Being*) or has the very concept of the subject undergone a change from an already novel conception which, in *Totality and Infinity*, had transformed the ontological tradition into an ethics of hospitality? The second type of question also involves the distance between the subject *qua* host and the subject *qua* hostage, but asks more specifically about the primacy of the "welcome" or "reception" in light of the cluster of concepts (responsibility, persecution, being in the accusative, obsession, etc.) that is introduced after *Totality and Infinity*, specifically in *Substitution*, written in 1967, the core text from which *Otherwise than Being* was later elaborated. In the "reverting" (*retournement*) or ethical movement of subjectivity, does the welcoming remain primary, or is there some earlier moment? What is the role of the idea of election and of the political as expressed during these years?

Derrida declares himself incapable of developing the questions during the lecture, but wishes to reinforce them with two references to — and quotations from — "Substitution" (chapter 4 of *Otherwise than Being*). What interests Derrida here is the idea of election preceding (but a precedence that apparently cannot be thought of in terms of the temporality of clocks, being "pre-originary") the welcoming of the subject. For (142) "has not the Good chosen the subject with an election recognizable in the responsibility of being hostage, to which the subject is destined, which he cannot evade without denying himself, and by virtue of which he is unique?"[37] Levinas gives the name *à-Dieu* ("to-God") to the experience of the affirmation preceding my "welcome," and creating me as unique. This initial "yes" is from the other. In the following quote from a footnote by Derrida (142–43 n. 61), there is a greater degree of recognition and acquiescence than any text of his hitherto.

> The *Adieu* does not wait for death but calls, responds and greets in the relation with the other insofar as it *is* not, insofar as it calls from beyond being. To God [*À-Dieu*] beyond being, where the *yes* of faith is not incompatible with a certain atheism or at least with a *certain* thought of the *inexistence* of God (beyond being). We will look more closely later at the use Levinas was able to make of this word *à-Dieu*. Though the experience of the *à-Dieu* can remain silent, it is no less irrecusable. It is from within this experience that we speak here, even when we speak in a whisper, and it is toward it that we will return, toward this infinitely difficult thought to which Levinas gave, in the French language and by means of its idiom, with its idiom as destination, an exceptional chance, a rare economy, one that is, in a word, at once unique, more than old, inaugural, and yet also replaceable: always translatable by paraphrases, of course, and as such always exposed to inanities.

There has been to my knowledge relatively little discussion of the *à-Dieu* in Levinas (Jean-Luc Marion's *God without Being* would constitute an exception), though it is probably as important as the *zum-Tode* (to-death) in Heidegger's philosophy.

Next Derrida examines the problem of the Third, i.e. the third party, and the entrance of justice. He points out that, despite a concession Levinas himself makes to a discussant in *Of God Who Comes to Mind*, justice, or rather the demand for justice, is already in the face of the other in the phenomenological analyses of *Totality and Infinity*. This corresponds to the presence of the third person, the He[38] within the "thou," which would constitute the full "you." It is the presence of "illeity" within the other that keeps it from being a "thou," which always runs the risk of assimilation into the same by not remaining sufficiently separate. This illeity, the separate, is the holy (saint), which is carefully distinguished from the pagan awe associated with the sacred — the sanctification of place. Derrida sees, below the Greek "ethical," which is a stop-gap solution,[39] the Hebrew holiness of the separated, the "kadosh."

Derrida also notes an anteriority of the passage of the holy, or the retreat of the other, in relation to hospitality. One of the indications he finds of this is the phrase "the trace of a withdrawal that orders it [the neighbor, *le prochain*] as a face." The translation is correct but necessarily misses the suddenness of the French "la trace d'un retrait **qui l'ordonne visage**" (my emphasis). The translation adds an "as" and uses the verb "to order" (following the Lingis translation, *Otherwise than Being*, 121). I am not sure that we should rule out, in translating this expression, the verb "to ordain," particularly since there seems to be a transformation of the "neighbor" that is reflected in a predicate nominative, thus: "that ordains him (or her) face." Derrida continues to explore the (paradoxically nonthematizable) theme of the face that is in the trace of illeity in the final pages of the section of "Meaning and Sense" titled "The Trace."[40] The trace is none other than the wake of the passage of God, and the face of the other as "visitation" is transcendence. Levinas's text in "The Trace" refers to Exodus 33 (the relevant verses are 17–23). God reveals himself to Moses, but only by shielding the latter from seeing his face directly, in order that he not die, for "man shall not see Me and live." Derrida enumerates (63–64) the "disjointed times" (but are they even **in** time?) that took place at Mount Horeb, or Sinai (the reception of the Torah, the appearance of God to Moses, etc.); and then moves on to the meaning of Sinaï today — the symbolic frontier between Israel and the other nations.

Derrida attaches great importance to Levinas's question/suggestion: "*A recognition of the Torah before Sinaï?*" His emphasis seems to derive from a concern for the universality of Levinas's message. This can also be seen in his lengthy footnote (145 n. 71) on Islam and the concept of substitution in the work of Louis Massignon.

Part 4 of Derrida's lecture turns to the "discreet though transparent" allusions by means of which Levinas directs our attention to current events and politics. Derrida shares with Levinas a heartfelt compassion for the stateless person, the refugee, and quotes, from *In the Time of the Nations*, Levinas's firm judgment against those who would deny the duty of hospitality. "To shelter the other in one's own land or home, to tolerate the presence of the landless and homeless on the ancestral soil, so jealously, so meanly loved — is that the criterion of humanness? Unquestionably so."[41] Derrida concurs, though not without some reservations. "Is Israel as isolated as Levinas claims?" Derrida asks, promising to take up the question later (78).

Part 5 is dedicated to Levinas's commentary on the state of Israel. Derrida at several points expresses his hesitations. It is clear that he believes Levinas to be equivocal in his comments about Israel, but the objections are postponed or left vague. The only interesting philosophical point that emerges from this section is that, by contrast with Kant, for whom the state of war was natural, the meaning of war seems to be derived from peace in

Levinas. However, Kant is speaking on a level of historical empiricism where the *a priori* of the utopia of the human in Levinas clearly is not situated. Derrida feels that it is the wrong place to examine the question of Israeli politics in detail, but asks: "[D]oes one have the right here to silence the anxiety of such an interrogation, before these words of Levinas, in the spirit that inspires them?" (81). He is concerned about the settlements on the West Bank, the use of torture authorized by the Israeli supreme court, "and, more generally, all the initiatives that suspend, derail, or interrupt what continues to be called, in this manner of speaking, the 'peace process'" (82). Are his comments those of an objective observer, or is his neutrality that of the truly "ne-uter," neither one nor the other because both: Derrida, an Algerian Jew, would be by his background doubly affected by this conflict between "Abrahamic siblings."

The sixth and last part of the lecture "enters into Jerusalem," that is to say, follows closely a talmudic reading of Levinas's titled "Cities of Refuge."[42] Derrida is at ease in this milieu of overdetermined signification, a palimpsest of inscription, an intertextual confluence run rampant. The degree of subtlety and complexity of Levinas's manner of commenting on this excerpt from the Tractate *Makkoth* 10a offers a congenial surface upon which to move toward a satisfactory conclusion. The theme, that of the "cities of refuge" (chapter 4 of *Beyond the Verse*) is one with which Derrida is familiar, since he himself has written about it, albeit from a different perspective (148, n. 113).

Derrida does not mention the allusion to "dissemination" in the new sense he himself has given to that word, alluded to by Levinas in this text. The allusion comes up in connection with a midrash[43] that reads "otherwise" a text from Ecclesiastes. Levinas writes, "The *Midrash* allows itself to be guided, when it wishes, by the physical form of the words. A way of reading that resembles the process of 'dissemination' in use today in certain avant-garde circles."[44]

To return to the theme of "cities of refuge" (referred to in Numbers 35:1–34 and Deuteronomy 4:41), Levinas praises the respect shown for the rights of both the blood relatives of the victim and the perpetrator of an "objective" or unintended manslaughter, by offering protection for the manslayer but not excusing the misdeed outright. The Torah thus recognizes a right (a "counter-right," actually) that protects the unintentional murderer against the "marginal right" of the avenger of blood. It also provides for a time limit after which the protected individual will have to seek safety in exile. The point is that even involuntary murder (manslaughter) is not totally excused. Derrida comments that

> Levinas insists on this double finality [the double goal of pro-
> tecting conflicting rights]. Indeed, it is there to remind us that
> there is no real discontinuity between voluntary and involuntary
> murder. Sometimes invisible, always to be deciphered, this con-
> tinuity forces us to infinitize our responsibility: we are also respon-
> sible for our lack of attention and for our carelessness, for what
> we do neither intentionally nor freely, indeed, for what we do
> unconsciously — since this is never without significance.

But this means that ultimately there is "only one race of murderers, whether the murder is committed involuntarily or intentionally."[45]

Next, Levinas's talmudic lesson shows how the talmudic text deals with the following circumstance. If a disciple is sent away to a city of refuge, his teacher (rabbi) must follow him, since he is granted "life," and life would be meaningless without the study of Torah. In the reverse situation, the *yeschivot*, or group of disciples, must follow their ostracized rabbi. But how can that be squared with the verse from Deuteronomy 4:44, which the talmudic scholars interpret to mean (by reading that verse as the continuation of the enumeration of "cities of refuge" named in the preceding verse and reading "the law" as "Torah" which in fact it is) that the Torah is itself a city of refuge? The talmudic text faces this difficulty by interpreting the study of the Torah as constituting protection from death as long as the attention remains fixed on the study itself. But we can become distracted! Is there not a midrash recounting how the Angel of Death sat in a cedar tree outside the house of study, causing the branches to produce a creaking sound which distracted the rabbi, at which point the opportunistic angel did his deadly work? Levinas is aware of the "specious" nature of some of these interpretations, but also of the edification of the lessons they make possible. He moves on, however, to a higher level. The humanitarianism of the laws are important, essential even: but the Torah itself has a higher teaching. For it is not the Torah that is essentially a city of refuge, but rather Jerusalem, the city of perfect peace, in which these antimonies are transcended. They are "transcended" but not totally left behind since Jerusalem is a double city — earthly and divine. Derrida comments that "[t]hough it exceeds the political ambiguity or juridical equivocation of which the 'noble lesson' of the cities of refuge still bears witness, the Torah, the Torah in Jerusalem, the Torah-Jerusalem, must still inscribe the promise *in* the earthly Jerusalem. And henceforth command the comparison of incomparables (the definition of justice, of the concession made, out of duty, to synchrony, co-presence, the system, and, finally, the State). It must enjoin a negotiation with the non-negotiable so as to find the 'better' or the least bad" (112). Here we have the spirit of Levinas's "for commerce is better than war,"[46] which is not a "meliorism" since it does not presuppose any immanent universal tendency for the world to become better, but perhaps bears within it a messianic duty of *tikkun olam* (repairing the world).

Derrida's lecture ends with a meditation on the various meanings of Levinas's *À-Dieu* (to-God), adding a new one that he believes he perceived over the last decade of Levinas's life, namely an *adieu* to life: "Vulnerability is being able to say *adieu* to this world. One says *adieu* to it in aging. Time endures by way of this *adieu* and by way of the *à-Dieu*."[47] Derrida goes so far as to identify death as the theme of Levinas's philosophical work: "And yet all of Levinas's thought, from the beginning to the end, was a meditation on death . . ." (120).

PART THREE

Commentary

L evinas's thought has left its trace in its most pregnant form in the original French texts, leading most surely to the potential "unsaid" that prolongs it and also serving as a "given" upon which future debates and interpretations will be based. Therefore I will at times supply both the original French and the English in this part, which is entirely devoted to commentary on specific texts. (Pagination given in the body of the text will always refer to the English version of the text being discussed.) While relinquishing any claim to synoptic or analytic "mastery" of Levinas's philosophy, textual interpretation enjoys a special place and deserves the last word.

In addition to his love of commentary, whether of talmudic or of philosophical texts, the motif of precedence granted to the other is also reflected in the following thoughts expressed by Levinas in the course of an interview.

> I found it very difficult to prepare my classes. I felt much better when I was carried by a text, in commentary. The construction of a systematic course — the anticipation of all the questions and objections — has always seemed to me to be abstract and artificial. . . . That sense of having overcome all the problems that you have to project when you are a professor is something difficult,

and a bit anxiety-producing as well. Everything that has been thought by someone else, on the other hand, even if it leaves unresolved questions, is welcome; it is much more exciting to prepare.[48]

He proceeds to compare the *explication de texte*, that venerable exercise of traditional French instruction, to "blowing on the embers to bring out the flame."

The following commentaries on texts presented chronologically will allow us to follow the development of some themes, such as the *il y a*, the original positing of subjectivity or "hypostasis," the analyses of time, the saying and the said, and philosophy as "indiscretion vis-à-vis the ineffable." The widest variety of literary and philosophical figures becomes grist to his mill — and this is doubtless why his reading of certain authors has been labeled one-sided, or even "violent." Rarely if ever does Levinas follow a line of reasoning for the sake of pure intellectual curiosity. The goal is always to push forward, during a philosophical career of over 60 years, an inquiry constantly building on its own achievements.

15. "De l'évasion" ("On Escape": 1935)

Levinas's first original work, "De l'évasion," was published in 1935 in *Recherches Philosophiques*. Bruno Roy, the director of Fata Morgana and a friend of Levinas's, asked permission to republish it, but Levinas demurred until, in 1982, a former student of his, the late Jacques Rolland, resurrected the work with commentaries and notes that so pleased Levinas as to convince him to allow the new edition.

The work begins by circumscribing the realm of "traditional" philosophy (and here Levinas seems to be using the term in its etymological sense of "handed down," i.e. the philosophy of the Western world beginning with the Greeks) to that of a "revolt" against being. That revolt is based on a discordance between "the brute fact of being" and human freedom. The resulting conflict, says Levinas, opposes the human person and world, not human and self. As we read on, it becomes clear that Levinas is moving in the direction of a critique of Western philosophy. To oppose "man to himself" would require a breaking up of the calm simplicity of the unitary self, which is at peace with itself. What is already adumbrated here is Levinas's critique of freedom (which can only be a "difficult freedom") and the inner rending of the self into the *moi* or selfish self and the *soi* or self responsible for the other — the "same" in the "other."

Levinas's view of Romanticism confirms his assertion. Since Romanticism is not a philosophical, but rather a broader cultural manifestation, Levinas is referring to a certain *Weltanschauung*, determined on the basis of a certain understanding of the relation between human beings and the world. This "bourgeois spirit and its philosophy" champions the self-reliant self, as manifested in the triumph of the will, effort, work, imperialism, and capitalism. Its lack of scruples is "the shameful form," the ugly aspect of its inner serenity or clear conscience.

Reading this early text in light of what followed it, how very clearly the later developments are already delineated in it! The main displacement that Levinas's philosophy will try to bring about is a shift from the human/world dichotomy to a human/human one, i.e. a splitting of the self, such that a philosophy of scruples — a philosophy in which we question our own intentions vis-à-vis other people, a moral philosophy, is developed.

In the "traditional" worldview, which reflects an understanding of being based on the physical object, any insufficiency is an insufficiency of being. Levinas already hints at something other, some other possibility, in the sentence "Their essence and their properties can be imperfect; the very fact of being is placed beyond the distinction between the perfect and the imperfect."[1] In other words, the notion of value and of the justification of being is secondary to the brute fact of existence.

But Levinas detects a contemporary malaise during those years between the two wars — a desire to escape, which he sees reflected in literature. It is the reaction to a sense of being riveted (*rivé*) to being. Passing in rapid review the difference between the desire of Romanticism to escape specific undesirable facets of existence and the "becoming" mode of the *élan vital* (becoming is not really an escape from being but just an aspect of it), he notes that this new desire has no destination but is just the desire to escape identity, the bond of the self with itself that is the very definition of ipseity. By tracing this desire to escape from being, Levinas will lead us to a renewal of the question of being *qua* being, an expression that signals the presence in Levinas's thought of Heidegger's work in renewing the question of being. Levinas refers in this text to this mode of leaving being by the neologism *excendance*, from *ex-* (out of) and *ascendere* (to rise); in later texts he will adopt a parallel term he borrows from Jean Wahl, *transascendance*.

The analysis of need in this work will subsequently find fuller development in the opening pages of *Totality and Infinity*, in the form of need versus (metaphysical) desire.

From an initial analysis of need, which is seen, contrary to popular belief, to be based not on a deficiency in our being but rather the presence of that being to itself, we move on to an analysis of pleasure. Pleasure is not a state but a process, the unfolding of which is part of its essential way of being. It is described as an evaporation of substance, and an inebriation, an abandonment, at the height of which being "is wholly disappointed and ashamed to find itself still existing."[2]

In this description of affectivity there is also the intimation of a new direction of thought that foreshadows the "otherwise than being" of Levinas's late period. The passage occurs in the course of the analysis of pleasure. It is revealing that the satisfaction of a need should be accompanied by an affective event, Levinas says, and it would be wrong to think of what satisfied a need as a simple act. Affectivity "is foreign to the notions that are applied to what is, and has never been able to be reduced to the categories of thought and activity."[3] Pleasure is the process of leaving being; it is affectivity precisely because it does not adopt the forms of being, but attempts to break them. But in the end pleasure is a deceptive escape from being because it fails. It is not deception because of the role it plays in life or its destructive effects or its moral indignity, but because of its internal structure. And at the moment of its failed triumph its failure is underscored by shame.

The style of the analysis in this portion of the essay is reminiscent of that of Max Scheler in his analysis of the emotions. Shame is based not on a lack in our finite being but on the attachment of ourselves to ourselves through time. We are stuck with what we have done, even after the motivations that would have made those actions comprehensible are no longer apparent to us. It is the solidarity of myself with myself that makes me capable of shame, as well as of responsibility for what I have done. The analysis of shame leads to analysis of the meaning of nakedness and poverty, which are also traceable to the concept with which Levinas began his analysis of the malaise of his time: the sense of being riveted to one's self, to ipseity, and the attendant need to escape this ontological impasse. The analysis of being that is a burden to itself is pursued further in the notion of nausea (three years prior to Sartre's novel of the same name, *La Nausée*, which was published in 1938). Nausea is a malaise arising internally from which there is no escape and which is therefore the experience of pure being itself. As Jacques Rolland points out, there is a strong affinity between Levinas's nausea and Heidegger's anguish: the former is the experience of "pure being," the latter of "nothingness." Rolland's notes also emphasize the connection between this rather grim description of being — especially "pure" being — and the *il y a* or the "there is," a term describing the anonymity and neutrality of being, the background being against which (in *Le temps et l'autre*, 1946/47, and *De l'existence à l'existant*, 1947) the subject emerges through *hypostase*. Rolland even goes so far as to indicate, as if with dotted lines, the future metamorphosis of the notion of "escape" or *évasion*. This term will be dropped in Levinas's later philosophy; it will become "the other in the same" and the transformation of the substance of the subject into meaning.

Levinas's main thesis in "De l'évasion" is that the need (which, as I have indicated, will be replaced in *Totality and Infinity* by metaphysical desire, as opposed to the more elementary "needs" of the living organism in general) to escape being is based on a sense of the overfullness, the extreme density or crushing weight of being, later termed the *il y a* or the "there is." This sense of the overfullness of being may be the ancestor of Sartre's density

of being in *Being and Nothingness*, which requires the nothingness of consciousness to allow for the freedom of human consciousness. Being is imperfect, not because finite but just because
it is being.[4]

This essay concludes by reemphasizing the ineluctable attachment of "Western philosophy" (the term is redundant in Levinas's
view) to being. It is as if to bestow being on something were a
stamp of approval, a recognition that is *de rigueur*, a mark of
respect. Even to think nothingness is to posit it in some sense, as
in Plato's *Sophist*. The *élan* toward the Creator was in a sense a
desire to exit being, but philosophy applied the category of being
to God as well, whose existence it then became important to prove.
Neither Romanticism nor idealism succeeds in breaking with
being; the latter's liberation from being was in fact an underesti-
mating of it. Yet Levinas expresses his admiration for idealism,
to whose aspirations he attributes what is of value in Europe.
Idealism, in its "first inspiration," was an attempt to go beyond
being. The piece concludes with the call to "leave being by a new
path, at the risk of overturning certain ideas that appear the most
self-evident to common sense and the wisdom of the nations."[5]
On this note the essay ends, without any specific indication of
how such a departure could be realized. Nevertheless it is clear
that this early essay is a movement "toward the outside," a movement that characterizes Levinas's work as a whole, even though
the meaning of that spatial metaphor, that "exteriority" is expressed
with increasing frequency as "the other."

16. EXISTENCE & EXISTENTS (1947)

This work was written during the war years, which Levinas spent in a prison camp in Germany. He mentions that circumstance to explain the absence of allusions to the most recent developments in French philosophy (the work of Merleau-Ponty and Sartre, which proceeded unimpeded by the German occupation: Merleau-Ponty's *Structure of Behavior* was published in 1942, Sartre's *Being and Nothingness* in 1943).

The introduction to *Existence & Existents*, as indicated by the original title, *De l'existence à l'existant* ("From existence to the existent," or less literally, "From being to beings"), sets out from the ontological distinction made by Heidegger between beings (*das Seiende*) and being (*das Sein*). Levinas shows the essential connection, but also the distinction, between being and entities that "are," by calling the former verbal and the latter substantive or noun-like. Being is fluid, an event; beings are instants, substantive moments, the emergence of entities and human subjectivity out of a background milieu — not of nothingness — but of a frightening, haunting and anonymous being/nothingness called the *il y a*, the impersonal "there is" of being.

Already in this introduction it is clear that Levinas wishes to distance himself from Heidegger. While acknowledging his debt, he also expresses "a profound need to leave the climate of that philosophy," without, however, leaving it "for a philosophy that would be pre-Heideggerian."[1] He then proceeds to group Heidegger with the broad tradition of Western philosophy that sees evil as a lack of being. Heideggerian anxiety, for example, is anxiety or fear of death, hence of nothingness. Nothingness is still dialectically connected with being, of which it is a defective mode. Levinas questions the view that evil is a lack. Does being not bear a vice other than its limitedness and nothingness, within itself?

Can the relation between the existent and existence be truly termed a relation? In order for such a relation to exist, it would seem that two existents, two entities, must exist. But that is not the case here, since existence does not exist in the same way that the existent or entity does. The human person can take up an attitude toward its own being. Such would be the struggle for life. But that is not a relation between being and a being: it is rather a being's attempt to prolong its state. It is the struggle of the already-constituted being to continue to be.

At this point we begin the analysis of tiredness, which is a relation of an existent with existence. It is as if there were a "contract" between the existent and existence which weariness would like to rescind. Similarly laziness, a hesitation positioned after the intention but before the accomplishment of the act, is a refusal directed toward existence.

Existence is dual, in that the *moi* possesses a *soi*: that is to say, I possess a self. Therefore rather than to say "one is," one should say "one is oneself." The French here is: *On n'est pas, on s'est.*[2] Existence is essentially reflexive. Levinas describes laziness as "a being fatigued by the future." It is as if the future had already been lived as a weary present. Levinas concludes this first section on the relation with existence by suggesting that perhaps for the solitary subject the future, a virginal instant, is impossible. The second section is devoted to "tiredness and the instant." Here Levinas notes that his method will be, throughout his research, to delve into the instant, in order to find within it a hitherto unsuspected dialectic.

As Robert Bernasconi has remarked in his introduction to the English translation of this work, there are traces of the circumstances in which this piece was written. He cites Levinas's description of the distance between the ego and the self as "less like liberation than the slackening of the rope that still binds a prisoner."[3] I would add to his observation the theme of tiredness itself, with the hand "that is letting slip the weight it finds tiring to lift," and so many other first-personal experiences in this short work that do not lose their poignancy for being expressed in a philosophical idiom.

The main characteristic of tiredness is a lag or a distance between being and itself. It constitutes the advent of consciousness, that is, the power to "suspend" being by sleep and lack of awareness (*inconscience*). But why does Levinas equate consciousness with sleep and lack of awareness? He promises us an explanation later on. Let us retain for the moment this unusual grouping, which seems to be made on the basis of human ability to introduce a distance between being and self.

The work of human beings is contrasted with God's creation, which is "magic." He is not the demiurge who creates by labor, but the one who speaks, creating by the word alone. Human work is tied to effort, which is to say to the instant — which Levinas contrasts with Bergson's *durée*, and with the time of play, which is not in fact a present, an instant, at all. It is the false note of the concert that refuses to die, to slip into the next without stopping. "The effort is the accomplishment of the instant." Levinas describes the act as the subject in relation to — struggling with — existence: the subject taking up or assuming that existence. This is the basis for the ancient curse of work. The present is a lag between the existent and existence. Here Levinas is attempting to describe his understanding of the relationship between the existent and existence, but at the same time suggesting the very formation of the existent out of a prior, anonymous existence. This apparition of an existent in existence, essentially act, is referred to as "hypostasis."

The second part of this work, "The World," takes up the notion of intentionality, but not in the "abstract" medieval or Husserlian sense. Intention for Levinas is much closer to the everyday meaning of the term, and it is motivated, not by care, as in Heidegger, but by desire. Objects exist, and we should note that they are not referred to in this work as existents (which term seems to be reserved for the human being) but just as objects, the objects of desire or intentionality. Further, the term hypostasis does not include the formation of objects, but only of the (human) existent.

Levinas's constant silent interlocutor is Heidegger. Thus, when Levinas remarks that "to be sure, *implicitly* we have always understood the meaning of the word 'to be' in its bare meaning," he is alluding to — and expressing reservations about — Heidegger's assertion that "we always conduct our activities in an understanding of Being."[4] Levinas's critique of implicit or unconscious knowledge is that it is thought of on the model of conscious knowledge. It would be another consciousness. But the essential difference between the two types of knowledge is, in Levinas's view, a moral one. Consciousness is sincerity; its field of action is that of intentionality and light. It is "before" the world, Levinas insists, that the unconscious plays its role. This view will have important consequences in Levinas's later analyses of the psyche, which is therefore to be thought of as situated on a metaphysical rather than a psychological plane.

In the following passage, Levinas is critical of the tendency to seek the deeper meaning of life in the unconscious, which is itself situated within the world.

> There is then a regrettable confusion in contemporary philosophy when it situated within the world the events which it has the incontestable merit of having discovered and designated by the purely negative term of the unconscious, and when it denounced as a hypocrisy, a fall, as "bourgeois" and evasion of the essential, behavior in the world, whose secular nature and contentment are simply counterparts of the very destiny of the world. **It is one**

thing to ask what the place of the world in the ontological adventure is, and another thing to look for that adventure within the world itself.[5]

But it is far from clear to what philosophers he may be referring. In the last sentence, which I have emphasized, the critique widens from one directed against the use of the concept or category of the unconscious, to a much broader critique of all philosophies that seek the meaning of the world in the world. Such a critique would include Merleau-Ponty, Sartre, and Heidegger if we take their philosophies as attempts to articulate such an "ontological adventure" within the world. Heidegger's correction of the "worldless" self of idealism would seem to put him in this category, although one must wonder, then, exactly what Levinas's charge comprises. In any case, there is a clear implication that being, or the ontological adventure, extends beyond the world itself. This critique seems to precede the time when Levinas will cease to claim the term ontological for his own philosophy. The "ontological adventure" will become an "intrigue of the infinite."

Levinas's constant use of the adjective "secular" (*laïc*) in this and contiguous passages suggests that he is objecting to the infusion of ultimate meanings into the phenomenology of everyday life. While praising Heidegger specifically for having distinguished between the concept of world and that of an accumulation of individual objects, he taxes him with failing to recognize "the essentially secular nature of being in the world and the sincerity of intentions."[6] For readers of Levinas's later work, in particular, the insistence on the secularity of our experience in the world seems surprising. This, together with the use of the word "magic" to describe the act of creation by the word of God, is in sharp contrast to the general tenor of the later writings. Levinas also praises Marxism for its straightforward or "sincere" recognition of human needs as ends in themselves, not as a moment in a circuit of circumspective care; he then points out that Husserl's reduction was intended precisely to disconnect the world from human purposes the better to reveal those purposes; for "it is not by being in the world that we can say what the world is."[7]

There are, in this section, anticipations of the more thorough analyses of the caress, the home, and food that will be developed in *Totality and Infinity*. A particularly striking formulation of love is: "The very positivity of love is in its negativity." This formula, italicized for emphasis in the original, is meant to distinguish between the positive nature of desires that can be satisfied (such as hunger) and the transcendence of love. The "tragically ridiculous" act of kissing, a simulacrum of eating, suggests a hunger for nothing (*une faim de rien*).

The next subsection, "Light," begins by evoking the light of the sun and of the intelligence in Plato and stressing the revelatory power of sight, whether in "natural" or mental seeing. Levinas sketches out the traditional access to the "outer" world and the notion that the self has an inside and an outside. Somewhat surprisingly, he claims that even Heidegger's Dasein has these two dimensions, and care, though it has no perceptual infrastructure, has its own way of illuminating the world. This associates Heidegger with the inside/outside dualism and with traditional philosophy, which approaches existence through the world. Levinas then elaborates on the theme of distance between the self and its engagement in things in the world. It is through light and sight that we can have a relation with the world of things and yet retain our freedom. The self steps back, so to speak, and has a *quant-à-soi*, a reserve, literally an "as for oneself."

To summarize, the existent separates itself from existence and forms a self through hypostasis. That distance has been described concretely through analyses of tiredness and of the present (instant). Consciousness is precisely this interval between self and world, this resistance to the anonymous existence that will be described more fully in the third chapter, called "Existence Without a World." I note that Levinas sees separation (a category that will be further developed in *Totality and Infinity*) as an achievement.

The first theme of "Existence Without a World" is our ability to disengage ourselves from the world. Art, for example, is able to interpose an image between ourselves and the real world. It reveals, in color, in sound, the elemental: that which is not yet an object. It reveals a certain sort of materiality, prior to the light or the nameable. This level is below that of "form," which has the function of mediating the passage from the external to the internal. Levinas writes that "[e]ven the most realistic art gives this character of *alterity* to the objects represented which are nonetheless part of our world. It presents them to us in nakedness, but real nakedness which is not the absence of clothing, but we might say the absence of forms, that is, the non-transmutation of our exteriority into inwardness, which forms realize."[8] This passage presents us with an early version of the notion of alterity that will play an ever-increasing role in Levinas's philosophy and the special sense of nakedness that surrounds or prefaces that alterity. In later passages, the nakedness of the face (minus the plasticity of it, the visibility of it) will signal the alterity of the other.

The second subsection of "Existence Without a World" is titled "Existence without existents." Here the *il y a* is described, impersonal being, anonymous existence. At this stage in his career, Levinas uses existence for being, and the existent for **a** being (in the sense of the human being). This is being-in-general, before the subject/object and before the interior/exterior distinction.

The *il y a*, the "there is," is compared to darkness and again to nothingness. But nothingness is a misleading notion because one normally thinks of it as that which bounds or surrounds being. At the end of this section Levinas presents a notion that bears some affinity, as we have already noted, to that of Sartre in *Being and Nothingness*, in which consciousness is equated with nothingness. Nothingness is not what limits the *il y a* on all sides since the *il y a* is precisely prior to any notion of limitation, but perhaps, Levinas says, it can be thought of as interval and interruption (in Being). We must ask "whether consciousness, with its aptitude for sleep, for suspension, for *epochè*, is not the locus of this nothingness-interval."[9] The similarity with Sartre's use of nothingness, or "holes" in being, to interrupt the density and immobility of being in order to accommodate consciousness is limited because for Sartre consciousness is pure mobility and freedom, the refusal to "be" anything in particular; Levinas's "consciousness," as described here, is capable of sleep — and sleep, inasmuch as it makes possible a distancing from the *il y a*, is a manifestation of freedom. The next chapter, "The Hypostasis," will clarify this relationship between consciousness and the *il y a* by introducing the concepts of "vigilance" or wakefulness (*la veille*) and "insomnia."

Vigilance, like the *il y a*, is impersonal. It is not my vigilance, but that of the night itself, that "watches." "I am, one might say, more the object than the subject of an anonymous thought." To the extent that I become conscious of myself as that object I am already moving away from the impersonal vigilance of the *il y a* which ebbs as it gives rise to consciousness. The "attention" of consciousness bears traces of its origin in vigilance, but to the extent that it can be willfully directed it is already detached from the impersonal — already the manifestation of a *moi*. From the point of view of consciousness, the *il y a* is obsession. This first section, titled "Insomnia," ends with some methodological considerations. First, the conditions for a phenomenological description are lacking since phenomenology supposes a subject to whom things appear. Levinas does not offer a different methodology, however. He simply makes the point that thought must go beyond intuition if it is to apprehend these impersonal phenomena "in certain awakenings of delirium, in certain paradoxes of madness."[10]

Section 2 of "The Hypostasis," titled "Position" (the action of positing), describes the interrelationship between consciousness and the unconscious, which is not the opposite of consciousness. Levinas begins by recalling the story of Jonas, who makes an impossible attempt to flee from the face of God. As the elements

are raging about him, he descends into the hull of the ship and
goes to sleep. Sleep is thus a dimension of consciousness into
which consciousness can disappear, and from which it can re-
emerge. There are many crossings between sleep and wakefulness, for there is a whole backdrop of unconsciousness, astir
with whisperings, behind consciousness. Levinas compares the
consciousness-unconscious manifold to the wink, which is made
up of a looking and a not looking. In concluding this section,
Levinas uses a term not unrelated to the wink that will reappear
in his later writings: the *scintillement* or *clignotement,* a twinkling, the pulsation of light that is also used to indicate the manifestation, in the modality of ambiguity, of the infinite or the
transcendent in being.[11] I attribute it to his familiarity with phenomenological description that Levinas is able to preserve the
modality of ambiguity — the wavering per se — not as a deficient
mode of certainty or a lack of clarity, but as an original structure
of presentation: that of the infinite in the finite, later referred to
as "the trace." In this case, faithfulness to the evidence of the
data has an importance that goes far beyond fastidiousness or
respect for Husserl's doctrine of equal rights for all data. It is
central to his understanding of religion, in that the modality of
the appearance of the Eternal is uncertainty.

The next subsection is "Here." Levinas admires in Descartes
precisely what Heidegger had deplored: the notion of a *res cogitans,* or "thinking thing." "For the most profound teaching of
the Cartesian *cogito* consists in discovering thought as a substance, that is, as something that is posited."[12] While Heidegger
believes Descartes is guilty of positing a "worldless" subject,
Levinas finds that, quite to the contrary, he has tied the ubiquity
of idealism to a "here," and made consciousness emanate from
something with material density, namely a head. But the head can
fall forward in slumber. Consciousness can sleep. This positing
of the subject in being is neither objective nor subjective but
the "subjectivation" of the subject. This reading of Descartes,

whose name has become almost synonymous with dualism, is an unusual one. Rather than emphasizing the intractable problem of interaction, Levinas insists on the fact that the notion of substance is common to both *res extensa* and *res cogitans*. He is reading Descartes more as a phenomenologist *avant la lettre*, and accrediting him with a faithful account of the impossible but phenomenologically true relationship between thought and position.

One might assume that the Heideggerian notion of the human subject as Da-sein (or "there"-being) would be quite close to Levinas's conception. But this is far from being the case: Heidegger's "there" already implies a world,[13] while Levinas's "there" precedes all time, place or understanding. It is the support, or basis, of the body — which in turn is not a thing, but "the advent of consciousness."

It is difficult to reconcile Levinas's admiration for Descartes' definition of the self as a thinking thing (in the Third and Sixth Meditations: *Sum certus me esse rem cogitandem*) and his emphatic denial that the body is a thing. What he admires specifically in Descartes' conception is (1) that it is first-personal and present tense, and (2) that it ties thought to place. He writes, "For the most profound teaching of the Cartesian *cogito* consists in discovering **thought as a substance, that is, as something that is posited.** Thought has a point of departure. There is not only a consciousness of localization, but **a localization of consciousness**, which is not in turn reabsorbed into consciousness, into knowing."[14] Beneath the English translation of "something that is posited," we have in the original *quelque chose qui se pose*. While it is true that in most cases such reflexives can be translated to the English passive voice, an important nuance is lost here, and it is one that may help square this text with the one that follows it a few pages later, in which it is denied that the body (and thus *a fortiori* thought) is posited. If thought or consciousness is something that **posits itself** rather than being posited, it is not difficult to conceive of the body as well as that which posits. As Levinas argues, "This is what makes the body the very advent of consciousness. It is nowise a thing — not only because a soul inhabits it, but because its very being **belongs to the order of events and not to that of substantives**."[15] Now Levinas's definition of "substance" as that which "posits itself" appears somewhat at variance with that of Descartes, for whom substance was that which requires no other thing in order to exist. Clearly existence *qua* the *il y a*, prior to hypostasis and its positing of entities, corresponds more closely to the Cartesian definition of substance *stricto sensu* as autonomous being. On the other hand, the oddly obsessive, impersonal existence of the "there is," indistinctly being and nothingness, is quite unlike any notion of being found in Descartes. Nevertheless, there is a certain consistency in Levinas's description of substance as a transformational positing, through hypostasis, of the a-spatial, impersonal *il y a* sort of being into existents: positing in the sense of an originative gesture, generative of locus altogether. The emotions undo the hypostasis of positing the self. They are the dissolution or the menace of dissolution of the self into the elements of the *il y a*.

The next theme to be treated is "The Present and the Hypostasis." The section begins with a résumé of what has been said about the subject and its "there." Sleep is a "withdrawal into the plenum," a formula whose appropriateness is derived from the notion of the sinking of the subject into the base, the "there." But the "thereness" of the inert, sleeping body has a precursor in the "there" that has been attributed to thought, to the subject, in the hypostasis.

The next subsection, "The Present and Hypostasis," begins by describing the present as "an ignorance of history," that cuts through the Gordian knot of time. The present is "a situation in being in which there is no longer being in general, but a being, a subject." Its evanescence is the price to be paid for subjectivity, i.e. for the transformation of the event into the substantive (thing) — a hypostasis. The present is described in terms that differentiate it sharply from the continuity of time, i.e. duration. This discussion continues in the next subsection: "The Present and Time." Levinas points out that the instant has always been understood in relation to time; he wishes to relate it to existence. "Every instance is a beginning, a birth." In a way that is presumably to be further disclosed, the instant is "par excellence" the "accomplishment of existence." In the following subsection, "The Present and the 'I,'" it becomes clear that the instant is to mediate the relation between existence and the existent: "What is absolute in the relation between the existent and existence, in an instant, consists in the mastery the existent exercises on existence, but also in the weight of existence on the existent."[16]

What is most striking about these descriptions of the present is Levinas's steadfastness and persistence in exploring their philosophical import or in investing them with such import. Already we find many of the key elements that will be developed throughout the rest of his career: the motif of "the return of the present to itself," which will become the notion of "recurrence" in *Otherwise than Being*; the theme of the self "riveted to itself," and hence the duality within the self of the *moi* and the *soi* (the ego and the self). Indeed, the present has many of the characteristics that will turn up later as attributes of being: "The present is pure beginning. But in its contact of initiation, an instantaneous maturity invades it; it gets caught up in its own game. It weighs upon itself. It is being — no dream, no game. The instant is like a breathlessness, a panting, an effort to be."[17] Here we have a vivid description of the way in which we become involved in life, but the description is not the psychological narrative of a life. It is rather the attribution of these so very general experiences of life to being itself. The poignancy of the moment is transferred to the modality of "essence" (Levinas's later term for being). The "effort to be" will become the *conatus essendi* (Spinoza's term) of being itself.

What might seem like an unacceptable level of anthropomorphism with respect to ontological description might seem less so, were we able to divest ourselves of the dominant mode of thinking about such matters that we have inherited from tradition. The unreflective causal framework according to which we ascribe such phenomena as effort, competitiveness, and the like to the "faculties" of the human being or to "character" may be more historically contingent than we realize. In any case, phenomenology, true to appearances, in describing the night itself as vigilant or honey as treacherous (in Sartre's *Being and Nothingness*), remains close to experience. It is true that Levinas, in attributing to being a certain inherent "efforting," has gone beyond mere phenomenological description, and begun to elaborate a metaphysical structure. Levinas's characterization of being seems to be both phenomenological and metaphysical: phenomenological in the way in which the material is presented (in the form of description and assertion rather than deductive reasoning), and metaphysical in the manner in which such concepts as infinity, being, and time are coordinated in a unitary account.

One of the unusual aspects of this overall metaphysical account is the secondary status of the origin. The terms "pre-originary" and "an-archic" seem paradoxical, because it would seem that there could be nothing prior to the originary. It is not my intent here to explore the necessity of such a notion, but just to put in proper perspective the statement from "The Present and the 'I'" that "The present — the occurrence of an origin — turns into a being."[18] In fact it is less clear in the original whether the present turns into **a** being or just into being (*se mue en être*). The "I" is ambiguous, or to use Levinas's term, *amphibologique*. The "I" is not a classifiable object. It is to be grasped in its transformation from event to entity, not objectively. The present and the "I" are closely related; both are identities by recurrence, a movement of self-reference. In concluding this subsection, Levinas returns to Descartes in order now to see what is being affirmed in the *cogito ergo sum*. It is the present, the "I" and the "instant" that constitute moments of the same event.

In the next subsection, "The Meaning of the Hypostasis," we

are given the elements of what might be termed an ontological grammar.[19] The two main terms, of course, are noun and verb. The *il y a* or the "there is" should be thought of as pure verb. But there is no way in which the purity of the verb can be denoted without some distortion, since verbs are really names for actions and thus already somewhat substantivized.

The hypostasis is then the production of a substantive from a verb. This event suspends the anonymous *il y a*, as it produces a private domain, the noun. Here Levinas compares his distinction between the *étant* or being (a present participle, i.e. a present that participates in the nature of both substantive and verb) as opposed to the infinitive "to be" (*être*). Heidegger, he claims, simply sets these two next to one another, the *Sein* and the *Seiende*. Levinas deduces one from the other, namely the substantive from the verb.

The last subsection of "Position" (which is part 2 of "The Hypostasis,") is called "Hypostasis and Freedom." It begins by reiterating the relationship between consciousness and sleep. Sleep is a form of freedom, but it is a secondary one. And the subjectivity that was achieved through hypostasis is not yet freedom. In fact there is something like a return of the *il y a* in the hypostasis of the instant. This hypostasis, in its participation in the *il y a*, finds itself alone, in an aloneness signifying a *moi* chained to its *soi*, and thus to being.

There is a freedom of knowledge and of intention that is not true freedom but rather nonengagement. It is what allows me to avoid the "definitive." But the definitive of solitude is not avoidable: that is, the definitive of my being riveted to myself.

Perhaps we are now in a position to approach the concept of the "definitive" with more assurance. The definitive refers predominantly to the attachment of the ego to the self in such a way that the essential solitude of the subject remains unbroken.

The world and light are solitude. By this Levinas appears to be giving subjective idealism its due. All meaning is projected by me. To reach others is the achievement of an ontological break. The relation with the other (*autrui*) cannot be thought of as being chained to another *moi*; nor is it the understanding of the other, which would dissipate his or her alterity; nor is it a communion with the other around a third term. None of these relations of light can help us here. It is in the dimension of *eros* and the feminine that the world is prolonged into a "behind the world." It is within this dimension that Levinas hopes, at this stage in his career, to go beyond phenomenology, which is bound to the world of light. (In later statements on this subject Levinas modifies this position, claiming that his philosophy is still, **in a sense**, phenomenology.) In that world, the other is an alter ego to be known through sympathy, which is a return to oneself. But this is not the true other.

In the third and last section of chapter 4 of "The Hypostasis," titled "On the Way to Time," Levinas presents us with a challenging formulation of the overall orientation of his investigations of time. He believes that "time does not convey the insufficiency of the relationship with Being which is effected in the present, but that it is called for to provide a remedy for the excess of the definitive contact which the instant effects. Duration, on another plane than that of being, but without destroying being, resolves the tragic [element] involved in being."[20] Let us formulate two questions that this rather sibylline declaration raises. (1) Why is the contact which the instant effects qualified as "definitive"? (2) In what sense can time be said to provide a remedy for the excess of the definitive contact which the instant effects? We have already noted that the definitive seems to refer predominantly to the attachment of the ego to the self, in such a way that the essential solitude of the subject remains unbroken. Hence we can answer the first question. The definitive contact which the instant effects (through hypostasis, or the positing of subjectivity) is that which bonds ego and self, that *solitude à deux* that defines identity and that also seems to underlie consciousness. We are invited to imagine a static bond without time and therefore "definitive." The instant without time would be very much like an endless status quo. The hypostasis has achieved this stability, but it is tragic in that it cannot change. Rather than being "frozen in time," it is frozen because there is no time.

The first subsection is "The ego as substance and knowledge." The ability of the ego to go through life retaining its identity is evoked. This phenomenon is sometimes looked upon as the constancy of substance with respect to changing accidents. This theory has been applied to both physical objects and the human self. Levinas rejects this way of conceptualizing the unchanging nature of the *moi*.

> We are inclined to take it [the identity of the "I"] as the identity of a substance. The "I" would be an indestructible point, from which acts and thought emanate, without affecting it by their variations and their multiplicity. But can the multiplicity of accidents not fail to affect the identity of the substance? The relationships of the substance with the accidents are themselves so many modifications of that substance, such that the idea of substance is going to enter into an infinite regression.[21]

The objection sounds weak since the notion of substance was elaborated precisely to explain the phenomenon of change; substance is, by traditional definition, that which does not change or that in which different "accidents" or predicates can inhere. There have of course been many serious objections to the notion of a substance that would itself have to lack all inherent qualities, in order to be a carrier of an infinite variety of possible ones. But whether the substance-accident model for the ego's identity is wrong for the reason Levinas gives or for some other one is not our main consideration here. The interesting point is: What is Levinas's counterproposal?

It is not the concept of substance that Levinas is objecting to, but that of the relationship between substance and accident. He believes that the subject should still be conceived as substance, but that the special nature of the relationship between substance and the objects of knowledge is such that it is possible for the subject *qua* substance to remain unchanged. This is because, unlike the case of physical objects with real qualities, the substance or self, through **knowledge** (*savoir*), relates to that which remains essentially outside. Here the word "secret" is associated with the self, a term in which the etymological sense of "separate unto itself" is doubtless co-intended. The epistemological subject, the knower, is consciousness and hence freedom. "The freedom of the 'I' is its substantiality; it is but another word for the fact that substance is not engaged in the variation of its accidents."[22] Hence the subject is the substance par excellence, and the "I" is not a substance to which the ability to think has been added; it is substance **because** it can think. Consciousness is this principle, remaining the same identity despite knowledge, thoughts or ideas, which to it are "accidents."

The next subsection, "The '*moi*' as Identification and Bond with Oneself," makes the point that the logical notion of identity does not give the background of the self's identity with itself. It was precisely the formation of a substantive, or noun, out of the verbality of the *apeiron*-like *il y a*, that produced (by hypostasis) identity out of a background anonymity. Hence Levinas's counterproposal is that the subject **is** in a sense identity. This identity is the work or product of the instant or the present moment, which ignores time. Its freedom with respect to past and future does not, however, include freedom from its unbreakable bond with itself. Here the duality of the self becomes apparent, as does the bond between its two parts. Contrasting the two classical French playwrights Corneille and Racine, Levinas finds in the latter convincing examples of the duality of the self. Levinas distinguishes this *solitude à deux* of the *moi* bound to its *soi* from the *ennui* (boredom) that seeks refuge from itself in sociality; it is also distinct from the relation to the other, which detaches the *moi* from its *soi*. This situation awakens the desire for escape, but since we take ourselves with us when we travel, no voyage into the unknown can satisfy it.

The next subsection is, literally, "The Thought of a Freedom and Time," or, a bit more English-sounding in Alphonso Lingis's translation, "Time and the Concept of a Freedom." The gauche literal translation does follow the order of presentation a bit more closely, particularly if we bear in mind that Levinas tends not to consider the present as time. The present is what closes its eyes to time. There is a thought of freedom in the midst of servitude, but that thought is just a thought, not an act. (This shows how metaphorical the expression "an act of thought" is, he comments.) Subjectivity pulls back from its engagement in existence in the present but cannot pull free. The divorce of the *moi* from the *soi* is illusory. Yet there is an intimation of true freedom: the thought of freedom "knocks at the closed doors of another dimension; it has a presentiment of a mode of existence where nothing is irrevocable, the contrary of the definitive subjectivity of the 'I' and this is the order of time."[23] This passage sheds light on the second question we asked: "In what sense can time be said to provide a remedy for the excess of the definitive contact which the instant effects?" Time is what frees us from the invincible vinculum between ego and self since "nothing is irrevocable." Time opens up a dimension of freedom from the definitive and that freedom is described in ethical terms or at least terms that suggest an ethics (and this will be confirmed in the next subsection); for if in time nothing is irrevocable, pardon or redemption is possible.

The next subsection is "The Time of Redemption and the Time of Justice." It introduces us to a completely new concept of time. More precisely, it redescribes a sense of time we are familiar with and contrasts it with one that is new. The guiding thread that leads us to these senses of time is the notion of "hope."

Hope is normally associated with futurity. But in Levinas's analysis hope is not just a certain uncertainty about the outcome of events: it is rooted in the gravity of the instant from which hope springs. "Hope is only hope when there is no longer room for hope."[24]

The future may bring a desired future compensation for present suffering, but that present suffering is like a cry that will reverberate forever. Such is the time, modeled on our life in the world, that Levinas calls "economic time."

Why this term? Because it is the time of compensations, in which we expect or demand recompense and keep track of what is "coming to us." The world is the possibility of getting paid. There is something a little superficial about this time, a naiveté in this ego whose sincere intentions exclude equivocation. This sort of time wipes away all tears or, more exactly, forgets about the unforgiven instant of pain for which nothing can compensate. The economic life to which this time corresponds is also the time of other equivalencies, such as the plate of lentils for which Esau sold his birthright. It is the secular world.[25]

But there is a sense in which no tear is lost, no death remains without resurrection. "The true object of hope is the Messiah, or salvation."[26] The caress of one who attempts to console us in our pain does not promise the end of suffering, does not refer to a time *after* the suffering is over. It concerns the present moment of suffering. It is outside economic time. To hope is to hope for the undoing of the irreparable, and it is directed toward the present. The recourse to an eternity is not essential to Levinas, though it bears witness to the impossible exigency he describes. The essence of time, Levinas suggests, is this requirement of salvation. It should be noted that interpretation of the meaning of time owes much to Franz Rosenzweig, a debt often acknowledged by Levinas. Here, more specifically, we see a reflection of Rosenzweig's identification of the future with redemption.

Before moving on to the next subsection, in order to avoid a superficial reading of this new and momentous concept of time, two points in the text require interpretation or at least elucidation.

The first concerns the givenness of this time. "For in the world time itself is given." And it is given in such a way that "the effort of the present lifts off the weight of the present." We are plunged into economic time by the nature of our present condition. The weight of this present may take the form of tasks to be accomplished in order to satisfy needs, the subjective form of which is desire, which we discover within and attribute to ourselves. Hence our efforts are enlisted in order to subsist in a world or situation not of our choosing but assumed and experienced as if it were so.

The second — sensitive and problematic — point in the text inviting interpretation is the use of the word "naïve" in this subsection. The ego, throwing itself willy-nilly into the compensatory system of economic time, is described as both "sincere" and "naïve." But can the implication be that the ego (or the aspect of every ego) that requires more, that refuses to forget "the unforgiven instant and the pain for which nothing can compensate," the holdout for Messianic time, is **less naïve**? Here we are in the area of interpretation rather than "explication" of the text. As I read this and related texts of Levinas, the ego finds itself embroiled in being — or, to speak in temporal terms, in the present, in actuality. The natural (inevitable or tragic) way of the naïve ego is to take economic time seriously, finding within it the means to manifest its own sincerity and moving in the direction of a good-faith worldliness or level of the blasé befitting man in the world. It is a direction that inevitably leads away from the uncompromising, inopportune truth revealed, for example, by that fastidious investigator of subjectivity, Marcel Proust. "Déjà homme par la lâcheté" (already a man, by cowardice), Proust says of Marcel in *Du côté de chez Swann*, when the young man prefers to hide in his room rather than witness the thick-skinned good humor of those who torment a sensitive aunt. Even in the religious realm manifestation transmogrifies. In the following text, in which Levinas rejects **on a philosophical level** the relation between being and beyond

being adopted by the "positive" religions (faith properly so called),
i.e. divine intervention or epiphany, Levinas shows his awareness
of the complex, tragic adventure of the naïve self as it is translated and thereby necessarily betrayed in the world.

> As a philosopher, one can seek a relationship between beyond-
> being and being other than the miraculous relationship of epiphany
> or intervention, in its enigma which is not a mystery, while leav-
> ing to faith properly so called hope and beliefs, the solution to the
> enigma and the symbolic formulas that suggest it. To the faith of
> the common man, no doubt. But the common man has, after all,
> other certainties, and his own problems. **Against the denials
> inflicted by failure, a simplicity of extreme complexity, and a
> singularly mature infancy, are needed.** That also is the mean-
> ing of the death of God. Or of his life.[27]

Naiveté seems, in one sense, to be true to itself only if it aban-
dons its naiveté progressively in the face of "the denials" of its
innocent expectations for justice and truth "inflicted by failure."
In order to retain its integrity, it must develop a system or non-
system of belief of an "extreme complexity," thereby retaining
an "infancy" of expectations that is "singularly mature." Such are
the spiritual living conditions that led to the nineteenth century
God pronounced dead by Nietzsche. Or is that perilous state of
worldly divinity God's life? (Levinas invites us to respond in the
affirmative: It is when God's reality is most doubted that God is
most alive.)

But there is another sense of naiveté that can hardly be so
termed since it has not been launched into being's "economic
time" at all, and therefore never enters into the naïve-sophisti-
cated (or naïve-callous) dialectic in the first place. Its exigencies
have remained intact; it is the "veritable object of hope," the
Messiah, or salvation.

The next subsection is "The *I* and Time." It is an attempt to
convey a sense of time different from economic time. Its traits
are (1) a death with every passing instant, such that there is a

new or resurrected "I," not tied to the past, not pulled into economic time; (2) a hope for the present; (3) an interval of nothingness between each instant; (4) an interiority of the I to time (in contrast with economic time, in which the I circulates outside and across equivalent instants to link them up, this time is lived more deeply as the ferment of time in the present); (5) an exigency for renewal that requires an otherness that it cannot itself generate. The result of these parameters is that the I is enclosed in the definitiveness of the present, and cannot traverse time alone. That necessary otherness can only come from elsewhere.

Now let us take up these elements in more detail. We begin with an affirmation of the new notion of time as introduced in the preceding subsection. The "next instant" is "an annulment of the unimpeachable commitment to existence made in the instant." Ethical terms begin to enter into the description. The next instant effectuates the "resurrection" of the I. The I "dies" in the interval and is given a new birth; it does not enter "unforgiven" into the following instant. This resurrection requires an otherness, coming from an "elsewhere." But Levinas's intent is not to replace "economic time," the reality of which is undeniable and the concrete milieu in which we live. But this new, interior time is not just another conception of time, either. It is a "better" time. "We ask then whether the event of time cannot be lived more deeply as the resurrection of the irreplaceable instant."[28]

"Time and the Other," the name of the next subsection, but also, incidentally, that of a short work by Levinas published the same year,[29] begins by pointing out that the I needs the other because it cannot negate itself. (Negation seems to be necessary for there to be time; this necessity derives from the new instant's replacement of the preceding one which it opposes or denies.) The I cannot find the requisite otherness in itself but must seek it in the other. The novelty of this approach is that it makes time (or at least this sense of time) the result of the social relation. In order to develop this temporality Levinas must find a way of framing a discourse between the subject and the other person. Heidegger's *Mitsein* is limited to another or others alongside me, a grouping around truth; what is needed is the face-to-face relation. Intersubjective space is asymmetrical, since the other is what I am not. Intersubjectivity is not just the application of multiplicity to minds. It is the work of Eros, by which distance is a modality of proximity and absence a modality of presence. What is thought of as being the failure of communication in love is in fact a positive element, and proximity is not a failed fusion.[30] Thanks to Eros it will be possible for the *moi*, in death, to leave its *soi* behind. The traditional notion of transcendence will not suffice; indeed it contains a contradiction since the self that leaves itself must take itself along with it or else sink into the impersonal. In asymmetrical intersubjectivity there is the possibility for the self to retain its structure of self without returning fatally to itself: to be fecund, to have a son.

In the conclusion, Levinas sets his own thematization of the present in the sense of the static instant in opposition to the general tendency of contemporary philosophy "from Descartes to Heidegger." That current, with its concern to avoid reification of the spirit, tried to develop a human way of being, or "existence" that would combine past, present and future in one thrust of existence without granting any special privilege to the present. Levinas summarizes and critiques this trend by saying that modern philosophy has sacrificed the substantiality of the subject to its spirituality.

Levinas claims that existents have being as an attribute (*pace* Kant). The existent is master of its existence, just as the subject is master of the attribute. It is in the instant that this domination takes place. This thesis may be one that we can count as having been abandoned by the later Levinas. Indeed it would seem that Heidegger would have a greater claim to being the philosopher of presence and the present than Levinas, unless of course we interpret presence as a being present to — or better, for — the other.

The picture that emerges from the last sections of *Existence & Existents* and the conclusion is of an ontological background event, hypostasis, that forms existents out of existence. This existence seems to bear similarities with the "unformed and void" of Genesis 1:2, as well as with the Greek *apeiron* or indefinite. But if this is a genesis of beings, there is no mention of any other sort of being but the human being, to the point that it seems warranted to take the term "existent" as designating human beings. This milieu from which beings emerge is the *il y a* — impersonal, menacing, and inescapable being, prior to being's exclusion of nothingness, prior to time, and to the inside-outside opposition. The idea of an "onto-logical event," which Levinas probably adopted from Heidegger, takes on very real proportions in the former. Hypostasis seems to be the ontological event that idealism does not take into account.[31]

It is quite remarkable that the general direction of Levinas's philosophical research should already be set to a considerable extent at this early date. Although much of the detail will change, and terminology will undergo major shifts, the interest in a Good beyond being, the asymmetry of the relation with the other, and the general movement toward an outside — be it outside of self or same, or outside being altogether — is manifest in this work.

17. TOTALITY AND INFINITY: PREFACE (1961)

The preface to this major work sets out by placing it within the framework of a question not addressed in the same terms within the work itself. The question is whether or not one is "duped" by morality. Thus the book could be considered an extended answer to the question of whether there is any reason to be "moral," whatever specific behavior morality may require of us. It resembles the Pascalian wager to some extent — but for Pascal all depended on whether faith in an afterlife (in which life's accounts would be balanced) was warranted. Levinas's question is not accompanied, in the preface at least, by an answer, but we are drawn into a number of related questions.

The preface proceeds from the initial question to that of war, since in times of war morality seems to be suspended in the overarching struggle. Not only does war suspend moral behavior; lucidity, says Levinas, may consist in the awareness of the "permanent possibility of war." The trial by force is the test of the real. What truth comes out in the trial by force? "Reality," no doubt, at least in the eyes of the proponents of what has come to be known in our time as "Realpolitik." When war breaks out, nothing, it seems, remains outside.

"The visage of being that shows itself in war is fixed in the concept of totality, which dominates Western philosophy." Hence totality is the aspect of being that is manifest in war. But just as "hard" reality was revealed to be pleonastic, so the face of being that is seen in war **is** being, the truth of being. And only the outcome, the objective fact of what will be, is of any importance.

Levinas speaks of the "ontology of war," and contrasts it with a "messianic eschatology." Philosophers are wary, playing it down the middle, deducing a final peace from reason. Eschatology for them is part of opinion, not philosophy. There is a way of misunderstanding prophetic eschatology, or a way it misunderstands itself perhaps, that would have eschatology adopt the ontology of totality that comes out of war. But the true significance of eschatology is elsewhere. "It does not introduce a teleological system into the totality; it does not consist in teaching the orientation of history. Eschatology institutes a relation with being beyond the totality or beyond history, and not with being beyond the past and the present."[1] Levinas rejects the popular understanding of prophecy that contacts being beyond the past and the present, focusing mostly on the future. Levinas's use of prophetic eschatology refers to a contact with being beyond the totality.

It is to be noted that at this stage of his thinking (1961) Levinas has not broken entirely with a positive use of the word "being." He calls for "a primordial and original relation with being."[2] Although a distinction has been made between eschatology's reaching being "beyond the totality" and its reaching it "beyond the present and the past," it is still being that is contacted. The "objective" totality, he says, is not the "true measure of being." What is needed is the concept of infinity. "Eschatology," he argues,

> establishes a relation with being *beyond the totality* or beyond history, and not with the void that would surround the totality and in which one could, arbitrarily, think what one likes, and thus promote the claims of a subjectivity free as the wind. It is a relationship with a surplus always exterior to the totality, as though the objective totality did not fill out the true measure of being; as though another concept, the concept of infinity, were needed to express this transcendence with regard to totality, non-encompassable within a totality and as primordial as totality.[3]

This metaphysical arrangement represents an interesting stage in Levinas's progression toward "the one," more fully elaborated and modified in *Otherwise than Being*. What should be noted here is that Levinas rejects a negation of being, a nothingness, as the milieu of externality, but the being he attributes to it is that of a "surplus." As Levinas begins to attribute to being more and more of the negative traits he associates with the (Hegelian) totality, he will be led to substitute an "otherwise than being" or a "beyond being" to this exteriority of the totality. But the idea of a surplus seems to be connected with a host of ancillary notions, such as the ex-ception, ex-cendence, and exaggeration or exacerbation as a technique, and these notions remain.

One senses in all this that Levinas is not committed to any of these metaphysical schemata irrevocably, but that his is a guiding intuition of what needs to be accommodated in such a schema. When a more appropriate structure is needed, it will be adopted, as is indicated in such declarations as "The idea of being overflowing history **makes possible** *existents* [*étant's*] both involved in being and personal."[4] It is what the structure makes possible, rather than the structure in and of itself, that determines the ontological configuration.

The recent French paperback edition of *Totality and Infinity* includes Levinas's preface to the German edition (1987), a four-page text that is extremely helpful in understanding more precisely what shifts Levinas's speculative structures underwent after 1961.[5] Levinas writes, "*Otherwise than Being or Beyond Essence* already avoids the ontological — or more exactly, eidetic — language which *Totality and Infinity* incessantly resorts to in order to keep its analyses, which challenge the *conatus essendi* of being, from being considered as dependent upon the empiricism of a psychology."[6] This statement would be at once a justification of the use of eidetic language (which is, after all, that of Husserlian phenomenology) in order to avoid "empiricism" (in response to Derrida's charge in "Violence and Metaphysics"?) in *Totality and Infinity* and an indication that such language would later be abandoned for yet another form of discourse. In any case, Levinas's decision to use *essence* in place of *être* after 1961 resolves a problem. No longer will Levinas say, as in *Totality and Infinity* (290) that "being is exteriority." The movement "toward the outside" that is the guiding one for this study will now be directed toward a "beyond essence" or an "otherwise than being." To simplify, we may say that "essence" is the more precise, limited subject of which the negative traits of being had hitherto been predicated: competitiveness, simultaneity, egotism, war. It may be that the term *essence* suggested itself to Levinas by his frequent appeal to the Spinozan term *conatus essendi*; whence also perhaps the emphasis on the verbal nature of the term as suggested by Spinoza's use of the Latin gerund.

The first "vision" of eschatology (hereby distinguished from the revealed opinions of positive religions) reveals the very possibility of "a signification without context." (23) These two interrelated concepts, that of a break in the totality, a rift, and that of a meaning without context (so antithetic and antipathetic to the structuralism of the era, which could be seen from a philosophical point of view as a somewhat dehumanized form of neo-Hegelianism) are essential to Levinas's thought. The Jewish person, the stateless person, still speaking, as he or she is loaded onto the railroad car bound for Auschwitz — is that face, that mouth, that person, not the "meaning without context?"

"The experience of morality does not proceed from this vision" i.e. the vision of eschatology, "— it *consummates* this vision." (23) The eschatological vision is, then, already a moral optics. (Later in the text the term "curvature of space" will be introduced to suggest how subjectivity constitutes this vision; this term, "curvature of space" in the sense of a moral optics is not used, to my knowledge, after 1961.) Levinas's project does not attempt to construct a morality upon reason, though he recognizes the "peace of reason," my example of which would be the European "balance of power" of nineteenth century diplomacy, and he does not undervalue the relative virtue of such accomplishments. Indeed, vision seems an odd choice for the faculty of moral discernment, since vision is synoptic, and orders a simultaneous view of persons and things.

Can this vision to be assimilated to "faith?" "Of peace there can be only an eschatology. But this does not mean that when affirmed objectively it is believed by faith instead of being known by knowledge."[7] Such knowledge emanates from a legitimized kind of "subjectivity." Morality understood in this way requires an extensive philosophical restructuring that includes "a defense of subjectivity," not as a "purely egoist protestation against totality," nor as "anguish before death" (as in Heidegger), but rather "founded in the idea of infinity." (26)

Levinas tells us that what he sets in opposition to "the objectivism of war" is "a subjectivity born from the eschatological vision," and his text distinguishes between the "subjectivism of the I" which is "refuted by war" and the subjectivity of peace.

The notion of infinity that Levinas proposes combines the categories of ontology and infinity, in the sense that the "production of infinity" is precisely the disproportion between a finite being and its "containing" of the uncontainable. Experientially that infinity is "the welcoming of the Other, as hospitality." "The idea of infinity is not an incidental notion forged by a subjectivity to reflect the case of an entity encountering on the outside nothing that limits it, overflowing every limit, and thereby infinite. The production of the infinite entity is inseparable from the idea of infinity, for it is precisely in the disproportion between the idea of infinity and the infinity of which it is the idea that this exceeding of limits is produced."[8]

The idea of the infinite is the way of being — the infinition of the infinite. The infinite is not first, showing itself afterward. Its infinition is produced as revelation, as a putting into me of its idea. Levinas started out this development by pointing out the double meaning in French of the verb *produire* (more or less as in the two senses of "to produce" in English, as in "to produce cars" and "to produce a witness"). It means both the realization of being and its exposition. This double meaning seems to be necessary for the development of the idea of the infinite. It is in part our finite nature (or the finite nature of thought) that is, in the conception of the infinite, the enactment (or production) of the infinite.

18. DIFFICULT FREEDOM (1963, 1976)

This collection of essays and articles, devoted either to Judaism or to Jewish themes (Jewish life in France, the relations between Jews and non-Jews, anti-Semitism, a commentary on the concept of Messianism, current events as they relate to the Jewish community, and a short autobiographical piece titled "Signature"), was originally published in 1963. References here are to the second edition (1976). I have chosen two texts representative of the broad spectrum of themes gathered in this collection.

"Messianic Texts"

This piece, the longest by far in *Difficult Freedom*, is a commentary on four passages from the last chapter of the talmudic tractate *Sanhedrin*. (Since the Talmud is itself commentary, the present text is commentary on [Levinas's] commentary on a commentary. Clearly, "intertextuality" is not a postmodern invention!) It was originally presented by Levinas in the form of two papers, delivered at the third and fourth Colloquia of Jewish Intellectuals organized by the French section of the Congrès Juif Mondial in 1960 and 1961. In his first footnote to this piece, Levinas explains the overall intent of his commentary. He compliments Gershon Sholem[1] for the historical accuracy he shows in distinguishing carefully between the apocalyptic notion of Messianism, which is mainly a popular one, and the rabbinic conception. But Sholem limits the rationalism of the rabbinic concept to a refutation of the miraculous, "as if, in the world of ideas, it were possible to rid oneself of some questionable values without becoming engaged in others. It is the positive meaning of the Messianism of the rabbis that I would like to bring out in my commentary."[2] This essay, which demonstrates great respect for and understanding of the philosophical significance of the Talmud, is followed by an essay on Spinoza that is highly critical of the latter's condemnation of the Talmud in the name of enlightened reason.

Rabbi Chiya ben Abba, in the name of Rabbi Yohanan, first maintains the thesis that there is a difference between the future world and the Messianic Age. The latter is the age referred to by the prophets and, in the fulfillment of their promise of a better humanity, it is characterized by the end of political violence and social injustice. The former appears to be situated at a different level, and is for "him that waiteth for Him" (Isaiah 64:3). "It concerns a personal and intimate order, lying outside the achievements of history. . . ."[3]

But Shmuel disagrees with the view that the Messianic era will be one of both political and social justice. He says that the only difference between then and now is that the domination of foreign nations will cease, for it is said in the Bible (Deuteronomy 15:11) that there will always be the poor. But, Levinas points out, this is not far from the text (Deuteronomy 15:4) which exhorts Israel that there be no needy among them, a text that Shmuel could not have been unaware of. Therefore we must interpret Shmuel's statement differently. He has a very different view of the nature of the Messianic age. While Rabbi Yohanan envisages the Messianic age as a time of spirituality without the contradictions connected with political and economic life, in which time will be spent in friendship, contemplation, and perhaps artistic activity, Shmuel's view of that age to come is that it cannot be devoid of economic life because spirituality is connected with giving, with not going to the other (person) empty-handed. Levinas takes Shmuel's thought a step further: "The Other is always the poor one; poverty defines the poor person as the Other, and the relation with the Other will always be an offering and a gift. . . . Spiritual life is essentially moral life, and its place of predilection is the economic sphere."[4] The difference between Shmuel's and Rabbi Yohanan's view of the Messianic era is strikingly similar to what Levinas considers to differentiate his view from that of Martin Buber. For Shmuel and Levinas, spirituality is essentially ethical, while Rabbi Yohanan and Buber believe in the ideal of a disincarnated spirit of total grace and harmony.

These two contrasting views of the Messianic age are presented in the Talmud as "two positions between which every thought somehow oscillates eternally."[5] The positions of Shmuel and Rabbi Yohanan are further differentiated by the question for whom the prophesies are intended. Rabbi Yohanan thinks they are for the perfect and just, while Shmuel thinks they are for the repentant. Both these views are within the Judaic tradition, Levinas points out, and should therefore not be used to characterize Judaism vis-à-vis Christianity, for example.[6]

But are those who have strayed and returned in a more favored position than those who remained faithful? Rabbi Abbahu says: "The place occupied by repentant sinners cannot be attained even by the completely righteous." This raises the *felix culpa* question and, Levinas remarks, "flatters our taste for pathos, a sensibility nourished on Christianity and Dostoyevsky." The Talmud recognizes the ambiguity of the problem and recognizes the strength required in either case, reconciling the two by citing Isaiah 57:19: "Peace, peace, to him that is far off, and to him that is near."

Having distinguished between the Messianic Age and the world to come, how is the latter to be characterized? Rabbi Yohanan said: "It is the wine preserved in bunches of grapes since the six days of creation." In this eschatological imagery, the last things are also the first. The future harkens back to what was before the beginning. But history was necessary: one must go through interpretation to go beyond it.

In his conclusion to the first half of the text (actually the end of the 1960 paper), Levinas makes an interesting point about the philosophical value of the Talmud, which certainly has not been universally recognized even by Jews. "But we set out nonetheless from the idea that this meaning is not only transposable into a philosophical language, but refers to philosophical problems."[7] This philosophical content doubtless correlates to Levinas's own tradition as a Jewish intellectual from Lithuania, the home of the Mitnagdim, those who set the study of Torah above all else and were noted for their intellectualist (as opposed to the more emotive or devotional Hassidic emphasis) form of Judaism.

But close textual readings should not be confused with "the historical method," for which Levinas expresses some reservations. While it opens up interesting and important perspectives, the historical method is wrong in thinking that, just as a particular word or construction cannot appear before a certain date, so too there are certain thoughts that cannot be thought, and that even *la pensée géniale* (brilliant thought, or "inspired," but without the specific theological implications sometimes attached to the latter term) is incapable of "anticipating the meaning of all experience." This is confirmed with a rather personal closing remark touching Levinas's own religious sensibility: "That confidence in the wisdom of the sages is, if you will, a faith. But that form of faith, to which I profess, is the only one that does not have to be kept discreetly to oneself, unless one has the shamelessness of the professions of faith that resound indiscreetly on every public square."[8]

The way in which language is used in the Talmud is to be understood as one in which the units are not words, but the verses of the Bible or indeed the Bible itself augmented by the Talmud, i.e. the Oral Tradition. In one sense it could be said that the pieces are bigger: whole verses are used in the argument or discussion. But the pieces contain more than the main argument: We are in the thick of meaning, we are bound. One side could only be right by overlooking some texts, i.e. could never be right in the sense of eliminating the other side, or, in many cases, the other sides.

A careful reading of Levinas's talmudic readings and of these Messianic texts, which are taken from the Talmud, will reveal the unity of Levinas's thought in a way that is impossible otherwise. The notion of election, of being chosen, is "perhaps, ultimately, the very subjectivity of the subject."[9] Who is the Messiah? In a daring interpretation of Rav Nahman's commentary on Jeremiah 30:21, Levinas, asserts: "The Messiah is Myself; to be Myself is to be the Messiah."[10] These interpretations take the form of central theses in Levinas's philosophical writings and should be understood in connection with the oft-quoted phrase from Dostoyevsky: "We are all guilty for everything and everyone, and I more than all the others."[11] The Messiah is the one who takes on the sufferings of the other.

The last section of these texts is titled "Messianism and Universality." It is a complex finale. The text it explicates begins with R. Simlai's question about a verse from the prophets. "R. Simlai expounded: What is meant by, *Woe unto you, that desire the day of the Lord! to what end is it for you? the day of the Lord is darkness, and not light?* (Amos 5:18)." The first meaning is doubtless to expose the hypocrisy of those who complain about there being so little justice on earth, whereas were the truth to be known those same self-righteous individuals would wish the day of judgment never came. But there is a deeper meaning as well. Levinas cites the midrash of the rooster and the bat. The bat does not await the light, nor would it serve him. The rooster has a surprising first place in the Morning Blessing: "Blessed art thou, Adonay, our God, King of the Universe, who gave the rooster understanding to distinguish between day and night." The importance of the rooster's ability to detect the coming of the dawn before it is visible symbolizes intelligence: the ability to discern the meaning of history before, rather than after the event. A cruel

Messianism, remarks Levinas. The Messiah is denied to those who are no longer capable of seeing the light even though the darkness may be burdensome to them. But now the text moves from that theme, via the notion of being prepared internally for the light, to the idea that the light is not universal in the logical sense of the term. Levinas finds in the texts discussed a distinction between two sorts of universalism. There is one "that might be called catholic, which is sought in political life and formulated by Aristotle." This is also the beginning of philosophy. "But it is precisely the destiny of Western philosophy and its logic to recognize that it is a political condition, to the point that the free expression of truth and the constitution of the universal State (through wars and revolutions) coincide. Enlightenment (in an obviously Hegelian movement) realizes the truth of the particular in a universal.

But then Levinas describes in a brief but neatly and strongly contrasting paragraph the situation of Judaism — cut off during the Middle Ages, convinced that empirical history, which befell it pell-mell, was devoid of meaning. This people who dwelt apart had a totally different sense of universality — one that had nothing to do with a process of synthesizing, of the elimination of the dross of particularities through the refining effect of confrontation — nothing to do with an epistemological melting pot.

This difficult and sensitive text leads to a contrast between "the prestige of exteriority" and the shining of an inner light. "At this point the real universality, which is non-catholic, can affirm itself. It consists in serving the universe. It is called Messianism."[12]

Levinas asks the obvious question. Is this a dangerous conception that would encourage any and all groups to promote their beliefs uncompromisingly, or is it, beyond such primitive subjectivism, a perception of the dangers of the politicization of truth and morality? Here a midrash is introduced. The first man was as big as the universe, for some stretching from earth to heaven, from east to west for others. Jewish universalism is that of the man who stands erect between earth and heaven while the other universalism is that of lateral consensus.[13] The lateral symbolizes politics, expansionism, and the exchange of ideas, customs and beliefs between particular groups.

"Messianic Texts" end with a question about the possibility of Judaism's thinking in terms of Messianism since Emancipation (i.e. since the French Revolution, roughly, at which time Jews were granted citizenship, first in France, then in other parts of Europe) and with a reflection on the situation and significance of the State of Israel. The two issues are linked in that in the first case it became difficult for Jews to continue to think that empirical history (as opposed to sacred history) is meaningless, and in the second case Jews are confronted with the task of reuniting "the irreversible acceptance of universal history with the necessarily particularist Messianism." The aspirations of Zionism are a "universalist particularism (which is not Hegel's concrete universal)."

What exactly is the difference between this "universalist particularism" and Hegel's concrete universal? The latter is a working out of the abstract universal through history to bring about an identity between nature and universal consciousness. It is brought about by the work of history through a dialectical process of assimilation and differentiation at increasingly higher levels of universality. Levinas's universal particularism is not dialectical but vertical. The absolute for him is the ethical, which he vigorously separates from the "cultural," which is relative. Levinas's philosophical endeavors may be seen as precisely the attempt to give universal expression to what is essentially (in its content) particular (and in this case Jewish). The conclusion of these "Messianic Texts" is in agreement with statements throughout Levinas's writing: the content of Judaism is ethical — but the Bible can be translated into Greek. This is a recognition not only of the historical fact of the Greek Septuagint, but also of the possibility of expressing the ethical message of Judaism in philosophy.

The Diary of Léon Brunschvicg

In a modest, personal article published in the journal *Evidences*[14] four years after the Liberation and five years after Brunschvicg's death, Levinas reclaims the neo-Kantian, that almost mythological figure of the philosophical establishment who formed a generation of philosophers at the Sorbonne (Merleau-Ponty in particular) for Judaism. The article was occasioned by the publication of a rediscovered diary. Aside from his being Jewish, what was the interest Levinas took in this mathematics-oriented cofounder of the *Revue de métaphysique et de morale* (1893), so distant in philosophical orientation not only from Levinas but from phenomenology altogether? He represented what the young Levinas had seen and admired, what had attracted him to France in the first place: justice (Brunschvicg was a Dreyfusard), academic distinction, and a certain serenity, or happiness mastered, if not declined. "I passed for a happy man; from the experience and memory of happiness, I hope I have retained the art of knowing how to do without it." That is but one item from the many quoted by Levinas from the (then) newly published diary of thoughts exchanged with the future historian Élie Halévy, the closest friend of his youth.

Devoting much of his time and energy to the direction of the ENIO (École normale israélite orientale) in the postwar years, Levinas felt some distress at the frequent assimilation of Jewish intellectuals, and wrote of many of them in a way that read into their intellectual positions something of Judaism. Vladimir Jankélévitch, whose works Levinas admired greatly, is a good example of this.[15] But some secularized Jewish intellectuals were too clearly opposed to Levinas's philosophical-ethical commitments to accommodate such a "recuperative" reading: this was the case for Raymond Aron, Éric Weil, and especially the structural sociologist Claude Lévi-Strauss.[16]

19. "Language and Proximity" (1967)

"Language and Proximity" was first published in the second edition of *En découvrant l'existence avec Husserl et Heidegger* (1967). It is not included in the English translation of selected items from that work (*Discovering Existence with Husserl*, 1998), but has been available in English since 1987 in *Emmanuel Levinas: Collected Philosophical Papers* (CPP). It contains, in an earlier and at times fresher form, many of the basic ideas that were subsequently developed in *Otherwise than Being*. It was the basis of the lecture the basis of the lecture "La Proximité," given on Nov. 29, 1967, in Brussels.[1]

Ideality and Signification

There are two temporal series: of events and of conscious acts. The story or fable can confer meaning upon the temporal dispersion of events and thoughts. It is the synchrony of the linguistic system that is able to accomplish this. Being is manifested in the theme. Logos *qua* discourse becomes indistinguishable from logos *qua* rationality. With the development of language there is break between the individual, the idiosyncratic, the personal, the particular inarticulate experience, and the universal or generally meaningful; a break that makes it possible for the individual to become part of the universal. There is considerable insistence on Husserlian intentionality in this section. To **take for**, to **take as**, to identify within the multiple, is thought as distinguished from sensibility. "Thought can therefore reach the individual only through the detour of the universal. For philosophy as discourse, the universal precedes the individual, and is, in all senses of the term, a priori."

The "Passive Synthesis"

At the beginning of this section we are invited to explore the possibility of a language "behind" the universality of discourse, a language that would envisage the singular. But, surprisingly, Levinas argues against that possibility. He argues that thought differs from the spontaneous feeling (*le sentir*), in which feeling and felt are confused or still fused in a drowsiness (*assoupisse-ment*), from which consciousness is the awakening. The felt must already have been lost in order for consciousness to find it again. Hence the singular is situated in the indistinctness of the feeler and the felt in such a way that even it would have to be transformed into the universal to become conscious.

The heading of this section, "the 'passive synthesis'" is a term borrowed from Husserl. If the activity of the full-fledged subject is synthesizing with respect to time, consciousness without a subject will be "passive activity,"[2] in which the activity is that of time. The distinction is made between athematic consciousness that passes like time, and objectifying consciousness. But then for Levinas all consciousness is not consciousness of something since there is a genesis of consciousness that stems from the original separation between feeling and felt, the consciousness of the "passive synthesis." If there is no subject, there is the creature at the moment of creation "without a subject to assume the act of creation." To assume, here, means to take upon oneself as one's condition.

The conclusion of this section attains a level of abstraction rather unusual in Levinas, a conceptualization reminiscent of Hegel. It concerns time and the dephasing of the present in order to generate a past and a future. "If the present did not diverge from its coinciding with itself, it would be neither temporal nor conscious simply by virtue of temporality. But if the present is present according to the mode of consciousness which time is, this is not only because time is the unrest (*inquiétude*) — the non-repose, the non-coinciding with self — of being, but because the instant that escapes itself is not pure negativity." What is the significance of this attempt to make consciousness inherent in temporality, at the lowest level, and of making the past something other than pure negativity of the present? "Across the indiscernible phases of its moulting into past, its 'passive work' of sinking into the past, it is — also passively — retained in retention and meant as identical, despite the silence of language at this level which sets forth identity in retention as identical, despite the non-recourse of this idealizing language to the system of verbal signs supplied us by the cultural heritage."[3]

We have moved, by means of Husserl's passive synthesis, from a rejection of the possibility of a language prior to that of universalization to an "idealizing language" that does not have recourse to verbal signs furnished by our cultural heritage (and commonly referred to as "a language").

Singularity without Universality

This section begins with the acceptance of the findings of the preceding one, according to which "nothing real, however rigorously individuated it [may] be, could appear outside of ideality and universality." But a portentous footnote states, "One can, to be sure, wonder if seeming and appearing, coextensive with being, exhaust the possibilities of the mind [*l'Ésprit*], that is, if the mind does not go beyond being. Western philosophy has been able to speak of this beyond, but forthwith took it as an Idea, that is, interpreted it in terms of being, thus subordinating God to ontology. Our effort proceeds in a quite opposite direction."[4]

Does not this reflection open the door to a blatant exception, if not contradiction, to the preceding determination that nothing real can appear outside ideality? Or is there a real beyond being? In any case, the notion of a beyond being is not indispensable here, since there is posited in these pages the possibility — the reality as well — of a singularity without universality. Speech is contact, and contact a transcendence without intentionality. Proximity is meaning per se, and intentionality becomes "ethics." Ethics, then, is contact, and subjectivity openness to (other human) beings. That is the "original language," the "basis of the other." And the precise point at which the intentional is transformed into ethics is the skin and the human face. "Contact" is tenderness and responsibility.

The term *kerygma*, which was already encountered three times in the first section of this piece, recurs here: *kerygma*, that which concerns proclamation or preaching, from a Greek word meaning herald. Levinas uses it to designate the assertiveness of identification.

Here the term "proximity" occurs (for the first time perhaps; it does not occur in *Totality and Infinity*). All the tentativeness and novelty of this first use of the word is present in the phrase "*Proximity* between myself and the interlocutor, and not our participation in a transparent universality."[5] This is not intentionality, not a subject-object polarity. It is the immediacy of contact, but not of spatial contiguity. "Proximity is *of itself* meaning."[6] It is an ethical element in which, for the moment, nothing moral is indicated, as Levinas points out parenthetically. The ethical is defined negatively, as a relationship in which the terms are related "neither by a synthesis of the understanding nor by a relationship between subject and object, and yet in which the one weighs on or is important or significant to the other, in which they are tied by an intrigue that knowledge can neither exhaust nor unravel."[7] The new notion of the ethical is further defined in opposition to the received sense of it. "The *ethical* does not designate an inoffensive attenuation of passionate particularisms, which would introduce the human subject into a universal order and unite all rational beings, like ideas, in a kingdom of ends."[8] This is a fairly broad characterization of a traditional view of ethics, although the "kingdom of ends" almost certainly refers to Kant. Noteworthy here is the distinction between being significant, weighing on, or being important to, as opposed to the theoretical or sapient. The affective displaces the priority of the cognitive.

Is it possible for phenomenology in the Husserlian sense to transform these affective elements into concepts without altering their nature? The problem that was raised earlier, that of the universalization of thought and language, seems to reappear here in the guise of a question about the status or nature of Levinas's own discussion of the problem.

The end of this section is filled with enthusiasm for the new revelation. The other is the human face. Contact is tenderness and responsibility: these two terms suggest a new category, one in which affectivity and ethics are conjoined. And yet, we are not led to morality of sensibility à la J.-J. Rousseau. Sensibility seems rather to be a precondition that had best not be thematized.

The term "proximity," which has little or no affective connotation in either French or English, is a term that requires some comment. It is an abstract term, and since it is generally used as a term of spatial relation, Levinas is obliged to insist on its new meaning here. What is meant by the expression "La proximité est *par elle-même* signification" (Proximity is *of itself* meaning)? It suggests a contextless meaning, perhaps even the context in which everything else takes on meaning. "The subject," we are told, "has gone into the opening of intentionality and vision. The orientation of the subject toward the object has become proximity, the intentional has become ethical."[9] Once the relation has been transformed from a theoretical (or epistemological) one to an ethical one, the way is paved for an ethics. The milieu of the subject is one that already has ethical meaning.

Language and the Sensible

Levinas begins by stressing that the immediacy of the sensible is the event of proximity and not of knowledge. He says that he has chosen the sense of taste because it is clearly related to eating, to hunger, etc.

Returning to the theme of the touch, Levinas cites the consecrated translation (into French) of Husserl's *leibhaft gegeben*, as *donné en chair et en os*, in English, "given in flesh and blood." You cannot approach an idea the way you can a physical thing. Levinas can overlook the proprietary sense that the sciences have granted themselves with respect to the physical world. What is new and interesting about Levinas's "sensible" is the fact that it is not knowledge, but closeness, presence. This section ends in making the distinction between the proximity to things, which is poetry (in what sense?) and closeness to the other.

Consciousness and Obsession

The distinction is made between the immediacy of proximity (and the other) and intuition, vision, or intentionality. "Consciousness is always late for its meeting with the close other."[10] Is love a tactile and pleasant sensation or a way of seeking one who is, to the utmost degree, already present? But is the other an absence or rather the presence of the infinite? The other is ordered on the basis of the absence in which the Infinite approaches, on the basis of its non-place. It (the presence of the other) is ordered in the trace of its own departure. The end of this section contains some remarkable descriptions of the other as absence or presence of the infinite.

The Sign

This section speaks of a sign given from non-place to non-place. It is decidedly a new and unusual sense in which the sign is being used, since it does not rely on a common language or culture. It may have something in common with a spontaneous, nonconventional sign, such as a movement one might make in the presence of another to make one's presence known. It is the saying prior to the said. The saying is a language before language. "The fact that a sign, exterior to the system of evidences, comes into proximity while remaining transcendent, is the very essence of language prior to every particular language [*langage d'avant la langue*]."[11]

The word "neighbor" is the usual translation of *prochain.* Neighbor (the modern French equivalent of which is *voisin*) is used, it is true, in the New Testament in the same way *prochain* is used in the French New Testament, with a sense of ethical responsibility. The point of the following passage is to avoid misunderstandings. The neighbor "does not appear. What sort of description could he send me ahead of time that would not strip him of his exclusive alterity? Absolving himself from all essence, all genus, all resemblance, the neighbor, the first one to come along [*le premier venu*] concerns me for the first time (even if he is an old acquaintance and old friend, an old lover, long caught up in the fabric of my social relations) in a contingency that excludes all *a priori*."[12] The neighbor is, then, in a sense, a stranger! The problem is of interest beyond the pragmatic level of translation, for it ultimately comes down to the question of the Levinasian meaning of proximity itself. On numerous occasions Levinas points out that he does not mean a spatial proximity. But, as Derrida says, if this is the case why use such words as proximity, height and so on, merely to cross them out immediately afterward as being inadequate? The answer to this question is to be sought, I believe, in Levinas's understanding of essential meaning.

In the first essay contained in *Humanisme de l'autre homme*,[13] Levinas develops a theory of meaning that effectively eliminates any distinction between the figurative and the literal. He denies the theory according to which meaningless data is endowed with meaning by the perceiving subject. "Pure receptivity, in the sense of a pure sensible without any meaning, would be only a myth or an abstraction. . . . Mikel Dufrenne, in his fine book, *The Concept of the A Priori*, was able to show that the experience of spring and childhood, for example, remain authentic and autochthonous, over and beyond seasons and human ages."[14]

Marking the evolution of Levinas's thought, the term *fraternité*, which plays an essential role here (e.g., "Our analyses have brought us to see fraternity with the neighbor as the essence of the original language. . . ."[15]) seems to give way to some degree to *proximité*.[16]

From Obsession to the Hostage

The connection between fraternity and proximity is clarified in the following sentence: "Responsibility *qua* obsession is proximity: like a blood relationship, a bond prior to any elective affinity." Levinas describes proximity as the condition of being a hostage. It is the "condition of the creature in a world without play, in the *gravity* that is perhaps the first coming of signification to being *beyond* its unthinking "that's the way it is." The condition is that of the hostage, a condition in which being is "backed up to itself," and is "the non-being of being"; it is "not nothingness" but "beyond being."[17]

Levinas contests the naturalistic theory according to which war was at the beginning of all, and the ego carries attributes such as pity and empathy as moral traits. The ego is hostage in that it empties itself of its being.

It is Only a Word

A question is asked at the beginning of this section. Is language the transmission of messages, thought independently of that transmission? Or would language bear a positive event, preliminary to communication, that would be "approach" and "contact" of the proximate other and in which would reside the natal secret of thought itself and of the verbal utterance that sustains it? Levinas attempts to describe a language without content as pure "proximity." But what is said in language soon displaces this proximity with theories (knowledge, truth) that **posit** the possibility of proximity.

Levinas speaks not of a birth of language and of thought, but of a **latent** birth. A birth would be an "arche," and the entry into being: the Saying is the an-archical, beyond and always already prior to being. Proximity is an event, but an **evanescent** event, which is **immediately** submerged by the tide of knowledge (*savoirs*, i.e. technical or systematic knowledge, such as explanatory, causal theories, including truths about the origin of proximity). "But," he writes, "can thought and truth force the other to enter my discourse, to become an interlocutor? The evanescence of proximity in truth is its very ambiguity, its enigma, that is, its transcendence outside of intentionality."[18]

The first saying says this saying itself. Yet the saying and the said cannot be the equivalent of each other. The last paragraph of the essay may be paraphrased as follows. Although the first saying says its very saying, the two are not equal. The saying bursts through what it says ("the totality it embraces"). In thematizing that very event of the breakup of its stated totality it forms yet another totality, which it equally escapes. "Someone has escaped the theme." In fact, "the original saying (*dire*) is delirium (*délire*)." Coherent thought enforces coherent discourse, but in doing so it understands (*comprend* as understands and/or contains) the extravagance it opposes and thus already recognizes its enigma. "This first saying is to be sure but a word. But it is God."[19] Levinas's problem is to reveal how the transcendent is revealed within the logos, the system or totality (the world, being). The ultimate *explicans* is, but cannot be, part of the total *explicanda*: it is part of the *explicanda* since what is to be explained is the totality, which would not be the totality if the *explicans* were separate from it. At the same time the *explicans* must, by definition, remain separate from the *explicanda* if it is not to become itself part of what is to be explained. The culprit here seems to be the concept of totality itself. If the totality (not *a* totality) is all-inclusive, it cannot admit of transcendence. It must be immanent and finite, or can only be, at best, Hegel's false infinite (in Levinas's texts, the *bad* infinite).

The *explicans/explicanda* binary rests upon an epistemological structure that presupposes a necessary separation, distance and difference between knower and known. Although the paradigm has always run into some difficulties, the escalation or exacerbation of the problem brought about by positing the totality as the *explicanda* leaves few attractive options. Either transcendence will have to be accommodated within immanence, or be cancelled altogether, making knowledge and truth something on the order of a subjective illusion.

The word God at the end of the text is less surprising if we remember that God (is) beyond being, and thus that which escapes the said par excellence. God (is) that "someone" who has (essentially past tense) escaped totalization/thematization. If drawn into the said, i.e. the realm of being, God becomes "but a word."

20. "And God Created Woman": A Talmudic Reading (1972)

[English: NTR 161–77; French: DSS 122–48]

As is the rule in Levinas's talmudic commentaries, we begin with a text from the Talmud, in this case the Tractate Berakhot (Blessings) 61a. The first problem that the rabbis take up is one of spelling. Why does the word *vayitzer* ("he formed") have **two** yods (Genesis 2:7) instead of the customary **one**? Levinas's first remark establishes the relevance of the discussion to contemporary thought. "The pious, proper thought of the right-thinking ones no longer wonders about anything. Let them at least be prodded into thinking by a peculiarity of spelling." This return to the letter for inspiration, *obiter dictum*, is consonant with T. S. Eliot's inversion of 2 Corinthians 3:6: "The spirit killeth, the letter giveth life."

The first interpretation given by Rav Nahman, son of Hisda, is: "The Holy One, Blessed be He, created two inclinations, the good and the bad." This is indeed the usual interpretation, but Levinas points out that the word *yetzer* really means creature. The proof is in Isaiah 29:16:[1] "The creature (*yetzer*) said to the Creator he [the Creator] understood nothing." Though made from clay, the human being is created differently than a clay vessel. "What is the human being? The fact that a being is *two* while remaining *one*. A division, a rupture in the depth of his substance or simply consciousness and choice: life at the crossroads. . . . Consciousness and freedom would seem to be the definition of man;

234

in short, reason."[2] We should take note of a certain wavering in Levinas's text: "would seem to be. . . ." There is a latent question here. Is the rift within the human being "a rupture in the depths of his substance" or "simply consciousness and choice," i.e. reason?

The importance of this question in Levinas's philosophical works is evident, as is his decision in favor of rupture. Levinas rejects the Aristotelian definition of the human being as *animal rationalis*. In this talmudic reading there is no sharp division between human rationality and the rational behavior of animals. The distinctively human lies in a dichotomy deep within human subjectivity, more fundamental than consciousness and intentionality: it is the possibility of the substitution of self for other.[3] A return to the biblical text carries the inquiry further. "Rav Nahman bar Isaac objected: If this is so, then does this mean that the animal which (he made), *vayitzer* (Genesis 2:19, where *vayitzer* is not written with two yods), does not have good and evil inclinations, though we can see that an animal can destroy, bite, and kick?"[4] If the initial interpretation of the two yods was correct, and it means that the human being is distinguished from the animal by freedom, consciousness and reason, why does it seem that animals have at least some level of choice and consciousness? And yet when *vayitzer* refers to animals, it is written with only one yod. We must conclude that there must be another basis besides consciousness and reason for dividing the human from the rest of creation. Hence a new interpretation of the two yods in Genesis 2:7: "The two yods must be interpreted according to Rav Simeon ben Pazzi; for Rav Simeon ben Pazzi said: woe is me because of my own evil inclination."[5] As Levinas explains, the word *vay-yitzer* broken down into two elements could be interpreted as "woe to the creature," since *vay* is an interjection like *alas!* in popular Jewish speech. Here the interpretation is, Woe unto the creature, for when I obey my Creator I am unhappy because disrupted by my creaturely nature, and when I follow my creaturely penchant I am rendered unhappy by my knowledge of the Creator, i.e. his Law, which makes me unhappy in sinning. My nature makes me incapable of submitting to the Law without constraint.

This view is expressed philosophically in *Otherwise than Being*: "No one is good voluntarily." In a broad sense it is true to say that a certain eschatological thought about creation informs his philosophy. "The oneself [*soi*] is a creature, but an orphan by birth or an atheist no doubt ignorant of his Creator, for if it knew it it would again be taking up its commencement."[6] The allusion to taking up or assuming its commencement refers to the fact that the oneself is not the knowing, but the sensible self. If it were aware of its origin and beginning in the Creation, that awareness would place Creation in synchronic time and in the domain of being. We might say that what distinguishes Levinas's thought from the theology of creationism is that the former places creation in diachrony and beyond being. The creation is not an event that we could imagine taking place within the created world, or in time. This makes Levinas's "creationism" as philosophically respectable as Aristotle's conviction that the world has always existed, and will never cease to exist.

Returning to the talmudic mode of inquiry and text, it is striking that the duality of the two yods enables Levinas to introduce the idea of humans being solicited not only laterally (between conflicting passions) in their freedom to choose but also vertically, toward the lofty or base. "Between the Law and nature, between the Creator and the condition of creature, to be man remains as dramatic as the conflict between opposing passions." The human, concludes Levinas, is not freedom but obedience.

Yet another interpretation is introduced by Rav Jeremiah ben Eleazar. God created two faces on the first humans, for it is written (Psalm 139:5): "You hedge me before and behind; you lay your hand upon me." As Levinas understands the technique of the doctors of the Talmud, the purpose of quoting a text is rarely to establish a direct proof of veracity: it is rather "an invitation to search out the context of the quotation." The theme of that psalm is my inability to escape God's scrutiny at all times and in all places. It is obsession and election — the Jonah syndrome.

This means, in Levinas's view, the end of subjectivity, which is based on the secrecy of the closed-in subject. The subject has its *chez soi*, its own private haunt. Now, beneath the shadowless, noontime scrutiny of God from on high, there is no longer an interiority. Everything is outside, open. This is what is meant by two faces. I cannot keep things "in the back of my mind," for I have no hidden, inner reserve. Rather than having two faces, it is as if I were a continuous face.

The important role of the concept of the face in *Totality and Infinity* is of course well known. In that major philosophical work much emphasis was placed on the notion of separation as life.[7] It is that privacy, that separation, that is now, in the talmudic reading discussed here, described as the interiority of subjectivity, which is turned inside out beneath God's scrutiny. The problematic of "And God Created Woman" corresponds closely to that of a subjectivity sundered between the *moi* and the *soi* of *Otherwise than Being*, which appeared in 1974, two years after this work.

In interpreting Rav Jeremiah ben Eleazar's interpretation, Levinas encourages us to "free it from its theological forms." (By "theological forms" Levinas has in mind the forms and figures in the biblical and talmudic texts.) This is his way of prefacing his own interpretation, which adopts a manner of speaking very close to philosophical analysis. The other in the self, the responsibility of the subject for the other, the "for the other," is the way in which we are "invested" by God. "To be under the sleepless gaze of God is, precisely, in one's unity, to be the bearer of *another* subject — bearer and supporter — to be responsible for this other, as if the face of this other, although invisible, continued my own face and kept me awake by its very invisibility, by the unpredictability that it threatens. Unity of the *one* subject, irreplaceable in the impossibility of refusing responsibility for this other — closer than any proximity and yet unknown."[8] Several of the major themes to be taken up in the philosophic vernacular of *Otherwise than Being* are already present here and already formulated: the inescapability of my responsibility for the other, the notion of a proximity of a nonspatial nature, and the insistence that my relation to the other is not essentially one of knowledge.

Levinas uncovers the abstract nature of these seemingly concrete discussions of textual form. For readers already familiar with Levinas's conception of the human being as "hostage" to the other, as responsible even for what he has not done, an exegetical version of the same idea is given in Rav Ami's interpretation of Psalm 139:5, "You hedge me before and behind." "Behind" means "the last one created" (as man is the creation of the last, sixth, day while "before" means the first one to be punished since Adam was the first creature to be punished (not as a result of eating of the tree of the knowledge of good and evil, since there it was first the serpent who was punished, but in the case of the Flood — first by order of mention in Genesis 7:23). Man is therefore hemmed in before and behind since he is the first one held responsible for what preceded him (in the earlier days of the creation).

We will not retrace here the rest of the text in all its rich detail. By its intermediary Levinas is able to transmit his interpretation of the feminine, and to make the human emerge from a relationship considerably more complex than that of "complementarity."

In closing, let us consider an important aside within the text on method:

> The method I have always used — I do not know whether it meets
> the approval of the absolute Talmudists (I am only a very relative
> Talmudist) — consists in the following: each time a biblical verse
> is brought in as proof it is not likely that the sages of the Talmud

are looking in these texts, squeezed every which way in spite of grammar, for a direct proof of the thesis they are upholding. It is always an invitation to search out the context of the quotation.[9]

It is this solicitation of the text within its context, and the constant interweaving of the *interpretans* and the *interpretandum*, that characterizes the movement within these talmudic readings that I believe to have furnished the welcoming, fostering milieu so favorable to Levinas's most innovative and original ideas.

CONCLUSION

It is quite clear that Levinas has broken a major convention in his philosophical works, and that is to have spoken of God and of eschatological matters that are traditionally held to be more appropriate to theology than to philosophy proper. It does little good to adduce the cases of Descartes or Leibniz, or any number of other believing philosophers, because they are of a different age, an age in which science had not yet or only mildly constrained faith. It changes nothing to point to the passages in which Levinas himself shows his awareness of these circumstances. What exactly are the jarring elements of Levinas's thought *qua* philosophy?

Let me begin with what I have called "essentialism." I have tried to indicate along the way of this work what I meant by "essentialist," but since the word, like most, has somewhat of a record, I will specify again that I am using essentialism to refer to the primacy of meaning as described by Levinas himself, and which he designates as "sens" rather than the more culturally determined "signification." A Platonist in the pre-Aristotelian sense, that is, before the latter forced his teacher's Ideas to assume the disambiguated status of separate, **existing** entities of some sort, Levinas's essentialism could almost be thought of as a linguistic essentialism[1] — were it not for the fact that linguistics proceeds from the *fait accompli* of the institution of language while Levinas situates (if such a term can be used for so metaphysical a localization) meaning before language. Secondly, Levinas is unwilling to equate valid thought with that which exists (and with the present since for something to exist it must be present, be it actually so or in what is sometimes referred to as the "deficient modes" of the present, i.e., the retention or anticipation of what was or will be present). Thirdly, temporality is given in its meaningfulness rather than in time, i.e. manifested or immanent being. Pastness never "was," no more than futurity will "be," and these dimensions of meaning are frankly sundered from being (or "essence" in the Levinasian sense). All of the above specifications put Levinas squarely in the domain of phenomenology as the study of "essences" or *eidos*, of course. But Levinas's attention to the domain of the *a priori*, and even of an "arche" that he posits "before" the *a priori*, justify my allusion to Plato in this regard.

Perhaps the most important result of my personal inquiry — of which this book represents the tidied-up remains — is a better understanding of Levinas's philosophical itinerary. He set out (in "On Escape") with an urgent sense of the need to escape from the immanence of being. That period, which culminated with the publication of *Totality and Infinity*, that "essay on exteriority," was followed by a reorientation from exteriority to alterity. The change seems to have been the result of Levinas's desire to distance himself from ontological language and represents not so much a philosophical shift as a terminological clarification. Being had become exteriority;[2] but that being was only on the way to a more radical exteriority beyond being. The essential feature of exteriority revealed itself progressively to Levinas as otherness, and that aspect is therefore the one ultimately retained and thematized in *Otherwise than Being*.

To use an example that will be familiar to Christian readers, consider the philosophical essence of the parable of the Good Samaritan (Luke 10:29–37). The neighbor is not one who is geographically or biologically near, but in fact a stranger, and perhaps **the** stranger, since that otherness that is at the root of altruism is, as a "limiting case," the complete stranger. The neighbor is "the first one who happens to come along."

The shift in emphasis from outer to other, a legitimate *autrement dit* ("in other words") that Levinas clearly saw as being essential to the inevitable and endless process of expression of the said, reflects Levinas's increasing insistence on the priority of ethics over ontology. It also, I believe, directs his readers beyond cognition. This could not be better said than it has been by Francis Wybrands: "It does not suffice to understand Levinas to read him. To understand him is to remain in one's position as subject, master of meaning, whereas what is required of us is to perform the movement toward the other as it is accomplished by the text in one's own saying.[3]

NOTES

Notes to Introduction

1. I am not denying the importance of Heidegger's rejection of a "worldless" self, which Merleau-Ponty also rejects, to the point of denying, in the preface to *Phenomenology of Perception* (New York: The Humanities Press, 1962) that there is such a thing as an inner man (distinct from the world, at least). But Husserl's "Ineinander" and Merleau-Ponty's late philosophical use of such terms as "the inside of the outside" to describe vision, and his assertion that "reversibility" is "the ultimate truth" in *The Visible and the Invisible* (Evanston: Northwestern University Press, 1968) demonstrate the ongoing vitality, if not validity, of the inside/outside figure.

2. An account of the general reception of Levinas's philosophy in this country and elsewhere is outside the purview the present work, which seeks instead to give a general presentation of that philosopher. But I should like to nuance the contrarian account I have given of Levinas's thought by adding that discussion of his work in France and this country is lively, as attested by an increasing number of publications of journal articles and books; his thought is often discussed in existential and phenomenological circles, and there is an upsurge of interest in Israel (translations into Hebrew, international conferences in Jerusalem) and in Jewish academic circles in this country.

3. David Bannon, "Une Herméneutique de la Sollicitation," in *Les Cahiers de La Nuit Surveillée*, Emmanuel Lévinas (Lagrasse: Verdier, 1984), 100.

4. Robert Bernasconi, in "Almost Always More Than Philosophy Proper," (*Research in Phenomenology* 30 [2000]: 1–11) argues that phenomenology, in seeking the universal through the singular and the concrete, has moved philosophy toward "the recognition that the metaphysical ontic is irreducible," a position designated as the basis of "metontology." This means that phenomenology has been right "to take seriously what claims thinking — corporeality, language, history, experience — without immediately

identifying these things as limitations or as cause for worries about relativism." This opens the way for a new relationship between philosophy and culture, or "the nonphilosophical sources from which it arises." Bernasconi concludes by citing Levinas specifically as a prime candidate for this new way of hearing the philosophical voice. Levinas's protest at being labeled a "Jewish" thinker was motivated by his reluctance to be read in a way that would "limit or deny the universal pretensions of all thought." But "once it is recognized that it is a part of the strength of a thinking that is rooted in a language, a culture, and a tradition, however hybrid or nomadic, then these labels can be heard differently." It is in this spirit that the present work avoids the temptation to reduce Levinas's œuvre to "philosophy proper."

5. EL 38, quoted from Jerzy Jarzebski, *L'Évolution de l'image des confins dans la littérature polonaise après la Deuxième Guerre mondiale,* in Daniel Beauvois, *Les Confins de l'ancienne Pologne* (Lille: Presses Universitaires, 1988).

6. EL 50.

7. For more details on this period of Levinas's career, see E 115–21.

8. EL 125. The bulk of my information on Levinas's career has been gleaned from Anne-Marie Lescourret's biography.

9. DLT 10.

10. CPP 100.

11. TAI 24; TI xii.

12. For a rapid overview of this critique, see E 122–23.

13. In answer to a question about the relationship between his philosophical and his "Judaic-Talmudic" writings, Levinas answered: "The difference is in the manner. What is communicated in the Jewish writings by warmth must be communicated in philosophy by light." ELSA 98.

14. ELVT 282. My translation.

15. Although in my rough periodization I set out from the *il y a,* it must be borne in mind that the concept of the *il y a* (the impersonal, the *tiers exclu*) remains a constant feature of Levinas's thought, constituting a subsection of the latter part (162–65) of OB. The *il y a, obiter dictu,* is totally distinct from Levinas's considerably later coinage and concept of *illéité,* which refers to a "Third Person" beyond being. See PA 111 ff.

16. There is an obvious objection to using the term "realm" for the "otherwise than being;" Levinas himself refers to it as "an-archic," i.e. without rule or principle or beginning. Bearing this impropriety in mind, and with the proviso that I will seek more apt terminology as this study unfolds, I let the "two domains" appellation stand for now.

17. EDE 168–69.

18. DF 171. Translation, somewhat modified.

19. See Levinas's *God, Death, and Time* (course notes, edited by Jacques Rolland), trans. B. Bergo (Stanford: Stanford University Press, 2000), 9.

Notes to Chapter 1: Totality/Infility

1. Enzo Neppi, in his article "L'Être et le Mal dans la pensée d'Emmanuel Levinas" (*Esprit* 265 [juillet 2000] 69–87), affirms too categorically that Levinas considers being to be evil, and otherwise-than-being, good.

2. David Banon, "Résistance du visage et renoncement au sacrifice," in *L'Herne: Emmanuel Lévinas* (Paris: Éditions de l'Herne, 1991), 406 n. 1.

3. Levinas himself , in his epistemological critique of knowledge as a form of "selfish" annexation or acquisition, has a very contra-Hegelian suspicion of the *Begriff* (from German *greiffen*, to seize, grab, comprehend) or concept (concept, from *cum-capio*, a grasping or seizing).

4. OB 7; AE 8. The translation of *indicible* as "ineffable" might be preferable to Lingis's "unsayable."

5. AAT xviii–xix.

6. "Infini" was first published in the *Encyclopedia Universalis*, vol. 16, 1968, 192–94; republished in AT 69–89 and AAT 53–76.

"Totalité et totalisation" was first published in the *Encyclopedia Universalis*, vol. 8, 1968, 991–94; republished in AT 57–68 and AAT 39–51.

7. AAT xvi.

8. It is probably never the case that an element of the system of one philosopher corresponds entirely to that of another, but the ontological/epistemological "economies" of Kant and Levinas are close enough to warrant careful comparison. See Catherine Chalier's study on the relationship between Levinas and Kant in *Pour une morale au-delà du savoir* (Paris: Albin Michel, 1998).

9. The French word *autrui* is the one Levinas uses to refer to the face-to-face encounter with one other person. It is different from *les autres* in this respect, since the others, or other people, implies a third-personal relationship, while *autrui* evokes a one-on-one or second-personal relationship. I shall, accordingly, use "the other person" to translate it.

10. Levinas is doubtless thinking of *Sein und Zeit* (Tübingen: Max Niemeyer Verlag, 1986), 425. It is noteworthy that Levinas's conception of time in *Time and the Other* (1946/47) is diametrically opposed to Heidegger's. Cf. TO 79.

11. This essay, originally published as "La philosophie et l'idée de l'Infini" in *Revue de Métaphysique et de Morale, n° 3, juillet–septembre,* 1957, pp. 241–53, is included in EDE and CPP.

12. F. A. Olafson's *Principles and Persons* (Baltimore: The Johns Hopkins Press, 1967) propounds this very thesis of (moral) autonomy as the proper tradition in which to place existentialism.

13. CPP 50. Adriaan Peperzak adds the helpful note here that underlying this statement on the resistance of the individual to philosophical thought is the tradition Latin dictum, *De individuis non est scientia*, and ultimately perhaps Aristotle's *Metaphysics* 999 a25–b5.

14. CPP 50.

15. CPP 51.

16. CPP 57.

17. CPP 57.

18. CPP 57–58.

19. CPP 58.

20. CPP 59.

21. OB 198, n. 2. The French (AE 173, n. 2) has: "cela n'est pas une réalité pour « fils à papa ». The "daddy's boy" is one who, taking advantage of his father's fortune, has had no real contact with the hard realities of the world of work and life as it is lived by most people. Levinas's point is that ethical necessity is as "real" as ontological necessity. I have altered Lingis's translation here.

22. For Levinas's own account of his use of this term, see AE ix.

23. See, e.g., F. A. Olafson's *Heidegger and the Ground of Ethics* (Cambridge: Cambridge University Press, 1998), 83 n. 14.

24. CPP 59.

25. *Hegel's Logic*, trans. William Wallace (Oxford: Clarendon Press, 1975), 138 (§94).

26. The text of this lecture is published as "'Between Two Worlds' (The Way of Franz Rosenzweig)" in DF 180–201; DL 253–81.

27. DF 190; DL 265.

28. PN 66–74, "Kierkegaard: Existence and Ethics," originally published in German in *Schweizer Monatshefte* 43 (May, 1963), as "Existenz und Ethik."

29. PN 66.

30. PN 69.

31. PN 72.

32. TAI 40.

33. On his opposition to Claude Lévi-Strauss in particular, see EL 360, 361.

Notes to Chapter 2: Same/Other

1. TAI 34 (translation slightly modified); TI 4.
2. TAI 307; TI 284. I have retranslated this sentence, taking more liberties than Lingis did, in hopes of clarifying the overall meaning. The quote within the quote is from Baudelaire's *Fleurs du Mal* ("Spleen" LXXVI), in *Oeuvres Complètes de Baudelaire* (Paris: Gallimard, Bibliothèque de la Pléiade, 1961), 69.
3. ENN 12 ("The *I* and the Totality," [1954]); EN 26.
4. ENN 18–39.
5. TAI 118; TI 90. My emphasis.
6. EAE 99.

Notes to Chapter 3: Saying/Said

1. This chapter owes much to the very helpful study of language in Levinas's philosophy by Étienne Feron, *De l'idée de transcendence à la question du langage: L'itinéraire philosophique de Lévinas*. See Abbreviations, above, under DLT for complete reference.
2. OS 145–50.
3. OS 148 (from Levinas's "The Transcendence of Words").
4. BPW 65–77.
5. ENN 103–21, esp. 103–08.
6. BPW 73; EDE 211.
7. BPW 73, translation slightly modified; EDE 212.
8. BPW 73; EDE 212.
9. PN 40.
10. PN 43–44.
11. OB 5–7; AE 6–9.
12. OB 5; AE 6. Translation slightly altered.
13. *Critical Inquiry* 17 (Autumn 1990): 65; IH 30.
14. OB 5; AE 6. Lingis translates this as "world behind the scenes."
15. OB 6; AE 7.
16. OB 6; AE 7.
17. OB 6; AE 7. My emphasis. The theme of the immediate moment of writing philosophy and its fall into the being of the Said recurs in OB 155, 167, 169; AE 189, 213, 215.
18. OB 7, translation slightly modified; AE 8. See also OB 156; AE 198.
19. OB 7, one word changed in the translation; AE 9.
20. OB 187 n. 5; AE 8 n. 4.

21. AE 199, my translation.

22. TAI 26; TI xiv.

23. OB 4, translation modified; AE 5.

24. OS 148.

25. *The Visible and the Invisible* (Evanston: Northwestern University Press, 1968), 155.

26. OB 169–70; AE 215–16. Translation slightly modified.

27. OB 170; AE 216.

28. OB 171; AE 217.

Notes to Chapter 4: Being/Beyond Being

1. OB 51; DLE 69.

2. OE 73; DLE 98.

3. OE 60–63; DLE 81–84.

4. TAI 3–5; TI 33–35.

5. OE 62; DLE 83.

6. EN xii.

7. As the author reminds us in a note at the beginning of his major work, *Otherwise than Being or Beyond Essence*, this new meaning of essence displaces its former one, which is henceforth designated as "quiddity" or *eidos* or "nature."

8. EN xii.

9. OB 3; AE 4.

10. See TAI 290.

11. DLE 98, 99.

12. TAI 301–02.

13. I owe this insight to Étienne Feron. See DLT, chap. 5, passim.

14. See EN 137; ENN 118. In this interview ("Philosophy, Justice, and Love," October 1982), Levinas specifically denies having "retained" the identification of the future with Redemption.

Notes to Chapter 5: Person/Thing

1. *Explorations talmudiques* (Paris: Éditions Odile Jacob, 1998), 47.

2. In ENN 36–38. The following short quotes are from these pages.

3. OB 5 (translation somewhat modified); AE 5.

4. PN 70–71; NP 82.

Notes to Chapter 6: Ontology/Metaphysics

1. EAI 38.
2. QEV 90; see IRB 45. N.B. I had already completed my research on the Poirié study, using my own "ad hoc" translations of it for the present study, before the publication of the definitive translation of the entire interview by Jill Robbins et al. in *Is it Righteous to Be?* (IRB). I have decided not to replace my translations with that one, however, with the thought that my interpretation may bring out more obviously the point I am making in a particular context. But in order that the reader with a keen interest in a specific passage may obtain a synoptic perspective, I supply page references to the Robbins translation as well.
3. This is the title of Edith Wyschogrod's study, *Emmanuel Levinas: The Problem of Ethical Metaphysics* (EM).
4. OB 11; AE 13 and QEV 92 (see IRB 47), respectively.
5. TAI 35; TI 5.

Notes to Chapter 7: Sacred/Holy

1. QEV 93; see IRB 47.
2. QEV 95; see IRB 49.
3. AEL 4.
4. There has been general agreement among translators to translate *saint* and *sainteté* as "holy" and "holiness." Sometimes this is awkward: for example, the term "sacred history" (rather than "holy history") in the sense of biblical history is consecrated by usage as the equivalent of the French "histoire sainte." A more serious difficulty is that English uses the term "holy places," while for Levinas only people are holy, never objects or places. Hence the reader should feel free to think in terms of saint and saintliness, which are etymologically closer to Levinas's French terminology. It is likely that translators have preferred holy to saintly simply because the former term is the usual translation of the Hebrew, and thus more readily associated with Judaism; saint and saintly are often associated with Catholicism. But the fact that saintly is always connected with a human being whose life is oriented toward the divine makes it, in my opinion, a justifiable translation as well. The essential point is, of course, that the binary opposition with sacred be maintained.
5. It was combined with his first anthology, *Quatre lectures talmudiques*, and translated as the second part of *Nine Talmudic Readings* by Annette Aronowicz (NTR).

6. The term oral Torah is a designation for the Talmud, because, though written down, it is the tabulation of discussion of the Torah by sages and scholars.

7. NTR 92.

8. OB 18.

Notes to Chapter 8: Judaism

1. 111; see IRB 62.

2. Seán Hand's translation, the only one currently available, should be used with caution.

3. DL 10.

4. See OS 47, sect. 8 and n. 4. For a more detailed account of *Difficult Freedom*, see below, chapter 18.

5. Good sources of information on the Colloque, as well as on the intertwining of the Judaic and the philosophical in Levinas's life and work, are Marie-Anne Lescourret, EL 129–82, esp. 167–82, Annette Aronowicz, NTR ix–11, and Perrine Simon-Nahum, "Une « herméneutique de la parole »: Emmanuel Levinas et les Colloques des intellectuals juifs," *Emmanuel Levinas, Philosophie et judaïsme* (Paris: In Press Éditions, 2002), 255–71.

6. ENN xi.

7. Rabbi Hayyim de Volozhyn, *L'Ame de la vie* (Lagrasse: Verdier, 1986).

8. QEV110; see IRB 61.

9. See "Ethics as First Philosophy," LR 75–78.

10. See DF 16–19.

11. The Aggadah, or Hagaddah, is the term used to designate apologies and parables that express the theological and philosophical parts of the Talmud.

12. NTR 182; DSS 155–56.

13. Georges Hansel, *Explorations talmudiques* (Paris: Éditions Odile Jacob, 1998).

Notes to Chapter 9: Hypostasis, Grammar, and Thematization

1. OB 36, translation somewhat modified. AE 46.

2. Guy Petitdemange, "Emmanuel Lévinas: Au-dehors, sans retour," in *Répondre d'Autrui: Emmanuel Lévinas* (Boudry-Neuchâtel: Éditions de la Baconnière, 1989), 79. My translation.

3. See, for Levinas's interpretation of Plotinus, ENN 133–36 (EN 153–56); also AAT 6–10 (AT 29–33).

4. EAE 103 (EE 170).

5. This paragraph is based on EAI 47–52 (EI 37–43).

6. OG xv, translation modified; DD 13.

7. OB 185; AE 233.

8. Originally published in *Tijdschrift voor Filosofie* 3 (1963). Included in EDE 187–202. In English, "The Trace of the Other," trans. by A. Lingis, *Deconstruction in Context*, ed. Mark Taylor (Chicago, University of Chicago Press, 1986), 345–59.

9. EDE 199, my translation.

10. This quote and the one that ends this paragraph are from AT 95 and 96, respectively.

Notes to Chapter 10: Proximity and Temporality

1. BPW 65.

2. BPW 178 n. 10. The text Levinas refers to is "Transcendence and Height."

3. BPW 27.

4. CPP 115.

5. HAH 45.

6. This and the preceding quote are from BPW 37.

7. BPW 38.

8. See *Archives de philosophie*, 34 (1971) 373–91. It is included in Anne-Marie Lescourret's anthology, *L'intrigue de l'infini* (Paris: Flammarion, 1994) 195–218, unfortunately out of print. The only significant differences between this prototext and the version contained in *Autrement qu'être*, 102–24 are the addition of the three last paragraphs of the first subsection ("*a. Proximité et espace*") and the addition of nn. 34 (on the difference between Hegel's and Levinas's use of the other) and 36 (on the question of the divinity of the "Dieu-Un.").

9. See OB 193–94 n. 1.

10. The text I am summarizing, AE 102, reads "Mais alors le terme de proximité aurait un sens relatif et, dans l'espace inhabité de la géométrie euclidienne, un sens emprunté." Lingis, very reliable on the whole, mistranslates the word "inhabité" as "inhabited"; the translation should be: "But then the term proximity would have a relative meaning and, in the uninhabited space of Euclidean geometry, a derivative sense." *Et Homerus dormitat.*

11. See Simon Critchley, *Ethics, Politics, Subjectivity* (London: Verso, 1999), 63.

12. OB 187 n. 4.

13. OB 272.

14. TI 235.

15. OB 258. Slightly modified.

16. OS 148.

17. Although *Totality and Infinity* is somewhat longer than *Otherwise than Being* (113,000 and 93,000 words, respectively) the difference is not great enough to distort the results of the word count.

18. Guy Petitdemange, "Éthique et transcendance. Sur les chemins d'Emmanuel Lévinas," *Recherches de science religieuse* 64 (Jan./Mar. 1976): 60. Cited by Jacques Rolland, *Parcours de l'infini* (Paris: PUF, 2000), 17.

19. Recurrence comes up in a passage on p. 55 of *Autrement qu'être* (in chap. 3, "From Intentionality to Feeling") that was transposed from the 1971 piece, "Le dit et le dire." It is included in Lescourret's *L'intrigue de l'infini* (165–93). On p. 183 of that text, there is a footnote to "L'accusatif originaire de ce singulier pronom (The originary accusative of this singular pronoun, that is, "se"). The footnote reads, "See our study on 'La Substitution,' in the *Revue philosophique de Louvain*, August 1968." Thus it is clear that the concept of recurrence was adopted and developed by Levinas between 1961 and 1968.

20. OB 8; AE 10.

21. See BPW 82–87.

22. Alphonso Lingis, the translator of *Otherwise than Being,* translates *moi* as "ego" and *soi* as "self." This solution renders such passages as "la recurrence du moi à soi" ("the recurrence from the ego to the self," 144 and 113, resp.), rather more obscure than the original, because the *moi* is more personal and more "selfish" or "self-centered" than the *soi*, its more altruistic avatar.

23. OB 89–190, n. 33; AE 60 n. 33.

24. OB 56, trans. modified; AE 73.

25. OB 108; AE 137.

26. OB 114; AE 145.

27. TAI 34; TI 4.

28. OB 114, AE 145.

29. OB 115; AE 147.

30. OB 114, translation modified; AE 145.

31. OB 194 n. 10; AE 137 n. 10.

32. OB 108, slightly modified; AE 137.

33. OB 108; AE 137.

34. OB 108; AE 137.

35. OB 107, slightly modified; AE 136.

36. BPW 33–64.

37. TAI 261 et seq.; TI 239 et seq.

38. AE 166, my translation. I have supplied the word *si* (if) because I think the meaning requires it, but have no textual basis for doing so.

39. Levinas's terminology is not to be confused with that of the French linguist F. de Saussure, who uses synchronic to describe a crosssection of a language at one moment in time and diachronic to follow the development of a language over time.

40. See "The Trace of the Other," translated by A. Lingis, *Deconstruction in Context*, ed. M. Taylor (Chicago, University of Chicago Press, 1986) 345–59.

41. M. Heidegger, *Being and Time* (New York: Harper & Row, 1962) 32.

42. *Autrement que savoir: Emmanuel Levinas* (Paris: Éditions Osiris, 1988), 92. My translation.

Notes to Chapter 11: The Holocaust

1. Howard Caygill's recent *Levinas & the Political* (London and New York: Routledge, 2002) makes an important contribution to the examination of the intertwined philosophical and political aspects of this period of Levinas's thought. His first two chapters, "Presentiments of National Socialism" and "The Post-War Political" are of particular relevance here.

2. *Critical Inquiry* 17 (Autumn 1990): 63. The essay itself is on 64–71.

3. Martin Heidegger, *Sein und Zeit* (Tübingen: Max Niemeyer Verlag, 1986), 12. In English, "in its very Being, that Being is an issue for it." *Being and Time*, trans. Macquarrie and Robinson (New York: Harper & Row, 1962), 32. It is clear that Levinas already knew at this writing (1934) that Heidegger was at least a Nazi sympathizer. See "As If Consenting to Horror," (*Critical Inquiry* 15 [Winter 1989]: 485) in which Levinas states that he knew "very early, perhaps even before 1933 and certainly after Hitler's huge success at the time of his election to the Reichstag, of Heidegger's sympathy toward National Socialism."

4. *Critical Inquiry* 17 (Autumn 1990): 63.

5. The quotes contained in this paragraph are from *Critical Inquiry* 17 (Autumn 1990): 65–66.

6. This is the convincingly defended thesis of Merold Westphal's "Situation and Suspicion in the Thought of Merleau-Ponty: The Question of Phenomenology and Politics," in *Ontology and Alterity in Merleau-Ponty* (Evanston: Northwestern University Press, 1990), 158–79.

7. OB 4; AE 5.

8. "Sans Nom." It was originally published in 1966 as "Honneur sans Drapeau," or Honor without a Flag.

9. PN 120.

10. PN 15. Translation slightly altered.

11. ENN 91–101. Quotations from 91–101, passim.

12. See, for an attempt at a post-Auschwitz theodicy, Hans Jonas's *The Concept of God After Auschwitz*. Jonas questions the omnipotent aspect of God, and incorporates elements from Jewish mystics, such as the suffering of God and Isaac Luria's doctrine of Tzimtzum.

13. ENN 100.

14. *Emmanuel Lévinas, Qui êtes-vous?* (QEV); in English, see IRB 23–83.

15. QEV 125; see IRB 73.

16. There is another dimension of this difference between Levinas's and Buber's scriptural exegesis. Buber seems to be reacting to historical cruelty with a modern sensitivity; Levinas says (QEV 124; see IRB 73) "Let us not discuss history or historicity. The meaning of the biblical hyperboles is to be sought in the context of those hyperboles, regardless of the distance between the verses!"

17. QEV 130; see IRB 77–78.

18. EL 126–27.

19. QEV 130; see IRB 78.

Notes to Chapter 12: Levinas's Early Work on Husserl

1. PT 50 n. 3.

2. I.e. the "thèse d'université," also known as the "thèse de troisième cycle" or "petite thèse." His "thèse d'État," or "thèse de doctorat ès lettres," was *Totalité et infini* and was defended at the Sorbonne in 1961 before Jean Wahl and Vladimir Jankélévitch. Merleau-Ponty, who was expected to be at the defense, died shortly beforehand (cf. EL 217–18). Lévinas decided fairly early on in his career not to attempt the *aggregation*, a national competition granting state-supported academic tenure.

3. "Lévinas avant Lévinas : L'introducteur et le traducteur de Husserl" in PT 49–72.

4. QEV 73–74; see IRB 31–32.

5. OB 18.

6. OG 87; DD 139–40.

7. This quote, and those that follow in this paragraph, are from De Boer's question and Levinas's answer, in OG 86–90; DD 138–43.

8. The *Merleau-Ponty Aesthetics Reader: Philosophy and Painting,* ed. by Galen A. Johnson (Evanston: Northwestern University Press, 1993), 120; Merleau-Ponty, *Signes* (Paris: Gallimard, 1960), 104.

9. QEV 74; see IRB 32.

Notes to Chapter 13: Levinas's Critique of Heidegger

1. Levinas, "Martin Heidegger and Ontology," in *Diacritics* 26, no. 1 (Spring 1996): 11.

2. QEV 79; see IRB 36.

3. *Inquiry* 43: 3, 271–88.

4. EAI 37; EI 27. The other works mentioned are Plato's *Phaedrus*, Kant's *Critique of Pure Reason*, Hegel's *Phenomenology of Mind*, and Bergson's *Time and Free Will* (*Les données immédiates de la conscience*).

5. AQS 51.

6. Robert Bernasconi comments on this in his foreword to the latest reprinting of the Lingis translation of *Existence & Existents*, and Jacques Taminiaux has given a detailed account of Levinas's early, discrete but insistent revisionism in "La première réplique à l'ontologie fondamentale," *L'Herne*, Emmanuel Lévinas (Editions de l'Herne, 1991), 275–84.

7. See Jean Greisch, "Heidegger et Lévinas interprètes de la facticité," *Emmanuel Lévinas, Positivité et transcendance* (Paris: Presses Universitaires de France, 2000), 181–207, esp. 191.

8. This course, the first given by Heidegger in Freiburg (where he replaced Husserl), was titled "Introduction to Philosophy," and is available in the *Gesamtausgable,* vol. 27.

9. Included in ENN 1–11; EN 13–24.

10. ENN 3; EN 15.

11. TAI 46–46; TI 17.

12. *Critical Inquiry* 17 (Autumn 1990): 69–70; IH 39.

13. Levinas, "Martin Heidegger and Ontology," in *Diacritics* 26, no. 1 (Spring 1996) 11.

14. OB 28, n. 28; AE 49, n. 28. My translation.

15. In *Gesamtausgabe* 7, written in 1952, and included as chapter 3, "*Moira (Parmenides* VIII, 34–41)" of Martin Heidegger, *Early Greek Thinking* (New York: Harper & Row, 1984), 79–101.

16. In Heidegger's analysis of this same fragment (3) in *Being and Time* (H 171), *noein* is interpreted not as thinking but as seeing, apparently going back to an earlier meaning of *noein*: to perceive with the eyes.

17. Jacques Rolland, "Une logique de l'ambiguïté," *Autrement que Savoir: Emmanuel Lévinas* (Paris: Éditions Osiris, 1988), 51.

Notes to Chapter 14: Derrida's Reading of Levinas

1. I rely here on the number of entries between these dates listed by Roger Burggraeve's *Emmanuel Levinas, Une bibliographie primaire et*

secondaire, 1929–89 (Leuven: Peeters, 1990), an invaluable aid to Levinasian scholarship.

2. This and all other numbers introduced into my text in this chapter refer to Alan Bass's admirable translation of "Violence and Metaphysics," which constitutes chapter 4 of Derrida's *Writing and Difference* (Chicago: University of Chicago Press, 1978), 79–153.

3. WD 110. "Ce n'est pas moi qui me refuse au système, comme le pensaient Kierkegaard, c'est l'Autre" (ED 162). Derrida is quoting this statement from Levinas (TAI 40; TI 10). A better translation would probably be "It is not I who am refractory to the system, it is the Other." The idea is not that I actively refuse or do not refuse the system (as a willing or unwilling agent), but that my condition as subject is less resistant to Hegelianism than the absolute otherness as conceived by Levinas.

4. Alan Bass's version of the phrase in question, "the egoistic cry of a subjectivity still concerned with Kierkegaard's happiness and salvation" unfortunately reinforces Derrida's misinterpretation with a mistranslation. Derrida has omitted the comma before the words "de Kierkegaard" from the original; the comma is not essential to a correct reading of the text, but its omission seems to have opened the door to Bass's erroneous translation. The very literal translation I have given in the text above, is my own — but is in fact inferior to the less literal one of Al Lingis's: "the egoist cry of the subjectivity, still concerned for happiness and salvation, as in Kierkegaard" (OB 305). Lingis has translated "égoïste" as "egoist," a term more commonly used in philosophy. But an "egoist" is one who acts according to self-interest **in principle**. I prefer "egotistical," because the Levinasian subject acts according to a spontaneous selfishness.

5. PA 15.

6. Derrida lists the works of Levinas he read as a basis for his article, the last in date being *Difficult Freedom* (1st ed., 1963). He also mentions two articles, "La trace de l'autre" and "La signification et le sens," but says that his essay had already been written when they appeared. It is therefore almost certain that he was unaware of "Existenz und Ethik," which did not appear in French until its inclusion in *Noms Propres* in 1975, followed by another piece on Kiekegaard, "À propos de Kierkegaard Vivant." See PN 66–79.

7. PN 71; NP 83.

8. TO 75–76; TA 63. Cohen's translation differs slightly from Bass's.

9. HAH 15–70; CPP 75–107.

10. TAI 38–39; TI 8–9.

11. Derrida's characterization of phenomenology here is quite streamlined for polemical purposes. For a more nuanced exploration of what

phenomenology is, see Merleau-Ponty, *Phenomenology of Perception* (London: Routledge & Kegan Paul, 1962), vii–xxi.

12. RL xiii.

13. RL xiii.

14. PA 86.

15. PA 140.

16. *The Provocation of Levinas: Rethinking the Other*, ed. Bernasconi and Wood (London: Routledge, 1988), 169. The interview, by Tamra Wright, Peter Hughes and Allison Ainley, took place in 1986, and constitutes chapter 11 of the volume cited, 168–80.

17. PA 179.

18. PN 62.

19. PN 57.

20. PN 57–58.

21. PN 58.

22. PN 59.

23. PN 59.

24. Jacques Derrida, "En ce moment même dans cet ouvrage me voici," *Textes pour Emmanuel Levinas*, ed. F. Laruelle (Paris: Jean-Michel Place, 1980). The English translation by Ruben Berezdivin is included as chapter 2 of RL (11–48), and a detailed discussion of it by Simon Critchley, one of the editors of the volume, titled "Bois — Derrida's final word on Levinas," is included as chapter 10 (162189).

25. RL 4.

26. RL 13.

27. RL 13; EDE 191 and HAH 45.

28. RL 163–89, *passim*.

29. The allusion I am thinking of occurs in a 1982 interview. "When I speak to a Christian, I always quote Matthew 25; the relation to God is presented there as a relation to another person. It is not a metaphor; in the other, there is a real presence of God . . . I'm not saying that the other is God, but that in his or her Face I hear the Word of God" (EN 110).

30. PA 20–23. See also PA vii, 3/. Rolland distinguishes between "the ethical," which is "the human" structured as the "inter-human," and is "morally neuter," and all the moral and religious issues that may be analyzed by drawing conclusions from that strictly philosophical domain of the ethical. I am not at all sure that Levinas would have concurred on this point, given his opposition to the thought of the "neutral."

31. Robert Bernasconi, "Whose Death is it anyway? Philosophy and the Cultures of Death," *Tympanum: A Journal of Comparative Literary Studies*, vol. 4. http://www.usc.edu/dept/comp-lit/tympanum/

32. GDT 5–53, *passim.*

33. AEL 21. Page references given in the text of this section refer to AEL.

34. TAI 155.

35. TAI 299; TI 276.

36. OB 112; AE 142.

37. Derrida is quoting Levinas, OB 122; AE 157.

38. What I have in mind here is the French *il* of "illeity." The French *il* can be construed as a "he" or an "it." My sense is that the third per-sonness contained within the *vous* (which makes it cease to be the more intimate *tu*) is a third person that is neither masculine nor feminine nor neuter — or at least not in a pre- or infra-human way.

39. *"un pis-aller."* A 113.

40. CPP 106–07 or BPW 63–64.

41. TN 98.

42. BTV 35–52.

43. The midrash (from Hebrew root *darash*, to search or study) is a genre of rabbinic literature that interprets biblical texts.

44. BTV 48.

45. BTV 43, quoted by Derrida in AEL 108.

46. OB 5, translation slightly modified.

47. Quoted by Derrida, from Levinas's *Of God Who Comes to Mind* (OG 83).

48. QEV 132; see IRB 79.

Notes to Chapter 15: "De l'évasion"

1. OB 50–51; DLE 68–69 (my emphasis).

2. OB 61 (trans. slightly altered); DLE 82.

3. OB 62 (trans. slightly altered); DLE 83.

4. DLE 93.

5. This term, "the nations," is the talmudic one used to designate all of humankind surrounding (but not including) Israel.

Notes to Chapter 16: Existence and Existents

1. EAE 4; EE 9.

2. EAE 16; EE 38. *On s'est* is not really translated by "One is one-self," which would be the equivalent of *On est soi-même.* In that case the verb does not express being; it is just a copulative, joining subject and attribute, or establishing an equivalence. But *on s'est*, a form that does

not normally occur, has the peculiarity of using the verb "to be" as if it were transitive, like "he ises himself," as if there were a transitive verb "to is." Only transitive verbs can be reflexive; hence, in order to indicate the reflexivity of being, it is necessary for the verb to be to become transitive. Sartre experimented with this thought by inventing (in *Being and Nothingness*) the form *ester*. This point, the reflexivity of being, plays an important role in Levinas's philosophy. It is at the basis of his notion of "recurrence" in *Otherwise than Being or Beyond Essence*, and in the relation between the *moi* and the *soi*.

3. EAE xi.

4. Martin Heidegger, *Sein und Zeit* (Tübingen: Niemeyer, 1986), 5; *Being and Time*, trans. Macquarrie & Robinson (New York: Harper & Row, 1962), 25.

5. EAE 33; EE 63–64.

6. EAE 34; EE 65.

7. EAE 34; EE 64.

8. EAE 46; EE 84–85.

9. EAE 60; EE 105.

10. EAE 63; EE 112.

11. See OB 152 ("a blinking of meaning"); AE 194 (*clignotement de sens*) and OB ("the scintillation of ambiguity"), transl. slightly altered; AE 206 (*le scintillement de l'ambiguïté*).

12. EAE 65; EE 117.

13. This is a debatable issue. On one hand, it could be argued that Heidegger describes Dasein and the world as "equiprimordial"; on the other, the notion of *Geworfenheit* and of the "always-already-thereness" of Dasein's experience of the world might lend support to Levinas's view of the "*da*" (there) of Dasein.

14. EAE 65; EE 117.

15. EAE 69; EE 122.

16. EAE 76; EE 132.

17. EAE 78, my translation; EE 135.

18. EAE 79; EE 136.

19. For more detail on Levinas's metaphysical employment of grammatical terminology, see chapter 9, "Hypostasis, Grammar, and Thematization."

20. EAE 86–87 (I have added the word in square brackets.); EE 147.

21. EAE 87 (The words in square brackets are mine.); EE 148.

22. EAE 88; EE 149.

23. EAE 90–91; EE 152.

24. EAE 91; EE 153. My translation.

25. Here, it is the secular world that is epitomized by economic time. But the ethics of divine retribution that it gives rise to, which is not absent

from the Hebrew Bible, has also been criticized by Levinas; particularly when human agents pretend to interpret the suffering of others as the effect of celestial sanctions. This extension of economic time beyond the secular or lay world is also noted in the text we are considering (EAE 93; EE 155): "Religious life itself, when it is understood in terms of the category of wages, is economic." This is not a reference to the fact that nuns get paid, but to the theological and ideological implications of economic time. See, e.g., Max Weber, *The Protestant Ethic and the Spirit of Capitalism*, Trans. T. Parsons (London, 1930).

26. EAE 93; EE 156.

27. AE 121, my translation. Cf. OB 95.

28. EAE 95; EE 158.

29. *Le temps et l'autre/Time and the Other* (TA and TO, respectively). These works should be studied in conjunction with each other, both because they cover much of the same ground and because they reflect a unified and unique ambiance of postwar experimental thought as Levinas points out in his preface to the second edition of *Le temps et l'autre* written 30 years later; it is included in Richard Cohen's translation, complete with a virtual *apparatus criticus*: an analytic translator's introduction, copious notes, and an index. Levinas also wrote a preface to the second edition of *De l'existence à l'existent* which puts the earlier work in helpful perspective to the later ones. Unfortunately the English translation, *Existence & Existents*, which is very reliable and augmented with an insightful preface by Robert Bernasconi, one of the leading experts on Levinas, and a helpful translator's introduction by Alphonso Lingis, does not include Levinas's preface to the second edition.

30. See "The Other in Proust," in PN 99–105, esp. 104. This piece was originally published in 1947, the same year as *Existence & Existents* and *Time and the Other*.

31. EAE 88; EE 149. The logical idea of identity is the one that applies to relations between entities, which are the resultant "nouns" or "things that are." Again, the "I" is substance, but it does not have thought as one of its attributes: it is substance **because** it thinks.

Notes to Chapter 17: Totality and Infinity: Preface

1. TAI 21, 22.

2. TAI 22.

3. TAI 22–23.

4. TAI 23, my emphasis.

5. The text of that preface is available in English in ENN 197–200.

6. ENN 198.
7. TAI 24.
8. TAI 26.

Notes to Chapter 18: Difficult Freedom

1. In 1968, Levinas will partially endorse judgment of distinguished historian of Jewish Kabala and mysticism Gershon Sholem a propos of Martin Buber's "existentialist" interpretation of Hasidism: see OS 8, 9.
2. DF 296–97 n. 1; DL 89–90 n. 1. Translation slightly modified.
3. DF 60; DL 92.
4. DF 62; DL 94. Translation slightly altered.
5. DF 64; DL 96.
6. The parable of the prodigal son (Luke 15:11–32) has been so interpreted. See Jill Robbins's study, *Prodigal Son/Elder Brother* (Chicago: University of Chicago Press, 1991).
7. DF 68; DL 101. Translation slightly altered.
8. DF 68–69; DL 102. Translation altered.
9. DF 96; DL 138.
10. DF 89; DL 129.
11. ENN 105 (also quoted in OS 44 and elsewhere).
12. DF 94–95; DL 136.
13. This theme will be developed further in another, later talmudic reading: "Beyond the State in the State," (1988). See NeTR 79–107; NLT 45–76. The text is a fanciful meeting between Alexander the Great and the sages of Israel. The verticality of morality is contrasted with the horizontality of politics on NeTR 84, 85.
14. "L'Agenda de Léon Brunschwicg," Evidences (no. 2/1949), reprinted in DL 63–71 (DF 38–49).
15. See "Vladimir Jankélévitch," in OS 84–89; HS 123–27.
16. Cf. EL.

Notes to Chapter 19: Language and Proximity

1. OB 193–94 n. 1. "La Proximité" was first published in 1971 in Archives de la Philosophie, no. 34 (1971): 372–91 and is included in Anne-Marie Lescourret's *L'intrigue de l'infini* (Paris: Flammarion, 1994) 195–218, a work that has become virtually unobtainable.
2. CPP 114; EDE 222.
3. CPP 114–15; EDE 223.
4. CPP 115 n. 5; EDE 224 n. 1.

5. CPP 115; EDE 224.

6. CPP 116, translation modified; EDE 225.

7. CPP 116 n. 6, translation somewhat modified; EDE 224 n. 1.

8. CPP 116; EDE 225.

9. CPP 116, translation somewhat modified; EDE 225.

10. My translation. EDE 229. "[L]a conscience est toujours en retard au rendezvous du prochain." Cf. CPP 119.

11. CPP 122; EDE 231–32.

12. OB 86 (trans. slightly modified).

13. CPP 75–79; "La signification et les sens, I, Signification et réceptivité," in HAH 17–23. An integral translation of *Humanisme de l'autre homme* has recently become available. See *Humanism of the Other*, trans. Poller and Cohen (Urbana: University of Illinois Press, 2003).

14. CPP 77, 78 (trans. slightly modified); HAH 19, 21. See also Levinas's essay "A priori et subjectivité: A Propos de la *Notion de l'a priori* de Mikel Dufrenne" in EDE 179–86.

15. CPP 122; EDE 232.

16. In TI, *fraternité* occurs 12 times, and *proximité* 7: in AE *fraternité* occurs 20 times, *proximité* 250.

17. CPP 123.

18. CCP 125.

19. CPP 126 (trans. slightly modified; EDE 236).

Notes to Chapter 20: "And God Created Woman"

1. Both the original, published by Les Éditions de Minuit, and the translation have verse 6 instead of 16; the latter is clearly what was meant, for Levinas gives a literal translation of the end of verse 16.

2. NTR 165, translation slightly modified.

3. See OB 59 for these contrasting views on the nature of human beings. Are they mutually exclusive, or do they complete one another in the ambiguity of sensibility? See OB 79–80.

4. NTR 165.

5. NTR 165.

6. OB 11, 105.

7. See TAI 109–21.

8. NTR 168 (trans. slightly altered).

9. NTR 166; DSS 130–31.

Notes to Conclusion

1. The Platonism of Levinas is very close to that discovered in Proust by Gilles Deleuze in the latter's *Marcel Proust et les signes*.

2. TAI 290.

3. Francis Wybrands, "La voix de la pensée, " in Les Cahiers de *La nuit surveillé, n° 3: Emmanuel Levinas* (Lagrasse: Éditions Verdier, 1984), 77.

INDEX